Understanding
Garden Design

Understanding Garden Design

The Complete Handbook for Aspiring Designers

VANESSA GARDNER NAGEL, APLD

TIMBER PRESS
Portland · London

For Michael, whose love and support
encouraged this book to come to fruition.

Published in 2010 by Timber Press, Inc.

The Haseltine Building
133 S.W. Second Avenue, Suite 450
Portland, Oregon 97204-3527
www.timberpress.com

2 The Quadrant
135 Salusbury Road
London NW6 6RJ
www.timberpress.co.uk

Text design by Susan Applegate
Printed in China

Library of Congress Cataloging-in-Publication Data

Nagel, Vanessa Gardner.
    Understanding garden design: the complete handbook for
aspiring designers/Vanessa Gardner Nagel.—1st ed.
        p. cm.
    Includes bibliographical references and index.
    ISBN: 978-0-88192-943-0
    1. Gardens—Design. I. Title.
    SB472.45.N34 2010
    712'.2—dc22   2009053692

A catalog record for this book is also available from the British Library.

Contents

Acknowledgments   7

Introduction   9

1   Beginning the Design of Your Garden   13

2   Documenting Your Site   25

3   Components of Your Garden   43

4   Putting the Components Together   65

5   Design 101   79

6   Finishes and Furnishings   115

7   Irrigation   143

8   Plants: A Structural Perspective   151

9   Garden Lighting   173

10   The Final Design   185

11   Construction: Working with Contractors   201

12   After Construction   217

Bibliography   229

Index   231

Acknowledgments

It took many people to bring this book to life. My husband, Michael, is my mentor and motivational guru. My daughter, Wendy, put the idea of a book in my head, with the rest of my family behind me all the way. So many friends provided support, but especially Michael Peterson, Clark Jurgemeyer, and kindred garden spirits Bonnie Bruce, Laurel Young, and Lesley Cox. They provided additional time and insight in the form of willingness to read the book's draft. My gardening friends, professional colleagues, and wonderful clients have provided immeasurable learning opportunities. Thank you to the staff at Timber Press, especially Tom Fischer, who allowed me to express my experiences and ideas as a book; and to Lorraine Anderson, who made this book comprehensible through her gift of editing. Special thanks to these contractors for providing their time and support: JP Stone Contractors; Dinsdale Landscape Contractors, Inc.; JSI Landscapes; Tryon Creek Landscape; McQuiggins Inc.; D & J Landscape Contractors; Winterbloom, Inc.; Drake's 7 Dees; Circadian Consulting & Design; Landscape East & West; EnergyScapes, Inc.; and Landscape Design Associates of Westchester, Inc. My appreciation would be incomplete without a thank-you to Beverly Martin, who advised me to write; to Allan Mandell, who taught me to mind each corner in a photograph; and to my mother and grandfather, who taught me to love plants.

Trillium kurabayashi is a nice surprise in early spring. Author's garden.

Introduction

Whether you are a novice gardener, are launching a career as a landscape designer, or install gardens, understanding the detailed process of planning, designing, and implementing the installation of a garden is an invaluable tool. Landscape design is an astonishing blend of knowledge. From visualizing concepts to using design principles to setting a stone, you will test your visualization skills repeatedly. The better you understand the entire process, the better the outcome will be.

When I began practicing landscape design, it was after a twenty-two-year career in commercial interior design. I had a bachelor's degree in interior design, but I returned to school to take classes in landscape design. What I discovered was an inadequate choice of reference books that tackle the entire process of landscape design. There are sources that address specific areas or topics. However, I could find no comprehensive resource useful to landscape design students, homeowners, and design-build contractors.

After I had been practicing landscape design for a time, my daughter called to ask for a book recommendation. She had been searching for a book that would help her get started with her garden. She said, "Mom, they all start somewhere in the middle" and added that "the middle" meant a discussion of basic design principles. She was looking for a book that truly started at the beginning. She recognized that something had to happen before thinking about things like form, texture, balance, and other design principles. After

A series of zigzag raised beds along the south side of a house provides an attractive kitchen garden just outside the kitchen door. The arrangement not only provides additional planting space but also prevents the space from feeling like a bowling alley. Garden of Darcy Daniels. Photo by Darcy Daniels.

I enumerated several tasks that would help her begin the planning of her garden, she said, "Mom, you need to write that book." Thus began my book-writing journey.

It was with my daughter in mind and my own experience as a landscape design student that I wrote this book. The book begins by answering the question, Why design? This question haunted me for most of my interior design career. Beyond my enjoyment of what I was doing, how did it benefit the people who used the space? I always hoped that my professional design organization would find a way to evaluate how design benefits people. Where were the measurements that defined the value of design?

A meeting at a high-tech firm's offices to design their interior space revitalized my search. There I found a blue and gray environment that depressed me for the brief period I was there. What was this environment doing to the employees?

I began an evaluation of the benefits of color, and started to find answers in psychological journals and a couple of books about the psychology of color. This search predated the Internet, which meant it took considerably more time and effort to find resources than it does now. Learning about the value of color and its impact on employees helped me change a "blue and gray" organization into one that allowed an expanded use of color in the workplace.

How does landscape design benefit my clients? This continues to be an important question. I know that a layout that meets clients' needs helps them function better. I hope it encourages their interaction with nature. I hope it renews their spirits and gives them a keen sense of being alive. I hope it helps them connect to their greater purpose and inner excellence. Whether a garden is an idyllic setting or rows of crops, it elementally connects us to nature and to our planet. When my hands are in the dirt, someone once suggested to me, that is where I will find wisdom. Is this a provable statement? Perhaps not yet, but it feels right to me as a lifelong, devoted gardener.

This book also includes a chapter about construction and working with contractors. Oddly, this is a rarely touched subject, but it is a topic my clients ask about frequently. I wrote this chapter after creating a database of research with a variety of landscape contractors as a resource. The chapter also benefits from the knowledge I gained during my interior design career and working with many talented architects. The process of designing, creating working drawings and specifications, bidding, and dealing with the in-construction period was one I repeated incessantly in that work.

The last chapter in the book had to be one of celebration and being in the garden. While garden parties allow friends and relatives to share a garden, the open garden allows fellow gardeners to share the experience. I have opened my garden many times to such organizations as the Hardy Plant Society of Oregon and Master Gardeners, and to The Garden Conservancy Open Days Program. While I feel compelled to have my garden in its best condition, I do not believe that a garden must be perfect or that everything must be complete to invite visitors in. In fact, if construction is going on, so much the better. Open gardens are teaching opportunities. They offer an occasion for visitors to learn more about gardening. After gardening for about forty years, I confess I will never know all there is to know about gardening. However, I take delight in the ceaseless curiosity and the valued friendships of fellow gardeners everywhere.

In a well-thought-out border, each plant is visible against the others, will grow in the existing conditions, and with minimal pruning will work within the bounds of the space. Design by Lauren Hall-Behrens, Lilyvilla Gardens.

Beginning the Design of Your Garden

1

Why Design a Garden?

Think about the projects you do in your life. Sew a dress, build a house, take a trip—these activities usually succeed because of the planning you do before the experience. Planning and design are intention and purpose. They give a project significance.

Some people think design is too costly. Others think it too esoteric. Still others find it intimidating. However you think of design, it is indispensable to achieving a successful garden. A well-thought-out and carefully planned design will benefit many aspects of your life, including your physical health, your emotional well-being, and, yes, even your pocketbook.

The love of nature and plants often motivates us to fancy a garden that will improve and organize our surroundings. If you think garden design is all about the plants, think again. It is so much more. Design is an intangible. For that reason, people casually apply the word *design* as though it does not take much thought at all. Design is a creative endeavor enhanced by an open mind and a desire to go beyond humdrum.

In general, people find the term *design* ambiguous but understand the word *planning*. The two words are commonly interchanged as though they are synonyms. They are distinct. Design and planning embrace two intentions; you cannot experience one without the other. Planning precedes design. It is the time to prepare for design; to gather, review, and scrutinize information; to examine and define

What you will learn:

- the value of a garden design
- things to consider before beginning the design process

We see *Primula* every spring, yet because we are color starved at the end of winter, it is hard to bypass. Author's garden.

direction. Planning provides the basis to make decisions during design. Without planning, design is a little like trying to pull a rabbit out of a hat. It only works for skilled magicians.

A designed garden is as different from an undesigned garden as night is from day. An undesigned garden is created without much forethought about how layout and design integrate with the architecture of the home and its interior. A garden without design is often nothing but ill-conceived placements of foundation plants and turf, misaligned concrete, and the occasional swing set with a possible fence to, thankfully, hide some portion of it. A designed garden, alternatively, relates hand in glove with the architecture it surrounds. A designed garden succeeds because its planning considers the design as more than window dressing. A garden conceived through the design process is more than the sum of its parts.

Planning *plus* design makes a difference not only in the efficacy of moving about a garden and using its space, but also in the visual and emotional impact of being in the garden. Research shows that beyond the obvious aesthetic improvements, garden design provides psychological, physiological, sociological, and financial advantages. Whatever the current knowledge, we know that design is about purposeful, meaningful, and innovative placement.

Installing a garden with no deliberation is more expensive than taking the time to plan and design in advance. If you do not spend the time to understand what plants need in the way of general care or placement, you reduce the chance that they will thrive. Take the time to evaluate landscape materials, your property, how you move from one place to another, how you will use your property to its best effect. If you have high expectations, little knowledge, and a limited budget, expanding your knowledge will extend your budget and increase your degree of success.

A tree in a naturalized setting is a beautiful union of leaves, branches, trunk, and roots. Home of Maryellen Hockensmith and Michael McCulloch, AIA.

Beyond a hobby

"Historically gardens were used to discuss and evaluate society. Now most gardens are a hobbyist pursuit. They can be both," declares journalist Corinne Julius in the Royal Horticultural Society's publication *The Garden* (2007). Should we consider gardening as more than a hobby? Could there be more to a garden than gardening?

Because garden planning and design involve more than a casual series of decisions, individuals around the globe are asking the question, What is the meaning of a garden? Those who champion this investigation are on a quest to understand whether creating a garden is an art or a craft. Indeed, they purport that designing a garden goes beyond the plants. "You wouldn't go to a Mozart opera and talk about what fun he must have had putting all those dots so nicely on the page. But that's what we do with gardening," asserts garden writer Stephen Anderton (2009). Clearly, this intellectual pursuit may not appeal to everyone. Critics of this more esoteric approach suggest that emotions should drive the creation of a garden. They believe that one should reflect on what one finds appealing rather than dialogue about it. Perhaps this quandary merits debate as a means to expand our knowledge. What do we have to lose through discussion? Is the creation of a garden art, craft, or science? Perhaps it is all three, bound together as a tree trunk is joined to its roots and leaves.

How *do* we resolve what makes one garden well designed and another hopelessly tacky? Is the beauty in gardens, as in art, in the eye of the beholder? One thing seems certain. When we apply a skillful process of design to a garden, there will likely be greater agreement that the garden is beautiful.

Gardens for health

After reading the words of John Stilgoe, a professor of environmental studies at Harvard University, I recognized that the common view of design might be in a state of transformation. He said, "There is emerging medical evidence that the aesthetic end of landscaping turns out to be founded on medical reasons. You will feel better emotionally in a garden" (Colman 2003).

Indeed healing gardens are on the increase. Studies of patients in garden settings, particularly related to hospitalization, give us some valuable input about how people respond emotionally to a garden. Research reveals that patients who have a view of nature or natural elements recover more quickly, require less medication, and have fewer complications after surgery than those who do not.

And if healing gardens help sick people heal faster, how do gardens affect healthy people? Francine Halberg, MD, a radiation oncologist at the Marin Cancer Institute in Greenbrae, California, said of the healing garden there, "It offers a visual solace, a connection to nature, and a sense of peace. The spirit of the garden is growth and renewal, where one can feel connected instead of isolated." Deborah Burt, a volunteer on the healing environment committee at the Children's Hospital and Health Center in San Diego, California, said, "Nature heals the heart and soul, and those are things the doctors can't help. That's what this garden is all about—healing the parts of yourself that the doctors can't" ("Healing gardens," 2002).

Perhaps we might deduce that a garden could prevent sickness or heal parts of ourselves before we are able to detect disease. Indeed, documented investigation began as early as 1937 and is ongoing. Myriads of interactions occur inside our bodies every second. Researchers have proven that messages sent to the brain through vision have an effect on hormone production, autonomic body function, and ultimately our state of health (see, for example, Rossi 2004, pp. 68–69). It seems that what we see translates to every cell in our bodies. Perhaps if what we see has a positive effect on our psyche, that is what translates to our cells. So too, could a negative view affect us negatively. I always knew that well-designed spaces have a positive effect on people, but I never dreamed it might be something as vital as this.

Yet disheartening studies by Oliver R. W. Pergams and Patricia A. Zaradic (2008) showed that Americans are staying indoors more and more, by a considerable factor. This is particularly true of our children. Environmentally disconnected children equal a disaster waiting to happen. Pergams and Zaradic call the love of television and computer screens videophilia and write that "videophilia has been shown to be a cause of obesity, lack of socialization, attention disorders, and poor academic performance." Gardens are an opportunity to reconnect our children and ourselves to nature. This in turn holds the promise of inspiring us to care for our environment.

Gardening may not heal a sore back, but surely there is an emotional connection supporting the gardener's spirit. When I journey through my garden on an early spring day and discover the teensiest of buds, there is an unexplainable soaring in my soul that is enough to help me slog through another week of gray and rainy weather.

Numerous philosophers emphasize the importance of living in the moment and overcoming the obstacles of an overactive mind (Tolle 1999). If you have ever tried counting sheep at night because you are plagued with a to-do list running around in your mind, you have an understanding of what this means. Studies show that when we observe great beauty in nature, it quiets the chatter that is always bubbling away in our brain. Seconds later, our mind starts to think about it rather than merely experience

At Good Samaritan Hospital in Portland, Oregon, a garden invites staff and patients alike to experience the healing environment of nature. Legacy Good Samaritan Hospital, Stenzel Healing Garden.

it. We say things like, "It takes my breath away" or "It leaves me speechless." Sound familiar?

Do we inherently seek beauty to quiet our mind? To what extent does nature nurture us? Who among us would not benefit from a reduction in stress level? Are our eyes and brains capable of autopilot stress reduction? Can Mother Nature's beauty succor and sustain us, and reduce our stress? Radical concepts! It is common knowledge that when we reduce stress, we improve our physical well-being. Many people also believe that a quiet mind allows the opportunity for inspiration and creativity. A healthy body and a muse—what else does a well-designed garden offer us?

A personal statement

In a garden, we have the possibility of expressing our culture, our history, and the very essence of ourselves. Gardens can and should be a personal statement. Why would we want to have the same grinning gnome as our neighbor when there is so much that is unique to us? Does it make sense to duplicate that garden bauble that is so *irresistible* if it has nothing to do with our own personal experience and background?

We need to get over our fear of doing something original because the design police might come after us. If we follow sound planning practices and tried-and-true design principles, we can be confident that what we create will work. Then give the raspberries to disapproving critics. Creating a garden brings a tremendous amount of satisfaction when it is not only full of a gratifying collection of plants but also enriched with our own philosophy and memories.

Beginning Your Garden

Assume the design of your garden is a project. Before you begin a project, you define its scope. How can you create a successful design if you do not establish parameters? Consider it garden goal setting. It is no different from preparing a holiday dinner. You decide on recipes, make a grocery list, polish the silver, assemble each recipe, and serve the meal. With no planning, you would have your head in the refrigerator wondering what to serve.

Nature's beauty provides inspiration for our own gardens. Note the simplicity of plant material and massing of plants.

It is so easy to allow those little photosynthesizing vernal gems to sway our good sense. One walk through a nursery and we have a cartful of primroses before we can blink our eyes. We daydream about that blissful alfresco meal in the garden as we look out onto an incoherent and chaotic yard. Thinking beyond "I need some petunias in my garden this summer" brings greater rewards than a passel of brightly colored posies. Maybe what we need is Plantaholics Anonymous to keep us on track to meet our garden design goals.

The garden's context

We begin our list of objectives by looking at a broad perspective or the big picture of our garden setting. What is the context of our garden, and why is it important?

Study the location of your future garden. If you lived on a country estate, would you design a garden suited to a downtown condominium? The largess of a country estate would dictate a very different type of garden from what would suit the fishbowl of a tiny condominium space. The style of each may also be different, dictating more garden dissimilarity. Having a home in the middle of a forest is vastly different from having one's neighbor 10 feet away with a 50-foot fir tree. Consider a garden that has fire-retardant characteristics if you live near or in the woods.

Study your environs. Can you borrow a view from your neighbors, a park, or a forest? Imagine how your garden could harmonize with its surroundings. Is there a particular style or type of garden you like? Do you want the mood of the garden to be quiet and meditative or lively and entertaining? Do you have an existing garden to renovate or a blank slate with oodles of mud?

Complement to the built environment

Any good garden design should complement the architecture and interior space it surrounds. How many programs do we watch or attend that tout the importance of having a garden to enhance the curb appeal of a home? So too do we consider the value of our home when we plan for landscaping.

Whether a home is in an urban, suburban, or country setting affects the design of the garden. The closer the neighbors, the more the impact they will have on a garden. Issues of privacy and views tend to be more critical with a zero-lot-line neighbor (a house having one of its exterior walls directly on the property line) than if the nearest neighbor is a mile away. In an urban setting, people often walk to a park or a restaurant. In the suburbs those amenities may be equally convenient, or nearly so. Out in the country it may be more important to create your own amenities to minimize travel and enhance the usability of your property. The farther you are from your neighbor, the more self-reliant you may need to be. Perhaps a toolshed gains importance, as do places to compost yard waste.

Location, location, location

Any real estate agent will tell you that "location, location, location" is of prime importance in buying or selling a house. Too often, I see people make decisions about their garden without considering how their home fits into its local area—particularly their neighborhood. It is unusual to see owners overdo a garden. Frequently, owners install a garden below par for their house.

Keep your landscaping within the context of your neighborhood. Consider the street trees and the general ambience of the homes. Is it an old neighborhood or new? An older neighborhood might mean neighbors who have opinions about what you do in your garden—and are willing to share them. Is it a wide or narrow street, a cul-de-sac, or a main drag? The speed at which traffic passes by your home will likely affect the design of your garden. Is it a gated community with improved security? Depending on the level of safety, this could reduce your budget for security around your home.

Gated or not, many communities dictate requirements in the form of CC and Rs (covenants, conditions, and restrictions) with which owners must comply. The owner must usually present his or her garden design to an established committee for review and approval. The process is intended to uphold a level of quality to maintain home value, although some owners will still complain about restrictions. If you place a gnome, a pink flamingo, or a cactus in your garden, it could raise a red flag for additional scrutiny by unsympathetic committee members.

In addition to possible CC and Rs, local codes and possible easements may apply to your design. An easement usually allows an agency or entity access to or across your property. For example, a utility company may need to place equipment on your property. Every community has a building code that dictates things like the height of a fence, the setback (the distance between a structure and a street, sidewalk, or property line) of a new structure, or the type of tree planted in the parking strip. It is wise to meet with a local code official and review the laws that could affect your garden design before you complete the design.

You may discover that you have an easement on your property. This information would normally be contained in the papers that accompany purchase of your property and documented in public records, which are accessible through your local government. A permit is often required for certain types of construction—for instance, a swimming pool or gazebo.

While the permit cost and process might be something to gnash your teeth over, permits are intended to guarantee the health, safety, and well-being of the public, in addition to contributing to the community coffers. The agency where you meet with the code official is usually where you would also obtain a building permit. If your home is located in a historic district, you may have additional constraints. A design review committee may be required to review and approve your design as part of the permitting process.

Impact of your health

Remember to consider your age and/or your ability to access a garden when planning a garden. Common solutions for wheelchair-bound gardeners are to raise the level of the garden in the form of raised beds and to create ramps rather than stairs. Fencing may be required for the protection of toddlers. It is a good idea to review the requirements set forth by the Americans with Disabilities Act (ADA) when considering the accessibility of a garden. Even if no one in your household currently requires special means of access, visitors with a disability (or even you in a temporarily disabled state) would be grateful to be able to get to the front door and around the garden. Consider your ability to maintain a garden as you age. This may determine the sort of plants you select, the amount of lawn you install, or the type of paving you choose.

Be mindful of the allergies and asthma of the home's occupants when planning a garden. Windborne pollen and a plethora of fragrances can affect a twitchy nose. Asthma resulting from poor air quality is on the upswing. Some plants have a greater capacity to improve air quality. A plant's sap can cause a skin reaction. Poisonous plants have a varying degree of impact on small children and pets. Even plants that attract cats could be an issue for those allergic to them.

Sustainability

The issue of sustainability is in the mainstream conscience. Do you know what sustainability truly means? While we are still waiting for the best definition, the term "cradle to cradle" coined by author and architect William McDonough (McDonough and Braungart 2002) applies to being mindful of the origins and final destinations of any given material we deign to use. All of us are responsible for what we use on and from our planet. Now is the time to begin a lifelong habit as good earth stewards. To gardeners goes the challenge, "Never mind your thumb, how green is your heart?"

America has a sacred cow: the lawn. You might get your knickers in a knot about losing some lawn, but when you stop and think about what it takes to maintain it in pristine condition, is it really worth it? Lawns are colossal water guzzlers. Maintenance services usually use chemicals in the form of fertilizers, herbicides, and pesticides to get that perfect shade of green to which we are all so accustomed.

One of my clients and I had a disquieting discussion about her neighborhood, where virtually everyone could afford a landscape maintenance service to keep the lawns as pristine as a golf course. When we discussed the fact that so many services use toxic chemicals to achieve that well-manicured effect, she shared a personal experience. On walks around her neighborhood, she found large quantities of dead bees on the sidewalk. We concluded that there might be a correlation between the use of toxic chemicals and the demise of the bees. If ever there was a good reason to use nontoxic garden solutions, this is one.

More and more businesses are providing sustainable alternatives to unsustainable practices and products. Prices for these new options will come down.

Finally, we will have no excuses to avoid thinking globally and acting locally. Be curious about what is out there. Green-conscious business owners are developing new and improved methods to create and to maintain our gardens. Take responsibility for checking out what is available and apply that information during the planning of your garden design.

What to keep

Garden designers are often asked how much of an existing garden should be kept, rearranged, or changed. If you have inherited an existing garden and can bear the wait, it is useful to sit on it for a year. Take the time to document the plants that come and go during each season, unless there is some urgency to get started sooner. You may discover spring- or autumn-blooming bulbs that would not be visible if you moved into your home the preceding winter. Having a blank slate or a newly constructed home usually means getting some landscaping completed as soon as possible. The consequences of waiting tend to be a boatload of laundry every time it rains and cleaning the muddy feet of every child and pet that ventures outdoors, not to mention your own.

When to install

It is not necessary to install a garden project all at one time. Things must be done in a particular order, but installing your garden in phases may work better for any number of reasons. Budget comes to mind as a big reason for phased installation of a garden. Contractor availability can also drive the scheduling of some portions of garden installation. Often the time of year will affect how much of a garden we install at a given time. It is impossible to install utilities and underground work if the ground is frozen. Stonework and precast paving can be set in place during cold weather if the prep work is possible to do or installed earlier. Even concrete can be poured under certain circumstances during cold or wet weather. You can install deciduous bare-root plants and prune some plants before the end of winter while the plants are still dormant if the ground is not frozen.

What You Need to Know to Get Started

You will need to determine several things before you begin planning your garden. Who will make decisions and control the budget? Do you have a deadline or need a fixed schedule? Get these matters settled now, because waiting until later could result in an unpleasant situation or delay your project.

Who's on first?

Decide in advance how decisions will be made on your project, because there will be a lot of them. If one person will be making all the decisions, it is not much of an issue aside from the need to make the decisions in a timely way. When multiple decision makers have equal authority, it is very important to have a prior arrangement. Perhaps you draw straws for each decision. Perhaps you agree that each person will make a certain range of decisions. However it is decided, arranging in advance how conflicts will be resolved can prevent a divorce, a longer-than-expected installation, or a contractor walking off your job.

It may also help to understand how individuals make decisions. If experience says to you that one person may agonize over finishes for a month, plan to add another month to the schedule. Do not let decision making derail your project.

Handling the purse strings

The amount of money available for your project influences its scope. Do some homework up front to get some idea of what things cost. Nothing is more frustrating than developing a wonderful design you are in a hurry to install and not having enough money to get the job done. If you are working with a professional designer or architect, he or she will usually remind you that your grand ideas may get you a grand invoice. If you are phasing work because funds are not available all at once, you may be able to include certain items in the design that may not have been possible otherwise.

Having an approximate idea of how long you will own your home will help you decide how much to spend on a garden. If you purchase your home for

A stone wall installation shows the base of concrete masonry units with stone mortared onto its face. Assuming that the weather allows for mixing mortar and that any excavation work has already been completed, a contractor could install this portion of work even in winter. Design and construction by McQuiggins Inc.

quick turnover, curb appeal will be more important than meeting every functional desire. However, if you are in for the long haul, a larger budget may be more reasonable, especially if there are things on the wish list that would greatly improve your quality of life.

How you plan to use your garden will directly affect your cash outlay, perhaps dramatically so. Dedicated gardeners and owners who do a great deal of outdoor entertaining will usually have a significantly higher budget than a single businessperson who is out of town much of the time. Owners with teenagers are more inclined to consider a swimming pool than are families with toddlers. How you choose to use your garden will correlate with how much you will spend and with the garden's overall design.

It is normal to see clients' eyes roll back into their heads when landscape professionals explain the cost of landscaping. Here are recommendations about adding landscaping to your property:

- The American Society of Landscape Architects (ASLA) recommends that owners install a garden that is worth approximately 10 percent of the home's value.

- The American Nursery and Landscape Association states that landscaping can bring a recovery value of 100 to 200 percent when it is time to sell your home.

- The Gallup Organization says landscaping can add between 7 and 15 percent to a home's value.

Most people have specific functions in mind for their gardens, requiring some amount of paving or a water feature that usually raises the cost to the percentage recommended by the ASLA. If the house is on 5 acres, the recommended percentage may apply only to the area closer to the house, but there should be some consideration of how much property surrounds the house. Less land allows landscaping dollars to go a lot farther.

Establishing a schedule

Most projects have some sort of schedule, even if only in the owner's head. This schedule might affect decision making—if time is tight, quick decisions will help you stay on schedule. Do research. It will help you develop a realistic schedule. If you do not know how long it takes to install garden lighting, call an

TASK	WEEK 1	WEEK 2	WEEK 3	WEEK 4	WEEK 5	WEEK 6
Collect photos, gather data	• • • • •	• • • • •				
Preliminary decisions		• • • • • •				
Measure and photograph site	• •					
Draw base plan	• • •					
Develop concepts on plan			• • •	• • •		
Review paving materials, plants, decisions			• • • • • •			
Get preliminary costs; review budget				• • • • •		
Prepare final master plan					• • •	• •
Review list of contractors and qualifications			• • • • •			

Create a schedule by working backward from the date you want your project completed. If you find you have bypassed your current date, you know your schedule is not realistic. You will need extra help to get the work done, or you may need to change something to reduce lead time.

electrician who installs garden lighting. Tell him you are developing a schedule. Ask him for assistance. Let the electrician know you will call him when the time comes to obtain bids for the project.

If the garden must be completed by a specific date, it is a good idea to plan backward to establish a realistic schedule. Identify the date you can begin the installation of your garden and your completion date. Calculate the amount of time in between those two dates. Next, make a list of your tasks. Calculate how much time each task will take and add them together. Create a bar chart with this information.

If the time needed to do all of your tasks exceeds the amount of time you have available, you need to make some decisions. Determine if there are tasks that can overlap or if extra hands can complete some tasks more quickly. If this does not help, you will need to either extend your deadline or eliminate or change one or more of the tasks. It is especially helpful to calculate your schedule in terms of hours rather than days. Then when you need to calculate the cost of someone's labor, you can take his or her hourly rate, multiply it by the number of hours you have projected, and presto—you have an estimated labor cost.

Now that you have given some thought to your objectives in designing your garden, compile a scope statement—a list of general directions. No specifics are required at this point unless you want them included. To demonstrate what a scope statement might look like, I've written one for a hypothetical garden. This garden will serve as an illustration of each new development explored in the chapters to come.

Designing the Hypothetical Garden

The Scope Statement

The hypothetical garden exists only in my mind and on the pages of this book. The garden surrounds an average ranch-style house on an average-size urban lot. The siding is a combination of painted wood clapboard and stone; the hip roof is covered with dark shingles. The windows are primarily horizontal in character with dark bronze frames. The "owner" will keep the existing driveway. A concrete step exists at the front and back door. Either of these can be kept or replaced to make the design work. New paths are needed to get around the house. A fence surrounds the entire back of the property, and neighboring attributes include a stand of trees, among other things. One of the two trees in the front will remain. The parking strip is not part of the redesign. It is already parking friendly, relates well to those walking by, and contains drought-tolerant plants. The home is in a residential neighborhood with average foot and vehicle traffic.

For this hypothetical situation, I want a garden that

- is sustainable and environmentally responsible
- has contemporary style
- offers a mix of quiet areas and entertaining spaces
- has space to grow food all year
- includes hobby space
- has a space for the family pet
- allows for evening activities
- accommodates all guests, including those with physical challenges

Documenting Your Site

2

Assessing Your Site: What to Record and Why

Even if you can recall everything you have ever heard, read, or seen, documenting your site at the beginning of planning your garden is crucial. For some this can be an easy process; for others, quite an exercise. Measuring around existing trees and shrubs, in particular, can be more difficult than you might imagine. Even more demanding is measuring a steep slope with existing plants.

The more challenging your property, the more you may want to consider engaging the services of a surveyor. The property that my spouse and I own is half gently sloped or flat, and half a precipitous ravine. We have preferred to hire hearty souls with survey equipment to rummage around the ravine and to obtain measurements—especially of the degree of slope. Their efforts have been worth every nickel spent. Besides, sticky, thorny Himalayan blackberries grow down there.

You may have poison ivy, poison oak, poison sumac, or—quelle horreur!—kudzu, or possibly all four plus blackberries, in which case you deserve a great deal of sympathy. Your preference may be to remain unscathed by those herbaceous brutes. However, a surveyor may request that you provide due diligence in the form of plant abatement if the growth you have is excessively prohibitive. Anytime you have invasive nonnative plants, it is important to eliminate them anyway. Only cut back native plants as necessary for access. The point is that whether you hire someone else to measure your property or

What you will learn:

- how to assess your site
- how to understand and use architectural elements in your design
- how to document and measure your house and site
- how to create your existing conditions plan

The borrowed view through this hedge visually expands the garden's space. Garden of Doudou Bayol, Saint Rémy-de-Provence, France.

measure it yourself, you need sufficient access so that your measurements will be accurate.

In addition to measurements, you will need to assess other aspects of your home and site. Your site survey, as the process is sometimes known, begins with several essential objectives:

- **Determining your property's overall size and shape.** Notice any changes in elevation. Is your home on a hill or in a valley? How steep are any slopes around your home?
- **Getting to know your house.** Determine its height and shape. Is your house rectangular, L-shaped, or angular? Is your house a split-level? Does it have a daylight basement?
- **Relating your house to your property.** Where is your house relative to the street? How close is your house to property lines and neighbors?

Getting this information on paper is just the beginning of documenting all of the features that will influence your design. You also need to pay attention to things like where the sun sets, your soil fertility, the prevailing wind direction, and the impact on your garden of the neighbor's row of trees near your property line. These bits of information and more will give you a strong foundation for the design of your garden.

Document the quirky elements peculiar to your property, such as the place where the deer graze, where the water table is a little higher, or where it is just a little breezier. Discover the microclimates of your property, small areas that are affected in varying ways by exposure and drainage. Each side of your house has varying degrees of sun and wind. Other elements, like a concrete sidewalk, can affect the soil pH. The more complete your documentation, the better your garden plan and design will be.

Architectural Documentation

Did you know your house talks to you? Every detail and nuance of your architecture is a language spoken by your house. Now is the time to notice that language and determine what your house is communicating to you. It is important to note other structures and their details in addition to your house. This information will offer direction and maybe even inspiration for your garden design.

Your home's style

There are a myriad of architectural styles out there. It is useful to have a basic understanding of your home's style. Your house might have a single unadulterated style or it might be a combination of styles. It is all in the details. Those details may not fit neatly into any category. However, do not underestimate the value of distinguishing architectural details. Even houses that appear to be architecturally indistinct have important features to which you should pay attention.

One of my clients had a cottage that she considered indistinct in style. However, unusual brackets supported the extended roof along the east and west sides of her house. I used this cue to design details within her garden's hardscape. Sometimes windows have an arched top. Bringing that same arch out into the landscape as the top to a pergola or the curve in a patio marries garden to house.

The drawings shown here will help you understand the nature of architectural details and demonstrate how the style of your home can influence garden design decisions.

Note the elements that are particular to your home on the House Style Worksheet. You will refer to this information later during the planning process.

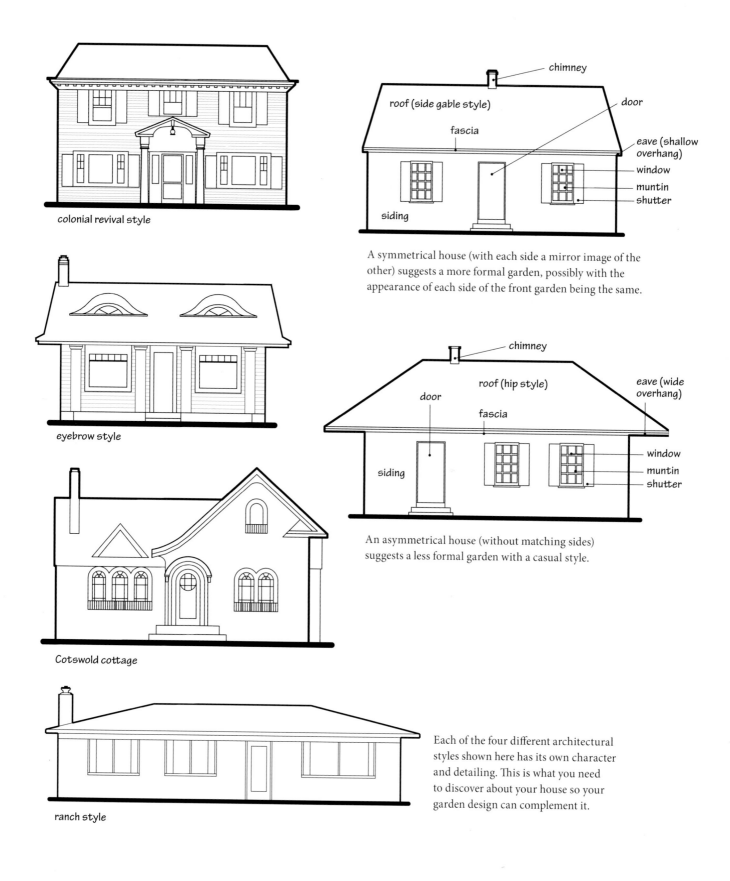

colonial revival style

eyebrow style

Cotswold cottage

ranch style

chimney

roof (side gable style)

fascia

door

eave (shallow overhang)

window

muntin

shutter

siding

A symmetrical house (with each side a mirror image of the other) suggests a more formal garden, possibly with the appearance of each side of the front garden being the same.

chimney

roof (hip style)

door

fascia

eave (wide overhang)

siding

window

muntin

shutter

An asymmetrical house (without matching sides) suggests a less formal garden with a casual style.

Each of the four different architectural styles shown here has its own character and detailing. This is what you need to discover about your house so your garden design can complement it.

House Style Worksheet

Number of stories

☐ one ☐ two ☐ split-level ☐ more than two

Roof pitch

☐ flat or slight pitch ☐ long and low ☐ high ☐ average

Roof type

☐ gable ☐ hip ☐ gambrel ☐ flat

☐ shed (a sloped roof with no gable, hip, or gambrel) ☐ combination of one or more styles

Eaves

☐ deep ☐ shallow ☐ none

Chimney

☐ central ☐ not central ☐ none

Siding

☐ wood clapboard ☐ vinyl ☐ aluminum ☐ vertical wood

☐ tongue and groove ☐ brick ☐ stone ☐ stucco ☐ half-timber

Profile

☐ long and low ☐ higher than wide ☐ width and height approximately equal

Layout

☐ symmetrical, rectangular ☐ asymmetrical, rectangular ☐ L-shaped ☐ U-shaped

Window style

☐ double-hung ☐ picture ☐ sliding ☐ bow or bay

☐ dormer ☐ round or angled top ☐ custom shape

☐ custom glass (stained or three-dimensional)

☐ combination—list _____

Door style

☐ solid, plain, no glass ☐ solid, ornamental carving, no glass ☐ plain, half glass lite

☐ ornamental carving, half glass lite ☐ full glass lite ☐ sliding glass ☐ Dutch door

☐ combination—list _____

Door material

☐ natural wood ☐ painted wood ☐ painted steel

Garage

☐ attached ☐ detached Other _____

Additional notes can include details such as window orientation (horizontal versus vertical, or perhaps they are square but grouped in a linear manner) and whether the windows have muntins (horizontal or vertical strips of wood or metal creating smaller panes within a window frame) that create intriguing shapes. Do interesting brackets support the roof overhang? Is there a round or square trim element? What is the overall character of your roofline: is it simple, or a complex array of peaks and valleys?

Note whether the front of the house has a formal symmetry or is asymmetrical. Take particular note of the color and materials of your house, because they will be important design factors when selecting materials for your garden. Your house may not be whispering all of these clues in your ear, but they are available to you visually. Translate what you see into hints for design direction.

Other structures

The details of other structures in addition to your house, such as a shed or detached garage, are important to pay attention to. How are other structures positioned in relationship to your house: perpendicular to it? at an angle? How noticeable are they in relationship to your house? Do they hide the location of your front door? If so, how does a visitor find it? Can you easily find the address numbers on your house?

Perhaps you have an existing arbor or gazebo that you may want to feature for its distinguishing characteristics. Note its relative importance in relationship to the details and placement of your house. Does the toolshed have a pleasing character or would you rather not see it? Does it look like your house or does it appear completely different? It may be necessary to disguise a structure if it is completely out of character with your house and it is not feasible to replace or relocate it.

Connecting the exterior with the interior

You cross a threshold each time you leave your house to go outdoors. A threshold is merely a line in space that exists while the door is open. It connects the walls of the house on either side. Why should this line dictate a change in character from the inside to the outside? If you use red, black, and yellow inside, consider bringing those colors outside to tie the interior and exterior together.

If you have modern furniture inside a modern home, why would you consider having a Victorian-style garden outside? Think about it in relationship to how you dress. Is your waistline the Maginot Line between your upper and lower halves? Of course not. We coordinate our shirts and blouses with our trousers and skirts, and our accessories with everything—not just what is above our waist. So too should we design our gardens with not only the exterior style of our homes in mind but also the interior. We look out our windows often, particularly during winter. How would it feel looking at a simple Asian sculpture through the window just past a highly ornamental Louis XIV chair inside? It is not that an eclectic approach is not plausible. However, we need to pay attention to basic design elements to make such a concept work. Maintain continuity of design within your entire environment, inside to outside.

Measuring Your House and Property

Now you are going to start getting some measurements down on paper and begin your existing conditions plan (also sometimes called a site plan or site survey). This section describes the tools to use, how to determine the scale, and how to take the measurements, whether you're measuring level ground or a slope.

Measuring tools

Before you begin to measure, you should have these tools on hand:

- At least one flexible measuring tape, 100 feet in length
- A 25- or 30-foot steel measuring tape to measure around structures or shorter distances
- If you plan to do the measuring by yourself, a stake or two to provide points to which you can return for repetitive measuring, such as during the process known as triangulation, which I explain later. Bamboo or metal BBQ skewers make good stakes—they are easy to poke into the ground and leave no visible hole after removal.
- A level, to determine degree of slope
- A yardstick, also helpful in working with slope
- A compass, one of each kind: to find north and to draw circles and arcs
- An architect's scale or ruler, to transfer site measurements to scale on paper
- Grid paper, which is more helpful than plain paper because the lines and squares guide your hand when drawing
- A pencil with an eraser
- Spray chalk, sometimes useful to mark a

Some basic tools for measuring property include (clockwise from left) grid paper, a pencil, a compass, a calculator, a rolling measuring tool, a quiver of stakes, spray chalk, a 100-foot measuring tape, an architect's scale, and a steel measuring tape.

reference point or grid lines to transfer locations to grid paper. Use chalk, not paint, to minimize your carbon footprint; it is also possible to use something like flour in a bag that has a small hole to dispense the flour.

- A camera, since photos to which you can refer save time—unless you prefer to run outside each time you cannot remember something. I find that photographs of key areas are good reminders to address something I might forget. Photos will help you note crucial details, such as the fact that one step is shorter than the other steps (creating the need for more caution than normal) or the sill height of a door's threshold in relationship to the ground level (important when deciding the thickness of paving material).

Determining scale

Before you begin to write down your dimensions, decide on the scale of your plan. Your paper may have a ¼-inch grid. The ¼ inch can equal whatever length you select. You may decide that the ¼ inch should equal 5 feet in order to fit your entire property on one piece of paper. Alternatively, you might choose to have each ¼-inch square equal 1 square foot. Express this scale as ¼″ = 1′0″, meaning that every ¼ inch equals 1 foot. If you use ¼-inch grid paper, that scale may work well for your plan. If you do not need to record much in the way of detail, you might be able to record your existing conditions at ⅛-inch scale.

Recording measurements

I find that the easiest way to document property is to begin by measuring around the house. Use a measuring tape to measure each side of your house and its nooks and crannies. Write down the measurements and then draw your house to scale on your grid paper with a ruler or architect's scale. If you allow each square on your grid paper to represent 1 square foot, it is simply a matter of counting off one square per foot or using the ruler or scale to do it more quickly. Note the location of each window and door. Locate the hose bibs, HVAC (heating, ventilating, and air conditioning) unit, and other utilities attached to or adjacent to the house. Situate steps and sidewalks adjacent to or attached to the house.

The next step in documentation is to draw the property line around your house. In order to do that, you first need to find the markers placed by county surveyors, which might be difficult. If you find it impossible, hire a surveyor to do a "point survey" for you for as many points as you need to complete the property line around your house. Once each point is located, measure the distance between them and note your measurements. Take note that the sides of your property line may not come together at 90-degree angles and the lines between them may not be perfectly straight. If you live along a curving street or a cul-de-sac, chances are the line between your front property markers is an arc or even a wavy line. Property maps are available in most jurisdictions. Whether obtained online or through a visit to your local agency recorder, they may give you additional valuable information, such as easements, that you will want to document.

Once you have drawn your house and measured your property line, you need to establish how the house is situated on the property in relation to the property line. It would be unusual for your house to be parallel to all sides of your property line. Without traditional surveyors' equipment, the most accurate way to locate the house within its property line is to triangulate points on your house in relationship to property line intersectional points. Triangulation is a method based on simple geometry that has you finding one unknown point on a triangle. Here is how to do it:

1. Select two points on your house (we will call them points A and B).
2. Measure from each of those two points out to a single point you want to locate on your drawing (point C, which could be a property line intersectional point, but I'll use a tree for the purpose of illustration). Record the distance from point A to point C and call it X. Record the distance from point B to point C and call it Y.

3. On your plan, draw an arc from point A using your drawing compass at the X distance.
4. Draw another arc from point B at the Y distance.
5. Voila! Where they intersect will be point C on your plan.

If you continue to do this with all other objects on the property, you will locate all the important items around which you will need to work. If your house is too far from some points on your property, use two new points to which you have already measured to locate additional items. You can create temporary points using spray chalk or a stake, if

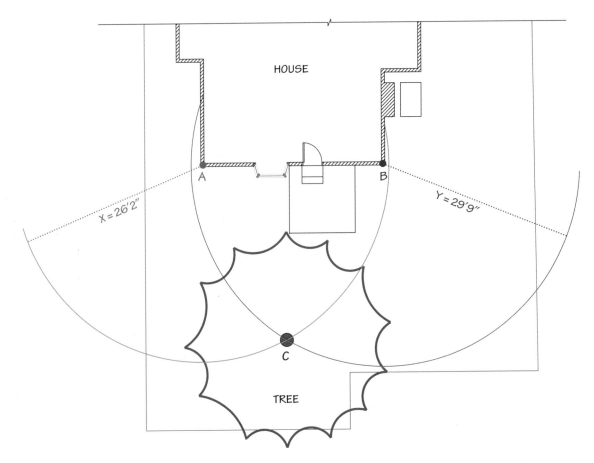

This is how you would triangulate a third point (C, the tree) from two points on the house (A and B).

necessary. However, it is best to use another permanently located object, such as a storage shed, patio, or post.

There is one other way to measure the location of major objects between your house and the property line: a simple linear system that works well for small yards with minor changes in elevation (less than 1 foot). The linear method may also be easier to use if you have many plants or small items around which to measure. Here is what you do:

1. Take your longest tape measure and lay it out straight on the ground, perpendicular from your house to your property line (assuming the tape extends that far).
2. From each object that you wish to locate on your plan, measure back perpendicular to your tape measure. Note the distance from your house and from the object. Add the object to your drawing in its measured location. Continue to do this until all of the major objects have been located.

Documenting slope

You will need to know your grade if you are going to have a ramp or stairs in order to move around a sloped area of your garden. It is also important to note that on a plan the distance of the slope is distorted—the steeper the slope, the more distorted. For instance, in the birds-eye plan view, the distance between points on a slope may show up as only 10 feet when in actual land distance it is 15 feet. This makes a difference when you are calculating how many plants you will need to keep your slope from eroding. Note that not all slopes are equal. One slope may have a continuous gradual decline while another may level out for a bit and then fall more steeply.

To measure slope, you can use a level, a stake, and a yardstick to do a very simplistic version. Remember that the steeper your slope, the shorter the level will need to be in order to use a yardstick. Vary the length of the level to suit your situation. Here is the method:

1. Find the high point on the slope. Hold your level out from the high point over a lower point until the reading shows that it is level.
2. Measure the difference in height between the level and the low point with the yardstick and record it.
3. Mark the low point with your stake. Note the length of your level. Is it 1 foot, 2 feet, or 4 feet?
4. Beginning from your stake, repeat steps 1 and 2 out toward the next low point.
5. Continue this process until you have reached your property line or the bottom of the slope.

Once you have your measurements, create a drawing similar to the one on page 34. Find the total amount of rise by adding together all the height differences you recorded. Find the total amount of run by adding together the lengths of the levels you used for each segment. To get the number of steps you will need in order to negotiate the slope, divide the rise by the height of an average step (7 inches). Divide the total rise by the result to get the actual height for each equal step. The tread depth will be divided equally over the total run by the number of steps.

Generally speaking, the most accurate way to calculate rise and run for stairs is to use a ratio of the rise to the run, arrived at by dividing the run by the rise; for example, 2 feet of rise and 30 feet of run results in a ratio of 1:15. In the example case shown in the drawing, for every foot of rise, there is a run of approximately 3 feet, 9½ inches, which makes for a steep grade. The grade called for by the Americans with Disability Act is 1:12, a gentler slope.

Usually, slope percentage (or grade) is used for

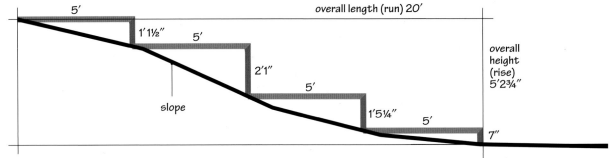

You can measure a slope using a level and a yardstick. In this example the level is five feet long. Determining the overall height (rise) and the overall length (run) is the basis of calculating the grade and the number of steps you will need in order to negotiate it.

purposes of grading. To find the slope percentage, divide the rise by the run and multiply by 100. Cut (excavating soil) and fill (depositing soil) is dependent on understanding the site's topography in order to calculate where soil must be removed or deposited. Consult a geological engineer to assist with calculations if you need them for grading difficult sites with steep slopes.

Completing Your Existing Conditions Plan

After you have drawn your house in relationship to your property line, position other existing conditions on the drawing. "Existing conditions" can include just about anything. It always includes existing structures, the property line, utility locations, hardscape (that is, sidewalks, driveways, and fencing), solar and soil conditions, and more. Document anything you are unable or unwilling to move that could get in the way of something else. Examples are plants you want to keep that would be nearly impossible to move or a sidewalk that will remain as is.

When I document a site, I use a digital camera to take photos of every imaginable detail that might be important. I photograph conditions at ground

level, such as the sill of a door or around the base of a tree. I photograph steps to show how many there are. I include photos of supporting columns, existing materials, neighboring properties, and favorable or adverse situations that could influence design decisions.

Other structures

Other structures in addition to your house are important to record. Take note on your plan of outbuildings such as a shed or separate garage. Jot down the location of each structure regardless of whether you plan to remove it or not. If you intend to keep it, pay attention to the details, as recommended earlier.

Plants you want to keep

If you have existing plants, you have decisions to make before noting them on the existing conditions plan. Deciding what to keep and what to eliminate is not necessarily easy. If you recently moved into your home, you may not have had the opportunity yet to identify or locate all of your plants, particularly if they were dormant over the winter. If possible, it is useful to keep some plants, because having older specimens in the garden helps the garden look fuller and more mature. It also helps your plant budget. More important, if you have native plants, they may be providing habitat or food for wildlife. If you are unsure, have a gardener friend or expert help you make the decisions.

When deciding whether to keep a plant, review its health. Is the plant vigorous in its current location or is it spindly? Do you see dead branches, signs of insect damage, or disease? Determine whether you find each plant attractive. If you do not care for a plant's appearance, consider whether it makes a good background plant for something else. Does the plant look good for only two weeks out of the year? Does it go dormant during the summer? If so, what is the feature that would cause you to keep it?

Carefully scrutinize each plant in a small garden, because you have less space to dedicate to plants. If you decide to eliminate a native plant, consider replacing it with another native plant. Native plants are not just the plants that would live there on their own without your help. Many invasive plants do that all too well. Make sure that if you are saving a native plant, it is truly native.

It may not be necessary to remove everything. If it is possible to relocate a plant, consider keeping it. Also, think about the degree of difficulty in relocating a plant. Any tree that has a trunk larger than 3 inches in diameter may be too difficult or too expensive to move. If you need to remove a tree and are unable to relocate it, you will need to cut it down or hire an arborist or tree service to do it for you. It could be more costly to postpone tree removal if plans for new planting or building include the area where a tree is currently located. Taking out the tree now will prevent damage to construction or newly installed plants later.

If you find it necessary to remove a very large tree (such as a 100-foot-tall fir tree in the Pacific Northwest), you need to have a clear area to fell the tree without damage to structures, overhead wires, or other trees, or remove it in smaller sections. Tree services usually will haul the logs away or grind the wood into mulch. In cases where tree services or contractors are able to sell the logs, they often make enough money to pay for their labor—or even to show a profit. Negotiate with the contractor to split the proceeds with you if they are greater than the contractor's charges.

You may need to contact local utilities to drop wires and cables during tree removal. Be sure to notify your neighbors in order to minimize inconvenience to them. In addition, you may need to contact your local code authorities to obtain permission to remove a tree. It is common for local jurisdictions to regulate conditions such as trees in wetlands or along a city street even if the tree is on your property. Your jurisdiction may require you to obtain a permit to remove a tree. Respect the fact that they are

Note the appearance of a deciduous plant in winter. Like this Harry Lauder's walking stick (*Corylus avellana* 'Contorta'), it may look nearly as interesting as the evergreen plants (or perhaps even more so). Author's garden.

attempting to help Mother Nature by saving mature trees. Trees are the lungs of our planet and provide abundant habitat for wildlife. Even dead trees provide habitat, although this is not a good reason to save a tree if it is a hazard or a significant eyesore.

Another thing to consider when determining whether to relocate a plant is who will move it, you or a contractor. If you move it, you will spend time, sweat, and possibly some money for the right tools. If a contractor moves it, he may charge you more than the plant is worth. Sometimes it is cheaper to feed the existing plant to the compost pile and purchase a new plant. In certain cases, you may be able to donate the plant to a worthy recipient who will dig and move the plant for you. The region where I live has a place to donate plants that sells them and uses the money to spay and neuter pets.

If you have limited space for your garden, consider whether you want a four-season garden. In a small garden, it is a luxury to dedicate space to plants incapable of running a horticultural marathon. In a larger garden, you have the luxury of including a plant whose only feature is a short period of peak bloom. You will get more bang for your buck if you have plants with at least three seasons of interest. For that fourth season, winter, evaluate plants based on whether they have evergreen foliage, exceptional bark, outstanding form, stunning berries, or midwinter bloom.

Take into account that plants that *die well* (meaning that as they become dormant each year, they are not unattractively messy) are plants you may wish to keep. Perennial and deciduous plants die back each season and should look good even when they are dormant. For instance, plants like grasses are often attractive in their dried form. Perennials may have attractive seed heads that also keep birds fed for periods during the winter. Dormant shrubs may

retain their colorful berries or fruits. Consider keeping anything that sustains wildlife during the winter, if possible.

When you've decided which plants you want to keep, add them to your existing conditions plan.

Views and/or borrowed landscape

Among other things you need to note on your plan is the direction of a great view—or of a hideous one you want to change. Designers of celebrated gardens make a point of using "borrowed landscape" or views of other properties. Is your view or landscape borrowed from adjacent property—a water feature, a forest, a cityscape, or a neighbor's lovely tree?

The nature of a view will influence your design. Views of water offer the possibility of reflection as a design inspiration. Views of a night cityscape and twinkling lights suggest that you plan opportunities to use the garden at night or that you design to reduce your own lighting in certain areas. Use views as an asset to make your garden appear larger. Do not fear hiding any part of a view. It is often more captivating to frame the best parts of a view while concealing other parts. Seeing vignettes of a larger view will encourage you to get out into your garden and look through the "window" or view frame for the big picture.

Conversely, you may have a view of a landscape that you want to hide, or you may need privacy on one or more sides. In this case, you will need to determine ways to disguise, conceal, or screen views.

Critters

If you have a larger property, you may have ravenous deer roaming through your yard. Believing that any plant is deer proof is naive. There are deer-resistant plants, but a young fawn or starving deer will try anything. It is more likely, with any size property, to have acrobatic squirrels, marauding raccoons, or voracious rabbits. Occasional visits by opossums, beavers, coyotes, or even bears and cougars may be a possibility in your area. Any or all of these may cause you to consider different types of fencing.

You may also have to modify a grand design for a pond. Mosquitoes can be a problem anywhere. Great blue herons and other water birds who love fish could discover that your new water feature is their buffet. How I wish I could miraculously deter the great blue heron that I occasionally encounter eying the fish in our pond! Your challenge will be to design around insatiable critters that think your garden is their dining room.

While you will want to keep some creatures out of your garden, you may want your garden to be a magnet to others. Research the requirements to invite butterflies, songbirds, amphibians, dragonflies, or beneficial predators like bats that may be in your surrounding environment. It is easy to incorporate into your garden little houses or habitats for the animals you want to encourage. Make notes on your plan of the native species in your area that you want to deter or attract.

Microclimates

Every garden has its own microclimates, meaning some areas get more sun or shade, more dryness or rain, more wind. As you document your site, it is crucial to take note of your yard's microclimates.

First determine the sun orientation and prevailing wind direction. Using a compass, note the direction of north and record that direction with an arrow on your plan. Then record where the sun rises, travels, and sets during summer and winter. Different seasons have varying degrees of shade and sunshine. Pay attention to the season in which you record your information. If you are recording information during the summer, expect that the deciduous shade trees will be bare in winter, allowing more sunshine into an otherwise shady area. Note your prevailing wind direction. You may have areas that are vulnerable to strong winds during different times of the year.

Next determine your humidity. Your weather dictates your relative humidity. Take note of this factor, because it will affect your selection of hardscape materials, furnishings, and plants. If you are unsure of the humidity in your area, you can learn what it is through local weather reports. The more humid the air, the more outdoor upholstery and wood decking could have mold or rot issues. Your humidity will also greatly affect the types of plants you will be able to grow. High humidity can often cause plant diseases such as black spot, rust, and mildew. Conversely, extreme dryness causes a diverse set of issues with which to contend. Exposed wood may crack or split more easily. You will have a different palette of plants to choose from. A specific place in your garden that retains water longer than other areas can be more humid than other areas on your property. Dry areas will have less humidity. Salt air near the sea will direct you toward plants suited to that environment.

Soil types

Your soil's type determines its ability to retain water. Fine particles of clay soil soak up a great deal more water than larger grains of sand. Soil with good amounts of humus and organic matter not only retains moisture but also provides good drainage. This is why compost is an important soil additive for many plants.

Beyond a soil's ability to retain water, there are other important soil characteristics to investigate. Knowing your soil's type will also help you know its angle of repose, meaning how much of a slope it can maintain. Sand has a lower angle of repose than does clay. This is important to know when you are dealing with slopes, terracing, and retaining walls.

Your plants will only be as good as the soil to support them, so having your soil tested is an excellent idea. You may want to have your soil tested in several areas to determine its fertility. Soil tests provide you with useful information like a soil's pH (acidity or alkalinity), identity of minerals and microbiota, and the percentage of each nutrient. Contact your regional department of agriculture or county extension service for information. They will give you specific instructions about the collection process, where to send your specimen for lab analysis, and the cost (if any), and explain how to read and use the results.

Knowing the pH of your soil is vital to growing certain plants. Synthetic fertilizers, concrete, pollution, and decomposing leaves are examples of things that affect a soil's pH. If your soil is acidic and you want to grow things like lilacs, lavenders, and hellebores perfectly, you will need to increase the pH, using limestone in one of its available forms. If your soil tends to be alkaline, you will need to lower the pH in order to grow rhododendrons, camellias, and azaleas. This is not as easy as raising pH. Ground sulfur, iron sulfate, urea, and other additives can lower soil pH. Most plants have a need for particular minerals, but nearly all plants have a need for specific microbes. If they are not present in the soil, plants will never do their best and may die. Perhaps the best approach is to use plants that do well without altering your soil.

There are several ways to test your soil's pH. You can use an inexpensive pH testing kit, litmus paper, or an electronic pH meter, or you can have your soil tested by experts. The pH test kit and litmus paper

direct you to mix your soil with a little water to get results. The pH meter is a probe you push into the ground.

Getting an expert soil test is not difficult. Like any test, it is only as good as the information tested. You can gather samples from various areas around your property and combine them to get an average condition, or you can test areas individually. Some areas may have certain soil characteristics that could sway the results—like where a fire pit used to be or where you just fertilized.

Chemicals, in the form of synthetic fertilizers, weed eradicators, and pest controls, can adversely affect the quality of your soil. They eliminate natural soil organisms that improve the health and tilth of your soil. Think of the times that you have had to use an antibiotic to eliminate the cause of an illness. Because the antibiotic is nonspecific, it also kills good bugs. This is similar to what happens when you treat areas of your garden for pests. You will need to reintroduce missing nutrients before installing new plants. Your local nursery probably carries a good source of assorted organic ingredients, such as mycorrhizae or trace elements, which you can add to each area as needed.

Drainage

In addition to knowing your soil's fertility, you will need to document your drainage. Drainage is the natural or artificial removal of surface and subsurface water from an area. Poor drainage can be an enemy of your garden, but it most certainly is to your house. You will need to correct poor drainage near your house. You may be able to work with poor drainage in your garden.

Walk around your site and take note of areas where water pools during heavy rains or quickly dries. Chances are you have varying degrees of drainage around your property. Pay particular attention to the entire area around your house. Water needs to drain away from your house near your foundation to prevent damage to your home. Ideally, water on your property should never become someone else's problem. If you have a drainage issue, make note of it on your plan. This will be essential to address during the planning stages of your garden. Drainage also plays a key role in determining the range and types of plants you will be able to grow.

If you have any doubts about the drainage of an area, have a percolation test done by a surveyor or a soils or geological engineer. If you do not need to worry about legal issues, your location jurisdiction can provide you with the method to do one yourself.

Utilities

Everyone has some form of utility on his or her property and/or house. Be sure to document all of the various utilities—overhead, underground, on your house, and farther away from the house. If you do not know where underground utilities are, call your utility and ask them to send someone out to mark them for you. It is disheartening when the tree you have lovingly cared for begins to grow more than expected—right into an overhead power line. Overhead lines can be difficult, perhaps impossible, to disguise.

Utilities also need to remain accessible. However, face it, utility boxes, cables, wires, and plumbing are ugly and often placed where they are difficult to disguise. Consider screening utility boxes with plants or a creative structure that allows access to the utility. If you note issues such as these on your plan, you will remember to develop solutions.

Influences from surrounding properties

You would have an unusual and lucky situation if you did not have something that either surrounds or is adjacent to your property that is objectionable. It could be traffic noise from a nearby road, a neighbor's ugly fence, or an overhanging messy tree. Do golf balls fly in on occasion? Do large trees cast a long shadow over the south side of your property? Do you need to keep your trees short to be considerate of your neighbor's view? Document what surrounds your property on your plan. Note their locations relative to your yard.

After completing your site survey, you should have an architectural review of your house, a drawing showing all of your existing conditions, and photographs to remind you of important factors you will need to consider. This information will accompany the list of features you require and desire in your garden, which you will compile next.

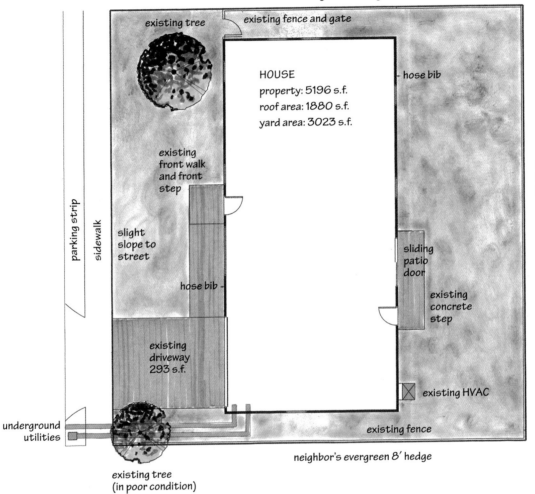

neighbor's evergreen trees

existing tree

existing fence and gate

hose bib

HOUSE
property: 5196 s.f.
roof area: 1880 s.f.
yard area: 3023 s.f.

ugly view
of neighbor's
yard

existing
front walk
and front
step

slight
slope to
street

sliding
patio
door

existing
concrete
step

hose bib

existing
driveway
293 s.f.

existing HVAC

underground
utilities

existing fence

neighbor's evergreen 8' hedge

existing tree
(in poor condition)

parking strip

sidewalk

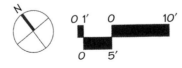

N

0 1'   0   10'

0   5'

Designing the
Hypothetical Garden

The Existing
Conditions Plan

The existing conditions plan for our hypothetical garden notes the direction of north
and the influences of surrounding neighbors.
There is very little elevation change; only the
slight slope to the street in front is noted on the
plan. One of the existing trees is in poor health
and will need to be removed, so I note this on
the plan. I make a note to myself that the prevailing wind comes from the east in the winter
and the west during the summer.

The existing conditions plan for our hypothetical garden shows existing plants and hardscape as well as noting facts about views.

Components of Your Garden

3

Your Garden Essentials

Plato said necessity is the mother of invention. He was on to something. Often the most creative ideas derive from the need to accomplish the simplest of tasks. Boiling water, a simple task, ascends to an art form when you do it with a gorgeous teapot. So too will you be able to translate the humblest of necessities in your garden into something to admire.

Components differ greatly from one garden to another under normal circumstances. Garden components also vary thanks to extraordinary conditions. During World War II, home-based victory gardens supplied families with food during difficult times. Even Eleanor Roosevelt created a victory garden at the White House and inspired First Lady Michelle Obama to do the same. Today's gardeners respond to a wider set of challenges: global warming, diminishing resources, environmental degradation, economic adversity, and increasing stress. However, great challenges offer great opportunities. A garden is your opportunity for positive action to resolve personal concerns and problems, which cannot help but impact what you include within your garden.

Like any garden owner, you must include certain necessities in your garden. Begin a list of your essential components. Keep in mind that the items for which your heart yearns may not be necessities. You will list desirable components later. Some things will consume space, while others may not. Some may be visible, while others may be the

What you will learn:

- how to itemize what you *require* in your garden

- how to record what you *desire* in your garden

- how to use rules of thumb to assign square footages to your garden components

- how to determine space for circulation

A vegetable garden can be beautiful, as in this example from Château Val-Joanis in Pertuis, France.

undetected supporting cast. Some of the things you must consider on your list of necessities are items dictated by your site, your family, your avocations or health concerns, and your need for storage.

Site requirements

Conditions that commonly affect your property or site have to do with weather, exposure, slope, soil type, utilities, neighboring properties, and access. The position of your house on your property also affects site requirements. The farther from the main road your house is located, the longer the drive must be. If it is a fair distance, you will need to provide parking for visitors and access for delivery trucks—from the mail carrier to a dump truck delivering concrete or mulch.

Drainage dynamics. Weather, slope, and soil type all affect drainage. Drainage is a critical factor for everyone but especially so in areas that get voluminous quantities of rain and/or snow. You already assessed drainage during your site survey. If you found a

problem, it may result from unexpected amounts of rain during any given event, low spots, compacted soil, too much pavement, incorrectly installed pavement, poor grading, or other factors.

Some cities promote the disconnection of downspouts. Water that used to go into a storm water collection system, and eventually to a treatment facility, stays on site. Water treatment facilities are expensive for municipalities and increase your taxes. It makes sense to encourage property owners to facilitate water percolation into the groundwater table.

Think about how you will handle rain falling on your nonabsorptive roof and pavement. Guiding it to your neighbor's property is not a solution. Consider diverting storm water to a rain garden, which is capable of containing an overflow of water and allowing it to seep gradually into the ground. A rain garden can be as simple as a 6-to-8-inch depression in the ground, or it can be an elaborate work of art. To implement a rain garden requires a percolation test and knowledge of the correct plants for this use. Because it is hard to know how much rainwater will

A rain garden in Portland, Oregon, is a natural. The concept, however, is universal. Toward the back of the walkway in this photo is a break to allow water to move through the path from the downspout to the rain garden. Garden of Jeremy and Angela Watkins. Garden design by Amy Whitworth, Plan-it Earth Design.

Working with Mother Nature

We live on a planet that is constantly evolving. As you plan your garden, you can do important things that will help your little corner of the globe. Research the native flora and fauna of your area. Create a list of native plants. Growing native plants, not just adaptable non-native plants, can have a positive impact on our shrinking, crowded world. By growing native plants in your garden, whether in a container or on an acre, you can help feed local insects, birds, and mammals and help prevent the extinction of more wildlife. Lists of native plants specifically for your garden and area are easily available from your local extension service and over the Internet.

A bird hose guide watches over *Trillium grandiflorum* in early spring. Author's garden.

Three Pacific Northwest native plants in a group—*Trillium grandiflorum, Polystichum munitum,* and *Erythronium californicum* 'White Beauty'— provide food and habitat for native creatures. Author's garden.

be produced by a single rain event, a rain garden should contain an overflow device that allows extra water to escape to the sewer system or another safe location.

You can also consider using some creative alternative to downspouts, like rain chains, to redirect water.

Rainwater collection. An alternative to water percolating into the ground is rainwater harvesting. If you live in an area that allows homeowners to collect

A rain chain is an ornament in any weather.

rainwater in barrels or large underground cisterns, you will have water for summer irrigation. Perhaps your city provides rain barrels or you have space for a larger storage device. I recall my fascination with the large ornamental terracotta cisterns aboveground in Florence, Italy's Boboli Gardens. Practical applications can be aesthetically attractive.

Underground tanks, bladders, or cisterns provide a superb resource for water storage and summer irrigation. This concept is an important one to consider early on in the planning stages, because the location of water storage will impact your garden layout. Storm water storage systems are becoming more widely available as demand increases. A range of materials and types are available to choose from, so choose knowledgeably after a thorough investigation into which type is best for your garden. The ultimate goal is to guide storm water to its ideal location for discharge or storage. Be sure to check with your local jurisdiction to find out if you can legally store your rainwater.

Calculate the rainwater-harvesting potential of your roof with this formula:

1. Multiply the square footage of the collection area (your roof) by inches of rainfall per year and divide by 12 to get the cubic feet of water per year that you can collect from your roof.
2. Multiply the cubic feet by 7.43 to arrive at the number of gallons per year.

For example, a 900-square-foot roof that gets 20 inches of rainfall per year will shed 1500 cubic feet or 11,145 gallons of water per year. (This calculation method is for horizontal areas and does not take into consideration system losses such as evaporation or leakage.)

Slopes. Whether you have a mountain or a molehill, slopes affect drainage, particularly if they are unstable. Erosion can occur when water drains over a sloping area. Eventually, unattended water will wear away the soil and create hazardous conditions for your home and garden. It is crucial to stabilize eroding soil before you install a garden. Recall the earlier discussion about angle of repose, where I mentioned that the degree of slope stability varies with different soils. Sandy soil, for instance, is not capable of maintaining as steep a slope as clay soil and requires more effort to prevent erosion.

You may need to engage the services of a professional engineer, depending on the severity of the situation. An engineer can determine the best method of stabilization and recommend solutions. More

Large cisterns in the Boboli Gardens, Florence, Italy, not only store water but also function as works of art.

An extreme slope such as this one can erode if precautionary measures are not taken.

A rain barrel can be directly beneath a downspout or in another location to which the downspout is diverted. Either way, it captures storm water runoff from the roof. Photo printed with permission of Rainbarrel Man Company.

knowledge of the condition increases the chance of success.

You may need to consider a retaining wall or a series of retaining walls in the form of terracing. Alternatively, you may be able to install plants combined with appropriate erosion-prevention engineering fabric, biodegradable natural fabric such as jute, or straw blanket barriers to mitigate erosion. Hillsides subject to erosion are good places for trees and shrubs, which can help soak up water and prevent soil erosion with their large, spreading root systems. Additionally, mycorrhizae in soils create a fibrous web that holds the soil together.

Utilities. The reality of property ownership is that you need to get utilities to your house, and they take up space—usually underground or overhead. They may include unsightly meter boxes. During your site survey, you noted all of these on your existing conditions plan. One of your needs is to keep these accessible and yet disguised, if not hidden. Another need may be to relocate a utility or to add onto one or more of them to accommodate a need or want in your garden.

Perhaps this is the time to consider placing overhead lines underground, at least from the pole nearest your house to the house. This could be particularly important if you want to grow tall trees that could interfere with electrical lines. Downed power lines caused by falling branches laden with ice are common during winter storms in areas with freezing temperatures. High winds could be another issue affecting power lines. Plan ahead.

Site access. Parking for visitors could be an issue. If you live too far from a street on which your visitors might otherwise park, you will need a place for them to park. You will also need access from the street to your house. More than likely, you will need a hard surface on which to park or drive. More sustainable options allow water to penetrate the surface, as in permeable pavers, packed gravel, or porous concrete. You will need adequate space for a vehicle, opening doors, and circulation around, to, and from the vehicle(s).

Curved drives have curvature requirements for turning radius, since no vehicle makes a precise 90-degree turn. The turning radius is important because it affects the speed at which a vehicle will be able to enter or exit the driveway. The longer the radius, the easier it is to make the turn. The optimum radius varies, depending on the vehicle. The range can be anywhere from 15 feet, 6 inches, to 50 feet.

Mind where you place trees or you might be dealing with this situation in your future.

Planning a driveway in a tight space occasionally lends itself to creative solutions, as in this one where the garden owners did not want to part with this tree. Garden of Mark and Terri Kelley. Garden design by Vanessa Gardner Nagel, APLD, Seasons Garden Design LLC.

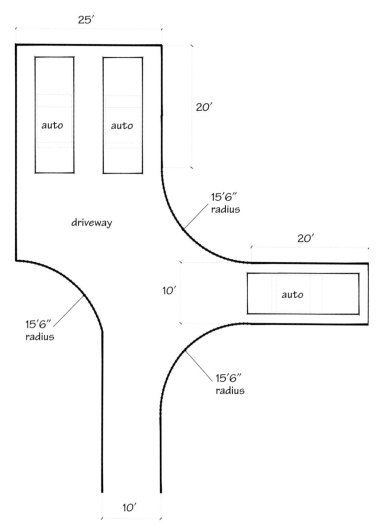

The critical dimensions for parking automobiles are shown here.

Family factors

Every family has its own dynamics. Yours is no different. Each member of your family should contribute ideas on how to develop your garden space. Engage them in the process as much as possible and they will have a vested interest in the garden. They will be more likely later to spend time in the garden and help maintain it.

Children. If you have children who will spend time in the garden, write down your children's ages and how many of their friends you want to have room for in your garden. If they are small children, how will you keep them safely in your garden? Will you be able to keep a watchful eye on them as they play? Line of sight is an important factor in locating children's play areas.

Most children would love a play area near their house. Many families have space for a lawn large enough to allow them to run and play. If your children enjoy a specific game or activity that requires a minimum amount of space—or even dictates the shape of the space—make a note of the size and shape required. If they want a play structure, look into the amount of space the structure consumes, what the spacing requirements are if there are several structures, and how much space they need around them for circulation and safety. Investigate the operation

and safety of each structure. Look into the recommendations of groups such as the U.S. Consumer Product Safety Commission. Because innovations in play structures are frequent, it is important to investigate the peculiarities of the structure you are mulling over.

If your children are interested in gardening, provide them with a space of their own to grow plants—especially the edible kind. You could inspire a lifelong interest and knowledge base that will also improve their diet and health.

Speaking of children and edible plants simultaneously, you may need to think about the proximity of your children's play area to the garden in general. That not-so-innocent-looking rhododendron

This backyard playground was incorporated into a garden within viewing distance of the children's grandparents at the kitchen window or on the outside deck. Garden of Kim and Kathy Christensen. Design by Vanessa Gardner Nagel, APLD, Seasons Garden Design LLC.

protects itself from being eaten by being poisonous. You may want to eliminate poisonous plants near a play area. Make a note of this if it is an issue. Some communities have "poison gardens" that allow you to view poisonous plants. They may also provide a list of such plants; or find such a list on the Internet or at your library. Some plants can aggravate allergies or asthma. If this is an issue in your family, you need to exclude or minimize plants that exacerbate those conditions.

Pets. Now is a good time to think about where Fido will hang out. If you have pets that spend time outdoors, you may want to provide some special areas for them. For instance, you may need a kennel for the dog or a pond for goldfish. They require space and utilities. They may need shade, an area with a hose that makes it easy for you to clean up after them, water, and food. Your four-legged friends may need easy access to the house or garage. They may also need an indoor space nearby to bathe or sleep.

If you need to provide protection for them because of your proximity to a wild area or restrain them to protect others, make a note of what is required. How will a fence help if your pet can dig under it or climb over it? If they need special equipment to keep them healthy outdoors, jot down the spatial and utility requirements for that equipment. Koi, for instance, need a more oxygenated and filtered environment than goldfish and therefore need space for more elaborate equipment. With regard to fish, you will also need to consider how many fish you would like to have. Inches of fish equate to gallons of water and dictate the size and depth of the pond you will need. The point is to make sure you fully understand the needs of whatever pets you have so you can assure them a safe, comfortable space that is easy for you to maintain.

The kind of outdoor pets you have will drive your

Nepeta ×faassenii 'Walker's Low' attracts Tashi (the author's cat), willing to lie on his back to get his fix of catmint. Author's garden.

Goldfish and koi cohabitate in a pond. Author's garden.

decisions about plants in their environment. If you have koi in your pond, you will have to anchor your water plants in their pots, because koi are curious creatures who will nuzzle your plants out of their pots. If you have dogs that like to crash around your shrubs, you will need sturdy shrubs, possibly with discouraging thorns, or plants that don't mind being stepped on. If you have cats, you may want to plant some catmint to distract them from other plants. Cats will also sit in your lower grasses, although I have found that my grasses typically bounce back after the cats have had their way with them. Different plants take up varying amounts of space, so it is helpful to have some idea if there will be plants serving a special purpose.

Necessary avocations

If there are hobbies you need to make room for the sake of someone's health and well-being or to earn additional income, list the requirements for each activity (for example, an outdoor exercise area, a carpentry shed, a beekeeping area). Consider how much space the hobby will occupy. Are utilities required? Think about maintenance issues with having the hobby outdoors. If you need to build a structure, it could require a special permit to comply with local codes and regulations. It is wise to check with your local jurisdiction during the planning stages of your design. At a minimum, you will also need to consider how to access the structure, its exposure to the sun, and how to get utilities to it.

Installing a greenhouse does not always mean the purchase of a manufactured kit. Here is a great example of a greenhouse built with recycled materials. Garden of Michele Eccleston, The Purple Garden. Photo by Brian Libby. Greenhouse construction by TJ Juon.

Outdoor work space and storage

If you are a gardener, you may need an outdoor work space. You may want the space to accommodate a compost pile or a greenhouse, tools and materials, or a workbench for potting plants. What are the requirements for each of these? Think about whether you will need electricity and water. Compost piles need to be a minimum size in order to function properly. Alternatively, will you purchase composting equipment? If so, how large will it be? Will you locate it so that the materials that go in and out of it are close by?

If you like to cook, want to trim your food budget, or need to control what is in your food, a kitchen garden may be necessary. Find out what will grow well in your garden and make a list of which foods you would like to grow. You can talk to your local extension service or master gardener to learn which food plants grow easily in your area. You can also find out by visiting local farmers' markets, if you are so lucky, to see the produce they bring to market. Don't forget to evaluate how to improve your soil to successfully grow edible plants.

What You *Desire* in Your Garden

You began your project by envisioning a garden. Now that you have documented your site and listed what you need, return to those dreams. This is the time when it is important to allow your mind to wander and invoke the muse. Thumb through gardening magazines and books. Collect the ideas that speak to your situation or that you just like. Visit other gardens, public or private, because these will have a wealth of ideas. Local arboretums are an excellent place to see just how large trees and shrubs can become in your area. There might even be a garden club you can join as a resource. Keep your mind open and discover your bliss. Brainstorm ideas with

your family and friends. Put everything on the table; do not eliminate anything you might want—*yet*.

What you require and what you desire in your garden will be a source of discussion if there is more than one decision maker. If you are wisely including every member of your family in the planning of

A tiny garden uses its space efficiently and beautifully for growing edibles, dining, cooking, and sitting, and includes a small rain garden in the foreground. Garden of Kristien Forness, owner of Fusion Landscape Design, LLC.

your garden, you could have countless wishes. Participants could be passionate or passive. You may need to compromise later. For now, include everyone's wishes, dreams, and desires.

Is a greenhouse, a space to start seedlings or overwinter tender patio ornamentals, something you want? Could a chicken coop help your food budget? Would a koi pond make your heart go pitter-pat? Does your property lend itself to the hobbies of bird watching, bonsai, or wood carving? Whatever floats your boat, give it some sail by investigating the needs attached to it. It will be important to have as much information as possible when it comes time to make decisions about what you will incorporate into your plan. Here are some important factors to record:

- the amount of space required

- the amount of time required to maintain the space
- rough estimates of installation and maintenance costs

Entertainment areas

Outdoor entertainment areas are a natural for any garden. Do you have the space for a bocce ball court, horseshoe pit, or croquet lawn? Does an outdoor fire pit or fireplace light your fire? Would an outdoor kitchen, pizza oven, or covered TV terrace whet your appetite?

Most people want an area or two for entertaining. The most important decision is the size of each area, based on the number of people you want to have room for or seat. You may have more than one

A fire pit makes a natural gathering area for chatting or cooking dinner over the open fire. Garden of Gordon and Laurel Young.

entertainment area, in which case you might want to separate them but still have easy access to them. Perhaps you need a deck, rather than a patio, to work with a slope. Maybe you can accommodate both a patio and a deck and have an interesting transition area in between or have them immediately adjacent to one another.

Consider spaces that can do double duty. Outdoor sports paving might double as a paved surface for something else–like a temporary greenhouse over the winter. A retaining wall or raised planter could be the perfect height for extra seating.

Areas of solitude

A garden is a wonderful place to escape to. When stress affects your life, you may need to get away and recharge your batteries. Can you imagine a private area for meditation or snoozing on a warm day? Even on a rainy or wintry day, the garden can offer us solace and a sense of calm. Our relationship with nature is a gift that keeps on giving. A paradise in your garden could prove to be a great place to vacation if you can't get away to a tropical island.

If you want your space to be private, you may need to develop a form of enclosure. You can always grow plants, but if you need something immediately, you may need to construct a fence, overhead trellis, or perhaps a gazebo. Local codes will likely dictate where you can locate those on your property if they are above a certain height. You may need to get a building permit through your local jurisdiction as well. Research the parameters and add those notes to your increasing amount of information.

A fountain of water, gurgling brook, or splashing waterfall makes a garden sing. Their music is soothing, comforting, and healing. They make a wonderful destination point in your garden or a delightful visual through a window in your house anytime of year. If you don't have much space, you can still include a small water feature. If you have little time for maintenance, make sure the water feature is easy to maintain. Even if your budget doesn't permit a water feature, the visual suggestion of a dry stream could contribute to a quiet mood.

Escape to your garden and your own tropical paradise. Garden of Susan LaTourette. Photo by Susan LaTourette.

Material preferences

Materials have a great deal to do with design; it is important to consider them in the planning stages because they can greatly affect your budget and design direction. You listened to the language of your house as you read the last chapter. You know its materials. You also know what you would like to have. Perhaps existing and desired materials do not match. With a little thought, could they work together? Maybe it just means adjusting the proportions to make it work.

What if you have considerable brick on your house and are reluctant to have more of it in the landscape?

Do not discount the idea of paying homage to an existing material in token form. Perhaps the nosing of some steps, the edging of a walkway, or the foundation of a piece of sculpture could be brick.

Do think about materials you like and have seen used successfully. Also consider who will be using the paved surfaces, because they may have special access requirements. Gravel may be a humble paving material, but many people enjoy the crunch underfoot and the casual nature of gravel. Do not substitute pea gravel for something like quarter-minus gravel. It does not pack down and it shifts—often with people walking off the path sloughing the pea gravel with

A bubbling water feature draws attention in the garden and invites a stop. Garden of Norm Kalbfleisch and Neil Matteucci.

them. Any gravel you find that contains the word *minus* in its description has fines, very small particles that help the gravel pack down to create a good walking surface. You may have decomposed granite, the ultimate gravel, in your area; it packs together so well that it begins to act like concrete. If not tightly compacted, gravel also offers drainage superior to that of many other types of paving. If you compact the subgrade and install filter fabric, you will reduce the amount of surface material compacted into the ground.

If you use stone or concrete, consider how you will offset the decreased drainage these materials often imply. Nonporous paving requires more subsurface preparation in order to manage drainage. Concrete paving in the form of ecologically friendly pavers and porous concrete may be an option. Stone paving might be set in gravel and sand rather than mortared. Slices of wood might be available on the property from felled trees. These make good casual stepping-stones or stairs if properly installed, sealed, and maintained.

If you know you *must* have stone, now is the time to find out if your budget is realistic, not after you complete the design and find that costs cause you to rethink it. Your budget may cause you some frustration in not getting what you originally desired, but it is more frustrating to have to return to square one because you did not begin with a reality check. You can also consider doing two designs simultaneously, one well within budget and another teetering on the brink of affordability. Prices rise and fall over the course of a year, with or without extreme economic conditions such as recession or inflation. Another option is to phase the installation of your garden, with higher-cost items planned now but installed as money becomes available.

Two stone columns represent a compromise on the part of three families that live on the property. One family wanted all rounded cobbles, while the other two wanted stacked, angular stone. The compromise was to combine the two in a pleasing proportion so one complemented the other. Column design: Vanessa Gardner Nagel, APLD, Seasons Garden Design LLC.

Vertical structures

Height in a garden relieves the banality of a single level. If you have existing mature trees, you have instant height. If you need to add something, consider the contribution that a fence, trellis, or other structure might make. You may need to have a covered area in your garden where you can sit on hot, sunny days or rainy afternoons. Perhaps a column or water feature can provide height. Changes in elevation may require a retaining wall that can be functional and artful simultaneously.

Garden maintenance

Remember that any materials you select will require some form of maintenance. Before you make a final decision on the materials for your garden, find out how to maintain each material. It could change your mind.

Be realistic about how you will care for your garden. Will you outsource care to a gardener or rely on

an in-house plant nerd? Evaluate your busy schedule and determine just how many hours are truly available to maintain your garden. If you travel a great deal during the summer, is it realistic to think you will spend much time working in your garden? On the other hand, perhaps you have summers off and want to handle all of the maintenance during the peak season. It might make sense to hire a maintenance service to do some of the work part of the year. Otherwise, your schedule or circumstances may clearly dictate the need to hire a maintenance service the entire year. If there is any part of the gardening experience that you think you can manage, do it. Any part of gardening will keep you in touch with your garden.

Always hire the right professional for the type of work you have. A lawn mowing service may formalize all of your casual garden's shrubs before you can say "clippity-clip" because they have little knowledge of pruning and it is faster to clip a shrub than to prune it properly. After a friend of mine purchased a new home, she called me, lamenting the meatball-like appearance of the existing shrubs. She insisted the previous owners gave what she termed "hedge Nazis" far too long a leash. The point is that garden services are not created equal. Make sure your budget is up to the challenge of hiring a maintenance service equal to the task of what you decide to include in your garden. If you do hire a service, prepare written instructions for them to save you some post-maintenance grief.

Using a Designer's Tools

When I was a commercial interior designer, I learned tips to determine spatial requirements. Spatial layout is crucial to the success of any garden design. However, before you can begin laying out a space,

The maintenance crew turned every shrub in this garden into a rounded mound. A formalized quick clip may do more harm than good. There is no substitute for proper pruning.

you need to separate the elements you want in your outdoor space on a function-by-function basis. This exercise is as simple as remembering to include space to allow a person to walk behind another person or to pull out a chair from a table. It is important because you want to have adequate space for each activity. I like to limit surprises to serendipitous coincidence as often as possible. Having adequate space to move through your garden will limit damage and accidents. It could even be critical to move equipment into your house from the curb. How will that old refrigerator leave and the new one make it into the house?

Designers use shortcuts to work more quickly and easily. Two important tools in a designer's mixed bag that will help you do the same are rules of thumb and a square footage study. For this planning component, you will do the following:

- Use and develop rules of thumb to calculate square footages for each function
- Add the square footages together
- Develop circulation square footage and add it to your total

Developing rules of thumb

Begin this exercise by reviewing your lists of essential and desirable items and your existing conditions plan. You must calculate square footage for each of the existing items that you must keep as is, either in the current location or relocated. For example, in the hypothetical garden, the driveway is an existing area that will remain as is; multiplying width by length, I calculated that the driveway uses 293 square feet. If you plan to enlarge or change an existing area, treat it as a future space using the rules-of-thumb method.

Before you begin to assemble your rules of thumb,

it is also important to explore the issue of how you live your life and the flow of space you create for your lifestyle. In the book *A Pattern Language* (Alexander, Ishikawa, and Silverstein 1977), the authors describe 253 basic functional elements or patterns that are complete as is, can combine with one another to fulfill the requirements of a more complex function, or show connections to one another. As an example, the authors suggest several other patterns to help create the pattern Sitting Circle, among them The Fire. They suggest considering The Fire for Sitting Circle because "this pattern helps to create the spirit of the Common Areas at the Heart . . . and even helps us to give its layout and position, because it influences the way that paths and rooms relate to one another." In other words, The Fire brings both psychological and physical elements to the Sitting Circle.

Well-thought-out spaces not only provide for essential physical elements but also consider the psychology of space. How comfortable would you be sitting with your back to a door or gate? Physically the arrangement may work, but our basic human instinct is always to *watch our back*. It is much easier, and more comfortable for us, to glance up rather than turning around to see who is entering our space. When you begin to create rules of thumb, remember that you will apply some psychology and interconnectedness when you assemble them within the context of your garden.

Rules of thumb make developing square footages for future spaces easier. The designer assembles the square footage for each item into a square footage study. This document allows the designer to review whether everything will fit within a space before she draws its layout. You will determine rules of thumb for each function. I illustrate some rules of thumb for various garden functions in this chapter. You will need to develop your own for some of the things you

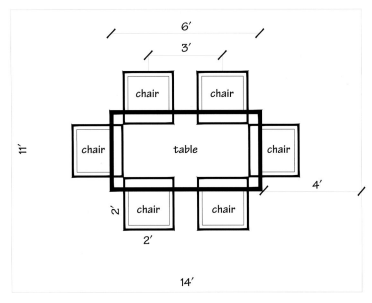

I developed this rule of thumb for the dining area.

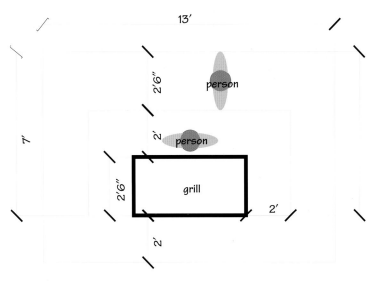

Here is a rule of thumb for grilling.

have researched and decided you need or want (for example, a bocce ball court).

For the hypothetical garden, I created one rule of thumb by assuming I needed an outdoor dining area to seat six people. The general rule of thumb is to allow 24 to 30 inches of perimeter around the table for each person. However, not all chairs are created equal. If you already have the dining chair, use the width of the chair and add 10 inches for each person. For my purpose, I assumed the chairs were 18 inches wide. I added 10 inches to get 28 inches per person around the table. This yields a minimum table perimeter requirement of 14 linear feet. A standard 3-by-6-foot table has 18 feet of perimeter, so it works.

Then because I must consider that chairs move in and out with people as they sit and that people need to get to and from the chairs, I allowed a 4-foot-perimeter space around the table. The perimeter allows people at least 24 to 30 inches to move around the table or through a space comfortably. Once I developed

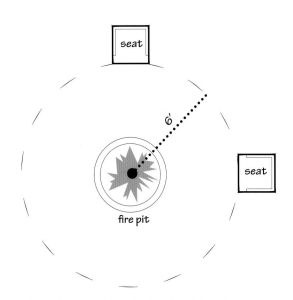

This is the rule of thumb I developed for a fire pit.

each space with its critical components, I multiplied the width and depth of the overall function to get square footage. Now I have an 11-by-14-foot space, comfortable to seat six people for dining.

Two keys to success for creating a rule of thumb are these:

- know the size of the objects you want to place within a space
- know how people move around each object

The figures show two more rules of thumb to get you started, for a fire pit and for grilling.

Assigning square footages to your garden components

Now that you have practiced with a dining area calculation, apply the same technique to the areas you want to include within your garden. Use the sketches provided in this book and/or work out your own if you cannot find one that applies to your situation. Multiply the width and length of each area to get the square footage for each of your rules of thumb.

List each function with its corresponding square footage and add the square footages together. Then add all of the functions together. On your list you may have two areas that are identical but separate, functionally speaking. Give each of those areas its own identity but use the same amount of square footage for each. It will be easier to keep track of them for the later diagramming exercises.

After you add the square footage for each of your functional spaces together, you will have the total square footage for functions only. It excludes one very important space: circulation.

Circulation, the forgotten space

Without circulation (or paths), you have no way to get from one space to another. Think about that path from the house out to the shed. How would you get to the shed if the path were not there? That said, there is nothing wrong with a space having more than one dedicated use. You may have a lawn for kids to play on that also acts as the route to the shed. Additionally, consider whether alternate paths make sense. Will there be a loop, cul-de-sac, or point-to-point access?

Calculating circulation is not necessarily a science. It is something of a learned art. Typically, circulation is expressed as a percentage called the

The layout of this garden path successfully weaves around the septic tank access, winding its way down a hill and to the terrace overlooking the river. Garden of Mark and Terri Kelley. Garden design by Vanessa Gardner Nagel, APLD, Seasons Garden Design LLC.

circulation factor. The lower the circulation percentage, the more efficient a space is, because there is less room devoted to it. In my experience, an average amount of circulation is roughly 25 percent. The larger each function is in a given amount of space, the less circulation space is required to get to each of them. If your areas are in the 500-square-foot

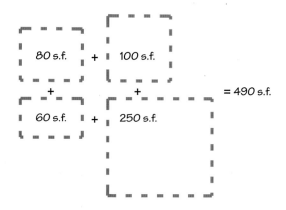

490 s.f. x 40% circulation factor = 196 s.f.
490 s.f. + 196 s.f. = 686 s.f.
500 s.f. (actual) – 686 s.f. (projected) = –186 s.f.

Here is an example of including circulation with all of the other garden components and comparing the total against available space.

or more vicinity, you can probably get by with less than 10 percent circulation. If you were to fit a lot of tiny spaces in that same space, you might need more than 50 percent circulation. Think about the circulation space required in a museum exhibit to circulate around each piece of sculpture.

If I had a fixed space and put as many 36-square-foot spaces as I could squeeze into it, this would result in a 37-percent circulation factor. If I took that same space and instead used 100-square-foot spaces, my circulation factor would drop to 25 percent. If I used 300-square-foot spaces, my circulation factor would fall to 7 percent.

When you have found the total square footage for your garden essentials and desirables and added in the circulation factor, you can compare this with the total square footage available. I find this exercise particularly valuable when I need to fit 10 pounds of function into a 1-pound space. The advantage of comparing the amount of desired functional space to the actual available space is evident. You will immediately know whether everything will fit without moving anything around or drawing one line on paper. It may also tell you that you need to make some decisions about what to cut.

The Components List

For the hypothetical garden, I have listed eighteen spaces of varying sizes that add up to 2640 square feet. The average of those spaces is 147 square feet, so the circulation factor is somewhere between 7 and 25 percent. This is where the art—or the educated guess—comes in. Since 147 square feet is much closer to 100 square feet than 300 square feet, I estimate a factor of 22 percent for the hypothetical garden. Twenty-two percent of 2640 square feet is 581 square feet. I add the circulation square footage to the subtotaled square footage of the functional spaces to get the total of 3221 square feet. Now I have a fully developed list of components (called the program) to use during the garden planning and as a handy reference during the subsequent design process.

The hypothetical garden has only 3023 square feet of available space. Thus, I have decisions to make.

The Hypothetical Garden's Components

ESSENTIALS	SQUARE FOOTAGE
1. existing driveway	293
2. HVAC unit	8
3. two garbage cans	8
4. rain barrel	4
5. kitchen garden (for fruits, vegetables, and herbs)	200
6. rain garden	325
7. dog run	150
Subtotal for essentials	988

DESIRABLES	SQUARE FOOTAGE
8. BBQ grill	91
9. lounge area to seat six people	120
10. dining area for six people	154
11. water feature	16
12. putting green	600
13. one quarter 14-foot radius fire pit area to seat ten people	154
14. 12-by-4-foot hammock space	48
15. meditation area	15
16. ornamental garden	350
17. bonsai display	24
18. 8-by-10-foot greenhouse	80
Subtotal for desirables	1652
Subtotal for essentials plus desirables	2640
22% circulation factor	581
Total square footage	3221
Available square footage of property	3023

Need to downsize desirables by 198 square feet

Putting the Components Together

4

Prioritizing Your Garden Components

Functionally speaking, now is the time to come to grips with your needs and wants versus your available space. Just because you listed a helicopter landing pad as desirable does not mean you have the space for one in your garden. If you have more available space than you totaled for functions, you do not need to prioritize your spaces, unless you want to for another reason. However, you may have less space than you need.

Before you burst your bubble because you cannot fit something you want into your garden, use a simple exercise that may eliminate your frustration. The essential items are not negotiable, which is why you listed them as essential. Instead, focus on the desirable items. Which ones must you have? Which ones are just nice to have? Review your entire list to see if there are things that might go together or use the same space if you tweaked the space just a little.

Multifunctional spaces are a good solution to not enough space. How many times have you used your dining table as a conference table or desk? If you have a handy 4-by-8-foot piece of plywood you can pull out of the garage in a pinch and if you can move a couple of things out of the way, your outdoor dining area might be able to serve more people for that once-or-twice-per-year event. Perhaps a bench could combine with a retaining wall for additional seating.

The hypothetical garden lists components requiring a total of 3221 square feet. The bad news is with only 3023 square feet of actual space,

What you will learn:

- how to prioritize essential versus desirable garden components

- how to determine, prioritize, and diagram adjacencies (what goes next to what)

- how to determine, prioritize, and diagram circulation (getting from one point to another)

- how to create a basic diagram of your garden's layout

Columns announce an out-of-the-way fire pit area that could pinch-hit as a lounge area. Garden of Dulcy Mahar..

A putting green is a poor candidate for multifunctional space, because its design includes variable heights and slopes.

I am short by 198 square feet. With insufficient space comes the necessity to prioritize the functions. I must decide what to leave out or how to use a space for more than one function. There are several options. First, I could downsize something like the putting green, which is hard to envision as a multifunctional space because of its height variations. I could also eliminate entirely something from the desirables list.

If I prioritize all of the items on the list, I will have a better idea of what I want to cut or use for multiple purposes. On the hypothetical garden's list of desirable items, I decide the first priority is the dining

This street-corner bench incorporated into the retaining wall not only performs two functions but also is a gesture to the neighborhood to come and "sit a spell." Garden of Lucy Hardiman.

Although it was part of a transitory show garden, this beautiful dining area would inspire anyone to dine alfresco. Design and construction by Barbara Simon, APLD, and Alfred Dinsdale, Dinsdale Landscape Contractors.

area. This area will likely get the most regular use compared to other functions.

The remaining desirable items are a lounge area for six people, a barbecue grill, a water feature, a fire pit, a hammock space, a meditation area, an ornamental garden, a bonsai display, a putting green, and a greenhouse. If I use the fire pit as the lounge area and eliminate 120 square feet, I only need to eliminate another 78 square feet. The greenhouse is approximately that amount. Do I really need a greenhouse? I do, to satisfy my desire to grow food year-round, but I could downsize it to 6 by 8 feet. I could also trim the ornamental border, but that would be a sizeable chunk of it. The largest area is the putting green. I decide that I would rather trim the putting green to 510 square feet. I may discover during the actual space layout that I could economize on space in some areas and pick up additional square footage at that time. However, now I am within the maximum space of 3023 square feet, and I have a final list.

Final list of the hypothetical garden's components

ESSENTIALS	SQUARE FOOTAGE
1. existing driveway	293
2. HVAC unit	8
3. two garbage cans	8
4. rain barrel	4
5. kitchen garden (for fruits, vegetables, and herbs)	200
6. rain garden	325
7. dog run	150
Subtotal for essentials	988

DESIRABLES	SQUARE FOOTAGE
8. BBQ grill	91
9. lounge area to seat six people (combine with fire pit)	
10. dining area for six people	154
11. water feature	16
12. putting green (decrease size)	510
13. one quarter 14-foot radius fire pit area to seat ten people	154
14. 12-by-4-foot hammock space	48
15. meditation area	15
16. ornamental garden	350
17. bonsai display	24
18. 8-by-10-foot greenhouse	80
Subtotal for desirables	1462
Subtotal for essentials plus desirables	2450
22% circulation factor	539
Total square footage	2989

What Goes Where: Adjacencies

Now that you have determined all the functions you will have, their size, and that there is adequate space for them in your garden, you need to determine their placement. Adjacency or closeness of various functions is the next point to consider. Will you walk from the kitchen to cook your food on the outdoor grill, through the woods, on into the rose garden, and beyond? Is this arrangement inconvenient or intentional? Should your outdoor grill be near the kitchen, where the food is stored? Look at how to place all of your functions so that it makes sense.

Start by drawing a big circle in the middle of a piece of paper. Label it "house." Around it, draw circles representing all the functions on your list—essentials and desirables. I suggest you also note locations inside the house circle representing some rooms that may have a relationship with functions outside. For instance, the dining area and barbecue grill will probably need to be immediately adjacent to the kitchen. You may need a dog run close to the garage or you may want to keep it as far away from the dining area as possible.

For simple diagramming purposes, I use four different line styles to indicate the priority of closeness.

Three lines represent the need for immediate closeness; two lines signify that functions can be slightly farther apart; one line, farther apart still. Dashed lines denote the wish for separation and no closeness at all. No lines indicate it is not important either way. Draw lines between all of the functions to indicate how close you want them to be to each other. This diagram, which may be complex with many circles, helps you determine the relative placement of all functions within your garden.

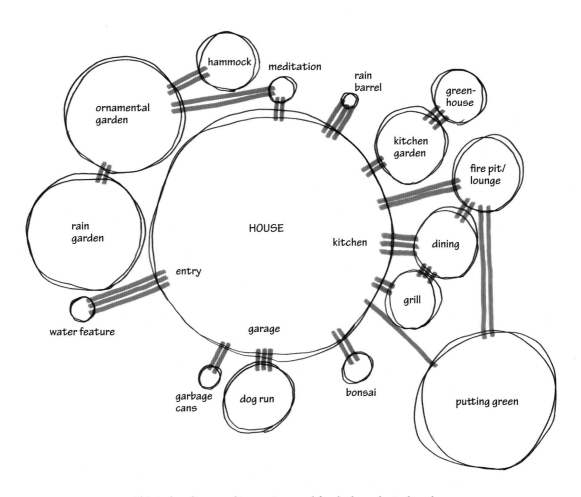

This is the adjacency diagram I created for the hypothetical garden.

Getting Around the Garden: Circulation

After determining where things go, the next step is to decide how to get there. Ideally, a path or walkway will provide subtle cues to guide visitors to their destinations. Other important considerations along circulation routes are accessibility and safety.

Subtle way-finding

Walkways, paths, and other means of circulation work best when you do not have to think too hard about where your destination is located. If you can easily see your destination from your starting place, it is just a matter of walking and watching your step. Otherwise, you are looking for signs to direct you. Designers like to use the art of "subtle way-finding." It is subtle because it relies on your intuitive ability to find your way around without needing signs.

The easiest time to begin placement of paths to assist with a visitor's instinctive sense is during the preliminary planning stages. As you place a walkway, think about it from the standpoint of how easy it is for someone to see his or her destination at the beginning of each path. This is especially true if you have an existing large tree or shrub or will consider having large plants that could block a person's view of the destination, such as your front door.

If you cannot see the destination, other subtle way-finding methods that designers use are the change or contrast of path materials, the width of a walkway, and the placement of focal points. I will discuss these in a later chapter before the final design is complete.

Accessibility

Accessibility involves the ability of people with disabilities to traverse a path. Even if everyone in your family is currently easily able to negotiate a path with steps or a steeper grade, there is no guarantee you will be able to do so if one of you sustains an injury or if age becomes an issue. If in the early stages of planning you allow the distance for a longer path with a gentle slope (a rise of 1 foot over a length of 12 feet makes a slope accessible, according to the Americans with Disabilities Act or ADA), you can accommodate future conditions. In addition, if someone is wheelchair bound, the width of the path will need to allow a wheelchair and there will need to

A fork in this path illustrates subtle way-finding. Stone edges the main path. Pavers turned on edge line the less-traveled path. Author's garden.

be a space to turn around (usually a 5-foot diameter circle, according to the ADA).

Safety

Safety along an outdoor path typically means a surface that is safe to walk, a surface that you can easily see (especially at night), and a way to safely negotiate changes in height. Subsequent chapters will cover surfaces and lighting. Here I will discuss slopes, steps, and stairs, because the early planning stages are the best time to address changes in height.

It is very common to encounter slopes in a landscape. Even smaller properties that appear flat can have a rise of 18 inches over a distance of 80 feet. A slope of more than 10 degrees may call for steps or a sloped walkway to make the change in grade easy for people to negotiate. The material of the path can also influence how easily a slope can be negotiated

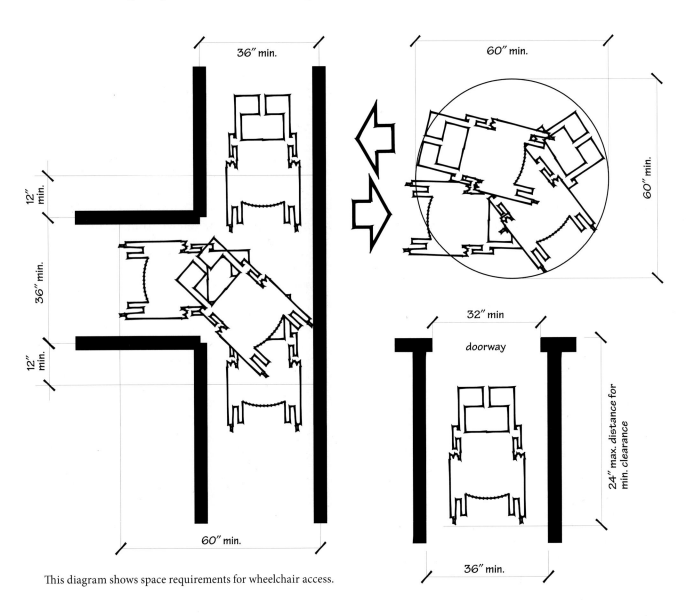

This diagram shows space requirements for wheelchair access.

without steps. Sloped gravel paths can be more slippery than a masonry path with the same degree of slope.

When steps or stairs are required, standard ratios are used to determine the "rise and run" or stair height and tread depth. You do not want a rise of more than 8 inches or a run of less than 10 inches. For the sake of safety, most steps are in the range of 6½ inches to 7 inches high, and most tread depths are in the range of 11 to 12 inches. If you have a series of steps, you must keep every rise and run the same; otherwise you risk creating a trip hazard.

Outside, it is more gracious to have deeper treads, because people tend to have a greater stride outdoors. A 2-foot tread depth would be ideal in many circumstances. However, the distance and overall height difference from one elevation to another drives the total length of a run of stairs, often setting the number of stairs, their rise, and the tread depth. During early planning is the time to find the place in the garden where the transition from one height to another can be made most easily, as well as to decide how to use the space most efficiently.

Diagramming Functions and Circulation

The final phase in the planning of your garden is to combine functions with circulation. A "bubble diagram" shows this information. Its name refers to its appearance: it looks like a series of bubbles overlaid on the site plan. Why do you do this rather than jumping right into laying out a plan? I assure you, you could spend hours moving things around on a plan if you do not take this important step first. It shows all of your functions with your existing conditions. It shows them in relationship to one another and your house. It shows where your circulation needs to be. It shows you the space remaining for your plants. It shows, in short, the pattern of your lifestyle imprinted upon your garden.

Before you begin your bubble diagram, take a copy of your site plan and draw lines from all of the entrances to the property to the doors of the house. What you are doing is showing the most efficient and direct way to get from point to point. I love looking at this kind of diagram, because it gives me an idea about the sizes and shapes of remaining space. It tells me where there may be a congested area, or where there needs to be an intersection. It allows me to direct where circulation needs to be before I overlay all of the functions. Yes, there will be some accommodation to the spatial bubbles. There will be circumstances that dictate a less direct route. However, if you can keep your circulation in its most efficient arrangement, you will have more space that is functional.

Because you created an adjacency diagram, you have a good idea of the placement of your functions on an actual plan. Now you will transfer the information to a copy of your site plan in the form of scaled, squared bubbles. In other words, if a function is supposed to require 200 square feet, create an area that is 10 feet by 20 feet. Using a calculator, you can fine-tune the sizes as you go along to accommodate the existing shape and space of your property. If you need a space of 200 square feet and the area in which you need to place it is only 9 feet wide, adjust the length of the bubble to make the space equal 200 square feet.

As you place your first bubble, recognize that this bubble leads the way for the others. It is best to begin with a bubble that has high priority, is close to a house entry point, and does not have much flexibility in its requirements. The dining area is a good example. Its requirements are rigid if you want the area to function correctly. If you want efficient circulation between indoor kitchen and outdoor dining,

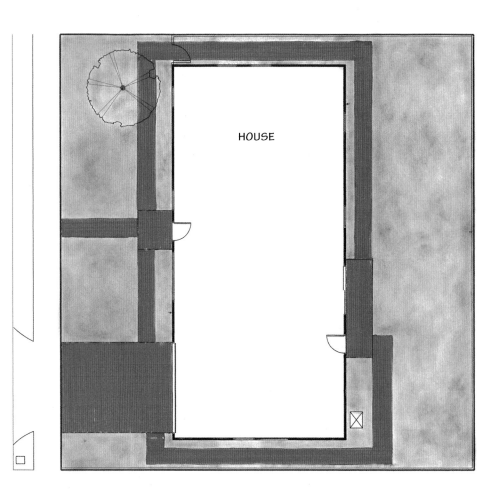

HOUSE

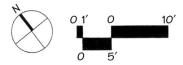

A circulation diagram with direct lines from point to point shows the shapes and sizes of spaces that remain once circulation carves up the property.

you do not want to travel far between them. It makes sense to locate the space as close to the house as possible. That said, there could be extenuating circumstances that would direct you to do otherwise. For instance, a neighboring two-story house may look directly out onto your ideal space, and you may prefer to have more privacy without the expense of constructing an overhead arbor. Then you may want to locate that space beneath the branches of an old tree farther away. Just be conscious of the fact that you have used more circulation space to go between spaces. If you could use the space for another function and it could still function as circulation space, that would be an efficient way to resolve the issue.

Follow the layout of the adjacency diagram as you add the next bubbles. At this point, ignore topography, or the fact that your land rises and falls slightly. Obviously, you cannot ignore a big cliff, but then you should not consider anything beyond that part of the garden unless you are prepared to include a substantial stair or terracing and have the budget to do it. One reason that the ravine on our property remains in its natural state is that it would be a difficult and expensive undertaking to terrace the space because of its limited accessibility. That is not the only reason, however. My spouse and I enjoy its natural state and like to see what nature does on its own down there.

One of my clients elected to add a substantial wood stair to get from the level of his house down to the level adjacent to the river. He uses a very large flat area at the lower level for his collection of zonally challenged plants. In addition to his plants, he installed a large patch of turf to create a natural amphitheater. He blended the edge of his property at the river with a variety of grasses. Now he harmonizes musical events with the river, the cliff, and remarkable plants. Another client worked around existing codes to install a deck cantilevered over a

river. A fire had destroyed the former owner's deck, and building officials allowed him to reconstruct it because the new deck was a replacement of the original deck.

Continue placing all of your bubbles until you are happy with their location. Once you have all of your bubbles in place, you will determine how to travel from one area to another. Are you able to use those initial direct lines of circulation? Is it easy to think of having an opening from one area to another as the means to transition from space to space, or will you need a less direct route? If the latter, make the route as short as possible—but use common sense. For example, suppose someone in your family or a good friend is physically challenged by a stair, yet that person will frequently use two adjacent spaces that are on different levels. Your route may need to be longer to allow for a ramp or sloped walkway than it would be if you allocated just a short distance for steps.

In some cases, the amount of space you have will allow for all of the functions you require or desire, but perhaps the way the space is divided as a result of the home's location on the property does not lend itself to placing some functions in the desired locations. For instance, what if the only place you can fit the fire pit area is in the front yard? Or what if the front yard is the only sunny place for a kitchen garden? It is important to look at space as just that—space. Do not let the existing use of a space redirect your thinking unless you are positive that you can either do without a function or swap one function's space for another.

It is no different from looking at the flexibility of indoor space. Just as you can have an office in what a real estate agent might call a bedroom, front yards can have courtyards or you can plant edibles among ornamentals. If it is imperative that you contain certain things within the backyard, you should calculate the square footage for that area separately and approach it as a separate project from your front garden. In the case of the hypothetical garden, I plan to maximize the use of space by being flexible about placement of different functions and by dividing some of my functional areas into smaller segments.

While you are arranging your bubbles, note on the edge of the drawing any design ideas or concerns you want to address later, during the final layout process. Additionally, as you are laying out the bubbles, refer back to the information you originally gathered. For example, you may have discovered earlier that your jurisdiction requires a setback for structures more than 6 feet tall. This requirement will affect where you end up placing a structure such as a greenhouse.

Now you can see how trade-offs, manipulation, and code requirements all come into play as you fit functions into a space. With your completed bubble diagram in hand, you are ready to gather ideas to stimulate the design yet to come.

The view of the river from this deck cantilevered over it is awe inspiring; the perpetual murmuring of the river, serene. Garden of Mark and Terri Kelley. Garden design by Vanessa Gardner Nagel, APLD, Seasons Garden Design LLC.

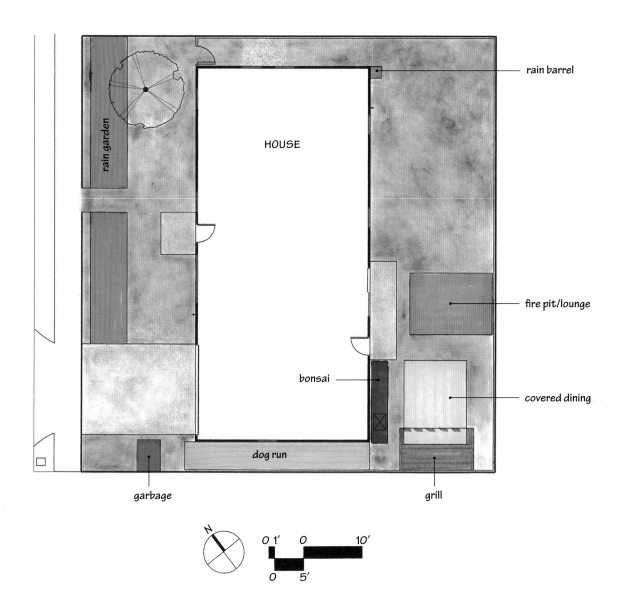

rain barrel

rain garden

HOUSE

fire pit/lounge

bonsai

covered dining

dog run

garbage

grill

N

0 1'   0   10'

0   5'

The first functional bubble leads to the placement
of the next, and so on. Subsequent bubble
locations follow the adjacency diagram's lead.

Designing the
Hypothetical Garden

The Bubble Diagram

In the hypothetical garden, I want to include a greenhouse. A 5-foot setback from the property line is required by the local jurisdiction for structures more than 6 feet tall. That means I must place the greenhouse at least 5 feet from the property line.

The hypothetical kitchen garden will have plants that require both sun and shade, which means I can make use of shady areas in the garden for a portion of the kitchen garden. I divide the kitchen garden into three segments: an herb garden close to the kitchen, a leafy greens garden along the northern side of the house for things like lettuce, and a garden for other veggies wrapped around the greenhouse, primarily in the 5-foot setback zone.

I place the rain garden out front, because if there is excess water during an event, the overflow will easily lead to the street and to the sewer system. Remember, what I am trying to do with a rain garden is to prevent water from having to go to the sewer system, so the overflow is for emergencies.

I locate the dog run along the south side of the house because the area is very close to the size I need, can also serve as a circulation corridor, and is adjacent to the garage. This location allows for a dog door, enabling the dog to go into the garage during inclement weather.

I had hoped to include the meditation area in the back garden, but there is just not enough space for it there. I decide to put it out front near the water feature, thinking I can create a courtyard effect with plants to shelter it from visitors heading to the front door. My ornamental garden is primarily left-over space and is more generous than I anticipated because there is less space devoted to circulation—an unexpected bonus.

The bubble diagram of the hypothetical garden shows its pattern of circulation and locates all the functional bubbles on the site plan.

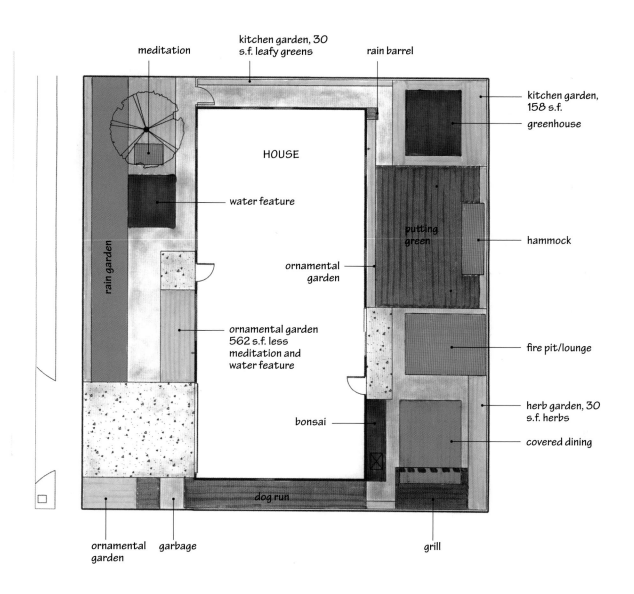

meditation

kitchen garden, 30 s.f. leafy greens

rain barrel

kitchen garden, 158 s.f.

greenhouse

HOUSE

water feature

rain garden

putting green

hammock

ornamental garden

ornamental garden 562 s.f. less meditation and water feature

fire pit/lounge

herb garden, 30 s.f. herbs

covered dining

bonsai

dog run

ornamental garden

garbage

grill

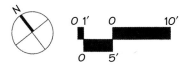

N

0 1'   0   10'

0   5'

Design 101

5

Why Basic Design Principles and Elements Are Important

Understanding basic design principles and elements is important to garden design. They are guidelines used to steer decisions and assemble varying components into an integrated and aesthetically pleasing composition. Basic design principles are universal, applying to all types of design problems. This is true even though following these principles may lead five different designers to come up with five different design solutions to the same problem, all of them viable.

Although all designers apply basic design principles, many do not do it consciously. There comes a point where a designer's aesthetic or sixth sense kicks in. Design skills become second nature. Intuition and experience become as valuable as knowledge of basic principles.

Among designers, varying definitions of design principles are easy to find and are often just a matter of personal expression, which can be confusing. What is important is to understand the characteristics and use of these principles. This is what will help you create a successful design.

Basic Design Elements: Color

In the array of basic design elements, color is unquestionably the most obvious and complex. While almost everyone sees the other

What you will learn:

- the importance of basic design principles and elements
- characteristics of basic design elements
- how to apply basic design elements to your design

An orderly rectilinear layout organizes numerous dynamic objects in this composition. Design by Daniel Lowery, APLD, Queen Anne Gardens.

design elements in essentially the same way, our genetic composition or DNA affects how each of us sees color. That said, the vast majority of us perceive colors very similarly, with imperceptible differences. It is easier for most of us to discern the difference between true hues—colors unaltered by the addition of black, white, or a complementary color. The more subtle or altered a color becomes, the more difficult it is for everyone to distinguish it in the same way. This insight helps me understand why there are people who try to match a shirt and pants that should not even be in the same closet together.

In addition to the influence of our DNA, characteristics of light affect our color perception. Light waves send messages to our eyes that the brain interprets as color. The amount, source, and quality of the light in which we view a color affects our perception of it. For example, yellow light makes the color purple appear brown. Natural light or white light reflected

A rainbow provides the perfect visual example of seeing the color spectrum as light.

from a red wall will cast a pink glow on surrounding surfaces.

The age of our eye also affects our ability to see color. Newborns possess color vision, with the exception of blue (Glass 2002). As we age, our eyes have more difficulty distinguishing subtle shifts in hue. In our fourth decade, our color perception typically begins to decline, though women are less affected than men. The lens becomes more yellow with age, so deficiencies in color perception are mostly in the short wavelength range, from yellow to blue. After the sixties, deficiency in the green range develops, probably as a result of retinal or more central factors (Timiras 2007).

Hue, Value, and Intensity

Regardless of how they are perceived, colors have three components: hue, value, and intensity. Understanding the influence of each component helps you understand how to use and manipulate color in your garden.

Hue is pure, unadulterated color—red, blue, green, and so forth. We can see pure color as light in a rainbow or prism. We can also see pure color as paint pigment or fabric dye.

Value refers to the degree or gradation of lightness to darkness of a color. This determines whether the color is a pastel or tint (light value) or a shade (dark value).

Intensity is how vivid or subdued a color is. Designers may also call this concentration or chroma. The degree of intensity of a color can be altered by adding its color complement. A color's complement derives from something called the afterimage. When one color overstimulates the eye, afterimages can occur. For instance, if you stare at the color red for a period and then look away to a white wall, you will see red's afterimage: green. This is a particularly useful concept when trying to prevent eyestrain, which ages our eyes. Practically applied in hospital operating rooms, for example, the color green allows the surgeon's eye to rest and refocus after overstimulation by the color red.

The value and intensity of a color affect visual scale. Dark or bright colors create more visual weight. If a pale pink ball feels too small or too light-weight, changing the color to an intense, deep pink will make it feel larger and heavier. A line will have more heft if it is black rather than gray.

Increasing the contrast of value and intensity also helps differentiate the hue of a color. A practical application is in areas of the garden where safety can

be increased by way of color cues, such as by care-fully choosing the nosing color on a stair tread. If the nosing clearly contrasts with each tread, the steps in a stairway's run are easier to see.

A selection of paint samples in the red family provides an example of the range of intensity within a single color. The intensity decreases from left to right.

The steps from white to black display the full range of a color's value.

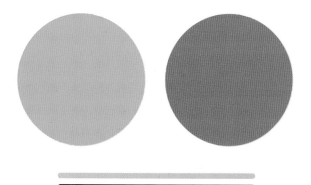

Two pink circles: the paler one feels smaller, the brighter one seems larger and heavier; the black line appears weightier and stronger than the gray line.

The nosing material of these steps contrasts with the tread material and surrounding patio, delineating a clear difference in materials. This improves the visibility of the stairway. A contrasting color would enhance the visibility further. Bellevue Botanical Garden, Bellevue, Washington.

The color wheel and color harmonies

The color wheel is traditionally the basis for many color harmonies. Its development was based on afterimages and the arrangement of colors as wavelengths, similar to a rainbow. There are numerous color theories, ranging from Boutet's color circles of 1706 to Goethe's color wheel of 1810 to the RGV (red/green/violet) color wheel of 1908. The color wheel we use today simplifies the use of color for many people, since there is an entire complicated science around the topic of color.

An oversimplified explanation is that we see color as pigment or as light. Most of us concern ourselves with color as pigment, which is how I will use it in the following explanation. Colors around the wheel are primary, secondary, or tertiary. Yellow, blue, and red are traditionally the primary colors, while orange, green, and violet are secondary colors. An example of a tertiary color is red-orange or yellow-orange.

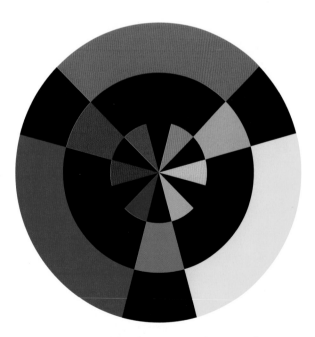

This color wheel has the primary colors around the perimeter and the tertiary colors at the center.

They are the colors between primary and secondary colors. A common technique for developing a color harmony uses colors in a logical sequence based on their location on the color wheel. A harmony's identity, such as monochromatic, analogous, or complementary, implies its composition.

A monochromatic harmony or scheme involves the manipulation of a single hue. What makes this scheme visually appealing is seeing the selected hue in a variety of values and intensities. A monochromatic red scheme might combine maroon (dark value, low-intensity red), pink (light value, medium-intensity red), and pure red (high intensity, medium value) flowers.

Analogous hues are next to one another on the color wheel—for example, blue-green, green, and yellow-green. Combine varied shades of green leaves for a cool analogous scheme in a garden of solitude to limit distraction, enhance concentration, and induce tranquility.

Adding a dash of warm color to our meditative analogous-schemed garden imparts just enough excitement to keep us from falling asleep and creates a complementary color scheme. (Notice how you can manipulate mood through color.) Complementary hues are temperature opposites on the color wheel. That could be red and green, orange and blue, or yellow and purple if only primary and secondary colors are involved. What makes this color harmony visually exciting is altering the state of at least one of the two complementary colors. For instance, red and green as pure hues remind us of Christmas. However, if I mute and tint the red to a pastel pink and darken the green to a deep forest green, you will be hard-pressed to recognize them as holiday colors.

Split-complementary harmonies are often popular because they are more complex. For example, begin with the color purple. Across the color wheel, its complement is yellow. On either side are yellow-

A scattering of wildflowers displays a range of reds, from pastel pink to true red to deep mahogany. Garden of Doug and Marcia Baldwin.

Yellow *Rudbeckia* and purple asters are a complementary flower color scheme. Author's garden.

Lush greens ranging from yellow-green to blue-green create a vibrant analogous color combination. Author's garden.

This *Choisya ternata* Sundance could be added to *Rudbeckia* and asters to create a split-complementary color scheme. Author's garden.

green and yellow-orange. Those two colors with purple create a split-complementary scheme. An example is a combination of purple asters with golden *Rudbeckia* and the chartreuse leaves of *Choisya ternata* Sundance.

Combining colors points up the fact that color is relative. Years ago, I worked for an architect who proudly declared, "I've never met a color I didn't like." I loved and agreed with his philosophy. He papered his office wall with overlapping photographs from the fashion industry, creating a marvelous collage of color inspiration. More important, he recognized that the juxtaposition of one color with another affects how we see the colors. The hotter

The darker and cooler the red foliage is, the more vivid the yellow-orange fall foliage of *Rhus typhina* 'Bailtiger' becomes. Author's garden.

an orange is next to a blue, the cooler the blue will appear. Seeing a color we like next to a color we dislike can affect how we feel about each of them.

Beyond the color *training* wheel

The first time I read that a designer did not use the color wheel concept, I was stunned. The color wheel concept has been around for a long time. This is what I learned in school. I began to wonder, Can we really get along without the color wheel and still produce a cohesive color palette? Should we use the color wheel only as training wheels for those terrified beyond white?

During the middle of autumn, deciduous plants do a slow striptease of their dazzling plumage; or in the case of several lusty blonde-leaved cherry trees in my garden, a heavy rain nearly disrobed them in one day. While I never considered myself voyeuristic, the array of colors outside my window captured my attention. In fact, Mother Nature tempts us to combine colors we might not otherwise consider, much like a kaleidoscope presents unexpected combinations of shapes and colors as we turn it.

After seeing magenta berries on a beautyberry mixed with the muted russet tones of the changing leaves of redbud, maple, and tree peony, I realized that this color combination, stretching a bit beyond the color wheel, did anything but clash. Not only did these colors look gorgeous together, they also looked fabulous with the limey yellow leaves of nearby bamboos. This was not just an inspirational but ephemeral outdoor color combination; it provoked me to rethink how to develop a color scheme.

For adventurous souls, going beyond the basic color training wheel is liberating. The arrangement of the colors magenta, russet, and lime is a split-complementary color scheme on the color wheel. While the color wheel provides a color selection background, what a simple color wheel does not exhibit is the more subtle aspects of color. It can limit our interpretations. If you consider other factors and set aside the design safety net, you can successfully combine many colors without ever glancing at a color wheel. How do you do that?

First, uphold a balance of shades, tones, and values. There is more information about unity and balance later in this chapter that will clarify how to balance a composition. For now, balancing refers to adding one color in a different shade, tone, or value to complement another color (not necessarily a different hue) in the same composition. For example, a small area of black will balance a larger area of light gray.

Second, view colors as belonging to either the yellow-tinted family or the red-tinted family. I would not be surprised if your eyes are glazing over at this point. The "deer in the headlights" look is common when discussing color. Although it takes practice, it is possible to differentiate colors of different tints. If you view blue and want to know if it leans toward yellow or red, you can use the principle that colors are relative. Place the blue in a group of blue paint chips and your blue's cast will become more apparent. The

Magenta berries on *Callicarpa bodinieri* var. *giraldii* 'Profusion' contrast with the muted russet tones of *Cercis canadensis* 'Forest Pansy', *Acer palmatum* var. *dissectum*, and *Paeonia suffruticosa* leaves. Author's garden.

Comparing a small black square with a large gray square demonstrates visual weight. The black square seems heavier.

These two blues—one from the yellow family (left) and the other from the red family (right)—differ in tint.

first time my college design instructor explained this to me, my eyes rolled up into my head, so my beloved spouse did not feel too bad when he had a hard time understanding it. Essentially, it is a contrast of the warmth or coolness of a color, respectively resulting from more yellow or more red. This does not refer to the hue of a color, like red versus purple. If you think of mixing paint, consider what would happen to the color blue if you mixed a bit of yellow or a bit of red with it. In the case of adding yellow, the blue would start to lean toward green. In the case of adding red, the blue would lean toward purple. When the tint is very subtle, it is harder to distinguish without comparing it to the pure hue.

Every color has a cool side and a warm side—even

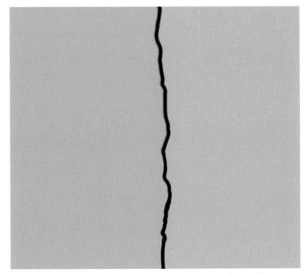

These two beiges—one from the red family (left) and the other from the yellow family (right)—seem to clash.

Factors that affect color choices

Many factors influence color selection. Recognizing these factors allows you to be more objective and intentional when selecting color.

- **Amount of light.** Knowing that the amount of light can affect color decisions, select colors under the conditions in which they will be seen. If you are older, you may want to invite a second opinion about your choices or ask someone else to make them for you.
- **Color names.** The names given to colors by manufacturers can affect our decisions. 'Tango Mango' sounds a lot more appealing than 'Mucky Mango'. I often wonder who picks those names.
- **Culture and belief.** Different cultures and beliefs also affect the use of color. Festive weddings in some cultures use the color

red, while the color white predominates in another. The colors purple, white, or black in differing cultures can signify death. Specific colors allow us to convey a message or set a theme in a design.
- **Preconditioning.** If your mother had wallpaper with maroon reindeer jumping through chartreuse flower hoops when you were young, you might hate that color combination as an adult. (Assume the worst when you wonder how I came up with this wallpaper description.) On the other hand, if your sister wore pink when you were growing up together and you adore your sister, you might love the color pink. Early childhood relationships to color often affect our unconscious decisions as adults.

blacks and whites. Clashing a warm, vivid orange with a cool, intense pink is an extreme example of combining two color types otherwise considered psychedelic. Many people have no problem looking at two colors and noticing they clash, but they may not be able to explain why. Often the simple answer is that one is a cool color (like taupe) and the other is a warm color (like khaki).

In the case of combining two colors that are usually seen as warm colors, like lime and russet, with what could be a cool color, magenta, the magenta would have to be on the warmer side to successfully complement the other two. A designer might say, "It needs more yellow." When you look out your window, you are likely to notice that Mother Nature does not use a color wheel. It does make a great learning tool, but maybe you can get by without one.

Basic Design Elements: Line, Shape, Form, and Space

Your vision and psychology daily assemble tens of thousands of lines into forms and shapes, yet how many lines do you consciously perceive? When you switch your brain off autopilot, examples of lines you might detect are the vertical line of a tree trunk, the horizontal line created by the edge of a table, or the wiggly lines of water weaving its natural course across soil.

You will also notice that lines have various characteristics. A line is either straight or curved, can extend in any direction, can vary in width, and can direct your view. A point moving through space becomes visible as a line at each new point it encounters. If you run into the line between the two points, the line will lead you to one of those points. A linear rill is a good example; it is able to lead you toward a pool at one end. Think of the lines you follow on a road, directing you to your destination. If you see a

columnar object, your eye has a tendency to follow the line of the object up or down.

Lines can be of any width or length. A garden hedge can be 6 feet wide and 60 feet long. A freeway is wider than several average city lots and can be hundreds of miles long. The lines of *Allium christophii* stems, from the soil to the starburst of its spectacular flower, are less than 20 inches long.

Lines create an emotional response. Zigzag lines feel dynamic and exciting but can increase tension. Horizontal, slightly wavy ribbons of passage feel restful and soothing but in some circumstances could be monotonous or put you to sleep.

Lines also divide space. A fence separates a large area into smaller areas. The crisp edge of a cut lawn distinguishes the lawn from the planted border.

The linear stems of alliums lead to their spectacular flowers.

Zigzag lines cause tension.

Curvaceous lines are soothing.

A line of sitting stones clearly defines the oval shape around the fire pit. Garden of Kim and Kathy Christensen. Design by Vanessa Gardner Nagel, APLD, Seasons Garden Design LLC.

When lines converge or intersect, they create forms, shapes, and planes, many of which are geometric: circles, squares, triangles, and so on. Used in combination with one another, these shapes create more complex geometry and visual interest. Lines can define form within space, as an elegant statue gives form to an otherwise vacant space.

Patterns of circulation

You learned during the development of your site plan that circulation is a primary concern. Circulation is provided for by a series of linear paths created by straight, meandering, parallel, or intersecting lines—each taking us to destinations within a site. A fence or hedge can crisply define circulation, or a garden seat can loosely define it. Consider the psychological impact of a narrow path with high walls on either side. Long, narrow paths are always a design challenge. Designers use many solutions to help break the length into bite-sized portions. Segmenting a long space creates space in scale with people, which is less intimidating.

Access through a garden in the form of a meandering path leads visitors around corners, creating mystery and curiosity. Rounding a bend in a garden also creates an opportunity for surprise, allowing circulation to enhance an element of fun.

Circulation can be on one plane or it can vertically take us to another plane via stairs or a ramp. Stairs create a diagonal, zigzag line. This creates a vibrant

The edge of a lawn is a dividing line between path and grass. Garden of Carol Kelly.

The interruption of the Italian cypress visually breaks the long path into smaller segments. Château Val-Joanis, Pertuis, France.

space if the line is exposed rather than enclosed. Even without the use of color to accentuate the stair, light and shadow will express the form.

Diagonal or variable curvaceous lines make a design composition more energetic. A path placed diagonally through a square space can be more dynamic and interesting than a path parallel to one of the square's sides.

Form and shape in the garden

Patterns of circulation create form that is readily visible in a plan or bird's-eye view. These forms need to relate to your house. Random curvilinear forms can be difficult to use in a small garden because they can weaken the garden's relationship to your house. In a small garden, a random layout can feel disordered. If you want a naturalistic curvilinear garden, create a rectilinear grid first that relates to the house. Use the intersecting points to lay out your curved line. This grid will help you maintain your garden's organic arrangement in proportion and relationship to your house.

Spatial form also creates emotional response. The formal geometry of a parterre garden would probably elicit a more reserved behavior from a visitor, while a looser, free-form garden would likely allow a less reserved reaction. Designers often use geometry that is more formal near a house, where more formal activities occur, and looser curvilinear forms farther away from the house in larger gardens.

You can use numerous shapes in your garden. If you choose to get much more adventurous than simple rectangles or curves, an excellent resource that describes the use of many forms in the landscape is *From Concept to Form in Landscape Design* by Grant W. Reid (2007). There you can explore layout themes using the ellipse, the meander, concentric circles and circle segments, various angles, the spiral, and more. An important issue no matter which forms you choose will always be the layout's relationship to the site and existing structures, such as your house.

Psychologically, your comfort with space plays a role in how you arrange forms within a garden area. When people lay out an area, they tend to fill the corners first. Perhaps our psyche wants to round out the shape of the space, possibly as a result of the tension that corners create. (A corner is just a part of a zigzag line.)

Lines can go in any direction. They can also connect to create shapes that are free-form or geometric. Lines define the edges of all shapes. Shape is two-dimensional. Form relates to shape but is three-dimensional. What surrounds forms or shapes, or is contained within them, is space. Space defines shapes and forms or vice versa.

When you combine lines, shapes, and forms, do so carefully. For example, a jumble of stone or plants creates lines and forms in many directions, which can make a design feel disorganized. Well-designed spaces relate and balance a limited variety of shapes and lines. A chaotic mix is overstimulating and often results when editing is not included in the design process. Create an orderly space by minimizing the arrangement of form and direction.

More Basic Design Elements

Besides color, line, space, form, and shape, there are a few other equally important basic design elements that you should be familiar with to apply to your garden design. These include proportion and scale, mass, focal point or emphasis, repetition and rhythm, movement, sequence or transition, texture, variety, contrast, balance, unity, and time.

Proportion and scale

Have you ever returned as an adult to your childhood home and discovered it to be smaller than you remembered? It is not really smaller, though; you are proportionately larger. Pretend you are four years old again. At that age, you are maybe half the size you will be as an adult. Your clothes, dishes, and toys fit your small size. Dressing up in your parents' old clothes is comical. So too, will a garden not *fit* if it is out of proportion to its surroundings or if its scale does not relate to its inhabitants. Try to recall how you felt in a space that was very large relative to you. Feelings that arise in this situation can include intimidation, discomfort, and an underlying sense of threat—or liberation.

How do we use proportion and scale to our advantage in the design of a landscape? What drives us to make spaces small and cozy or large and grand when we have the option?

In *The Biophilia Hypothesis* (1993), editors Stephen R. Kellert and Edward O. Wilson postulate that feelings about our environment are deeply rooted. In one chapter of the book, Roger S. Ulrich suggests that not surprisingly, early humans came to prefer environments in which their chances of survival were greater; thus, "people in Western and Eastern societies rather consistently dislike spatially restricted environments but respond with greater liking to settings having moderate to high visual depth or openness." A preference for the open savannah, however, could also change if an individual had a

A space seems larger to a child than to an adult because the child is proportionately smaller.

Note the difference in scale of a large garden and one that consists of a more intimate patio. An expanse of lawn framed by beautiful borders leads visitors to a lake at Killarney Cove Garden; an intimate patio garden graces the home of Anna Debenham and Charles Kingsley. Latter photo by Darcy Daniels.

Without much backdrop, this greenhouse looks people-scaled in this view. Garden of Doudou Bayol, Saint Rémy-de-Provence, France.

With the backdrop of the tall evergreen hedge, the scale of the greenhouse changes dramatically. Garden of Doudou Bayol, Saint Rémy-de-Provence, France.

traumatic experience such as a close call or an injury there.

In most cases, garden owners do not have the option of an open savanna. We usually must work within the framework of the property we purchase and restrictions imposed upon us by various entities, including local regulatory officials. Suburban and city regulations often require driveways to take up a disproportionate share of the front yard. Balancing the proportion and scale of a driveway's expanse with the rest of the front and/or side garden is always a challenge. So too will you need to consider the scale of objects in your design relative to one another.

If a garden is small as a result of a limited budget or large thanks to an unlimited budget, it can be out of scale to the users and the contents. Pay particular attention to the size of your house in relation to the size of your site. Are they in scale with each other or will they require your design intervention?

Mass

Mass relates to proportion and scale because here you consider using a quantity or mass of material— plants or hardscape (sidewalks, driveways, and fences). The use of a single plant or material in a large quantity creates a mass viewed more easily from a distance. If it is an evergreen plant, it will continue to have strong presence throughout the winter. Masses of plants simplify a planting scheme to better harmonize with a more intricate hardscape design.

The overall size of a mass of plants or hardscape is relative to its location, its use, and the size of the garden. One concern about massing plants is that oversimplification decreases plant diversity. A monoculture of plants does not provide wildlife habitat as well as a greater variety of plants. Consider massing native plants that provide food to more than one species of wildlife or that attract insects upon which wildlife feed.

The mass of a single plant makes a bold statement. Author's garden.

This container, with a study in blue, would catch anyone's attention. Note that the first plant your eye is drawn to is the tallest one. It acts as a focal point within a focal point. Meadowbrook Farm, Pennsylvania. Photo by Darcy Daniels.

Focal point or emphasis

A focal point is a place of emphasis, a point that draws attention. It can be any number of things: a plant with great structure or density, a piece of sculpture or art, a simple container with gorgeous plants. At least one place of emphasis is crucial to any design because it gives our eyes a place to rest. Without a focal point, a garden can be chaotic or boring—or worse, both.

Perspective also plays a role in the use of focal points by virtue of its ability to alter the scale of an object. If an object is closer to you, it will seem larger than it appears if it is 100 feet away. If you move closer to one object and away from another, your point of reference moves with you. When you place a focal point, remember to view it from multiple places in your garden, because its emphasis will change from each viewpoint. A focal point also alters perspective. Placing an object that draws attention by virtue of its color, form, or both at the end of a long path foreshortens the path, making the length seem proportionate to its width. This enhances our feeling of comfort traveling the path, because it does not seem as long.

Isolation also creates emphasis. For example, an object in the middle of an open space will be more obvious than one lost in the center of a jumble of plants. This is particularly important to remember if the object you want to use has considerable detail that will be lost amongst small leaves and dainty flowers.

You can also create focal points through color or size contrast. Most gardens have an abundance of green plants. A brightly colored turquoise garden seat will become a focal point amongst the green of the plants. When creating contrast through size, it is important to remember that a focal point is successful when it is in scale with its surrounding. If it is too small, it gets lost in the space and ceases to be

One simple but elegant pot in a sea of lawn is an unmistakable focal point. Garden of Ron Wagner and Nani Waddoups.

This colorful garden bench makes a welcome focal point. Château Val-Joanis, Pertuis, France.

a focal point. If it is too large, it overwhelms everything around it.

A frequent design faux pas is the use of too many focal points. A cute bird here, a funny thingamajig there, and a sweet little pot in between is more than our brains want to interpret at once. There is no place for a viewer's eyes to rest because they are too busy darting from one object to another. Too many focal points results from not knowing how or when to edit or from lacking an appropriate sense of scale. Appraise your garden as objectively as possible, considering the entire space, not just a view in one direction. Too many objects in one space diminishes the effect that each of them may have on their own. A single object has more power and can pull together an otherwise blowsy collection of plants.

On the same subject of too many focal points are focal points that have no relationship to one another. I have seen enough gardens that have a serene Buddha statue in one corner and a gnome 10 feet away. I want to encourage rather than quash anyone's creativity, but it does help your garden composition if you correlate your focal points—especially those you view simultaneously. Remember there can be multiple views, too, so evaluate the arrangement from all angles of the garden. If you must have something that is considerably different, find a special little place for it from which you cannot see any other clashing focal point.

Repetition and rhythm

While thinking of rhythm and repetition, I recalled the times I have sat on a train. That *clackety-clackety-clack* is a persistent background noise to every thought and conversation on the train. Music uses rhythm and repetition as an underlying force to unify its other components. So too do rhythm and repetition serve as background to garden design.

Rhythm and repetition are important to design because it would feel higgledy-piggledy to have every element in your garden be different. In fact, it could be so uncomfortable psychologically that you might want to leave the garden without necessarily knowing why. The best designs use the cohesive virtues of rhythm and repetition.

Rhythm implies that a regular beat, pulse, or cadence is occurring. It is what we tap our toes to when we listen to music. It is the beams in the patio cover or fence posts spaced at regular intervals. All the beams have a similar shape and size, as do all the posts. It is a common way to achieve rhythm.

Rhythm is easy to identify in a composition as repetitive and similar elements. Pointillism, a painting style that combines many colored dots that together read as a single color, is too subtle to be rhythm because all of the elements appear as one entity. However, if we were to space some toothpicks regularly on top of a pointillist painting, the similarity of the toothpicks, distinct from one another, would create rhythm against the colorful background.

Because the elements of rhythm consist of lines and shapes, rhythm has the same ability to evoke an emotional response. Rhythmic, angular objects are stimulating, while curvaceous objects are calming. Decreasing space between regular objects increases the pace of the rhythm, creating an energetic composition.

Repetition connotes that something recurs or replicates, without implying that there is any regularity to it. As in music, repetition does not need to be absolutely regular to create rhythm. While rhythm expresses itself through a fence, a hedge, or regularly spaced plants, you would see repetition in recurring flower colors, leaves, or plant shapes. Repetition is rhythm's subtler cousin.

Repetition often occurs at a small corner that coordinates with a larger corner, then twists to

Pots of *Taxus baccata* 'Fastigiata' in a regular line along a path rhythmically guide a traveler to the destination. Author's garden.

Repetitive arbors lure visitors through a rose garden. Photo printed with permission of Luther Burbank Home and Gardens, Santa Rosa, California.

become the edge of a table or the top of the back of a chair. It is like visible glue because it holds a composition together. The common shapes or lines gently lead your eye from one to another. Repetition is a strong unifying force because it uses similarly shaped elements in proximity to one another.

Can there be too much of a good thing? When do similar shapes and sizes, repeated colors, and the like cause an otherwise cohesive design to collapse? The answer is when they overpower everything else. If you cannot see the focal points for the rhythm, you have gone too far. If you have ever felt the overwhelming vibration of your house resulting from

nearby earth-moving equipment, you have an idea of a repetitive background gone awry. It distracts your attention, which is what rhythm and repetition should not do. They are supporting cast.

Movement

Movement in a garden can be literal or figurative. Natural breezes stir physical movement among leaves and branches, but movement is more than Mother Nature murmuring through your trees. Our eyes follow the line of a branch and then the outline of a house that intersects with that branch, and so on throughout a garden and continuing past the boundary of the property line. Beyond direction, lines create movement, which captures our notice. Rhythmic patterns cause our eyes to follow them. Strong color and form captures our attention. Creating visual movement in the composition of your garden adds a dynamic dimension to it, which puts a little sizzle in the steak. Pay attention to movement to enhance the level of vitality in your garden.

Sequence or transition

Sequence is about transitioning from one element within the garden to another—for example, from space to space, plant to plant, or plant to space. Some areas where transitions occur in a garden are from the street to the entry, from one level to another level, and from one specific area of the garden to another. People generally expect to move smoothly into and through a garden, without abrupt transitions. Even large gardens with distinctly different rooms have graceful transitions using a neutral zone for circulation. A change in the use of an area also dictates a transition (for example, a change from a more public dining area to a private area that requires solitude). If you want your environment to remain calm, use gradual transitions. However, design is all about intention. If what you want is a distinctly noticed

I took this photo in my own garden as fall was rapidly transforming flowers to seed heads. The lines of the grass blades move the eye, and the stems lean under the weight of spent flowers. The angles of the plant material make this view dynamic and energetic, with one planting pointing toward and contrasting with another. Repetition of the leaves of *Eupatorium purpureum* in the foreground and *Phlox paniculata* 'Nora Leigh' in the midground triggers our eye to move from one plant to another.

area, one way to get attention is to use an unexpected transition. But keep in mind that it could cause confusion, and use abrupt transitions cautiously.

Smooth transitions occur when elements from one area carry into another. Using the same paving, for instance, or similar plants or colors is important to maintain continuity in a design. Sudden changes in the paving material instinctively clue the garden visitor that there is something different happening. This concept is often used when the subtle message is "Stay on the path you were on. This is not the right path."

Texture

Whether we perceive it with our hands or our eyes, texture is all around us. When we are first born, our instinct is to touch whatever we see. We learn textures of objects and store them in our memory. Our reaction to a new object, even as adults, is to reach out and touch it. When I buy a new plant, I should look at the price tag first. Instinctively, however, my hands touch the leaves. We are used to coordinating what we see with what we feel with our hands.

The word *texture* comes from the Latin word *texere*, to weave. Perhaps this is why we so often think of texture relative to fabric. The broader meaning of texture from Merriam-Webster's online dictionary is "the visual or tactile surface characteristics and appearance of something." We feel *and* see texture.

When we see texture, we view it as one texture relative to another. Texture is fairly easy to see when comparing the leaves of plant material. Bold *Phormium* leaves adjacent to a delicate *Nassella* is an example of not only tactile but also visual textural contrast.

We see texture as a result of detail that creates a pattern. If you want something to stand out without changing its color, create strong contrast in texture, such as smooth against rough. The term "tone

An artistic garden owner created weatherproof ceramic leaves that the concrete contractor embedded in the colored concrete walkways, creating textural contrast. Garden of Fran and Sharri LaPierre. Design by Vanessa Gardner Nagel, APLD, Seasons Garden Design LLC.

This *Phormium* contrasts beautifully in texture with *Nassella tenuissima* next to it. Designed by Linda Ernst, Portland, Oregon.

99

on tone" describes the use of two degrees of sheen or luster in the same color—often shiny against dull.

A great way to see texture is to view it in black and white. We become dependent on color to help us differentiate one thing from another. Without it, we need texture to give us contrast and define objects.

Texture and pattern are linked arm in arm, like two friends. Texture is a pattern and pattern creates visual texture. Rough generally translates to bold, and soft to delicate. If we wanted to see the texture even more, we could vary the sheen of the pattern against the background. Glossy would translate as bold, while flat would be delicate.

Variety

"Variety is the spice of life," the old saying goes. We do not want to eat the same food every day—too boring. Mother Nature helps us out here with a wide variety of edibles. We do not want our house to look like our neighbors'; homes within our neighborhoods vary considerably in style.

If you look in your closet, you might see a fair amount of variety. Since you cannot (nor do you want to) wear the whole closet, each day you select a few things to wear that work together. How do you artfully create variety without wearing the whole closet? Use just enough color, pattern, form,

The black-and-white technique clearly demonstrates how texture differentiates each material in this path. Garden of Deborah Meyers.

Notice how this public bench, on a street in Rousillon, France, stands out from the background of the wall. Its visual texture is so different!

repetition, rhythm, scale, and/or texture to create interest. If you go beyond *just enough*, you risk creating confusion.

Contrast

Contrast is visible in many ways. We see the contrast of one color against another. We see it in texture and pattern. We notice it as proportion and scale. The degree of contrast is visible by virtue of simplicity versus chaos. If you include too much contrast in your design, you increase the chance your design will be chaotic.

Decrease contrast when something needs to disappear or be less obvious. For example, if you have an ugly yellow pipe against a black background, paint the pipe black or a dark color for it to vanish visually. Increase contrast to strengthen the visibility of items that you want or need to see. For instance, if you have a dark, smooth sculpture, you can increase its visibility by providing it a light, rough background. The amount and angle of light also contributes to how much contrast we perceive.

While the thought process behind design may seem complex, many of the best designs are simple. How do you simplify an assortment of items to prevent chaos? When is "the spice of life" too much of a good thing? As in any good recipe, the key is to keep it simple and blend well-matched items. The greater the degree of simplicity and organization, the more unified a design will appear to be.

Like singing a song with one note, too little contrast can be oversimplified monotony. It is critical to a successful design to find the right balance of simplicity and variety so that the design is apparent and not lost in the midst of too much detail. Appraising visual texture helps the editing process. Evaluate the sheen, the degree of boldness, the pattern of each plant in the garden. Consider creating masses of a few plants rather than a miniscule quantity of many plants to establish simplicity and minimize chaos. This is easier said than done if you are fanatical about plants.

Next time you go to go to the nursery to buy plants for a new border, try this exercise: after you have gathered a batch of *cannot-live-without* plants, set the group aside. Then move one plant over to a separate area. Add another plant, evaluating each relative to the whole design before you add the next one. Continue to add one at a time, keeping only those that work. Determine the dominant texture used to help all of the others work together. Savor the process as you would if you were creating an award-winning spicy barbecue sauce, adding just enough variety and textural contrast to make it exceptional. As in any good recipe, you never add the entire spice rack.

Balance

Balance and symmetry are virtually the same. They both imply a state of equilibrium. If our equilibrium is amiss, physically we lose our balance. We are comfortable in spaces that are in equilibrium. Balanced spaces put us in a state of equanimity, which is normally what we want to achieve. However, there are times when you intentionally want a space to be out of balance to achieve a desired effect. Knowing how it works puts you in control.

You can weigh objects on a scale to determine if they weigh the same. On this scale, a vertical support serves as the axis between the two sides. When you design your garden, you have to establish where that axis is located in order to balance visual space. Wherever you place your vertical axis in a design is where your attention naturally converges. There is also a horizontal axis, and balance occurs on both a horizontal and a vertical plane.

There are two types of balance: formal and informal. Formal (symmetric) balance usually means that each half of the whole is a mirror image. There is a more obvious axis in formal balance. Perhaps the sidewalk running directly to the central front door of a house is the axis. Formal balance feels calm and stable, but it can also feel too static. Informal (asymmetric) balance, where different things are occurring on either side of a not necessarily central axis, is more difficult to do well. Japanese design, garden and otherwise, provides us with masterful examples of informal balance.

Achieving balance in a garden is a little like walking a tightrope while we juggle a bunch of balls. The balls represent basic design principles, while the tightrope represents an axis. Balance suggests the state of being level or equal. Think of sitting on a teeter-totter: if an adult is on one side and a tiny child sits on the other side, the adult's rear end is on the ground. However, if several children were to sit on the other side, then the teeter-totter would lift the adult off the ground. You can apply that metaphor to balancing a design in a number of ways.

We achieve balance with a variety of elements and their inherent characteristics. Elements have shape,

In a good example of formal balance, an area of uncomplicated lawn balances the surrounding texture of plants and the raised seating area. Hardscape material, like gravel, or a low-growing, drought-tolerant ground cover can achieve the same effect. Garden of Michael Schultz and Will Goodman.

Recognizing visual balance and imbalance

Seeing equilibrium in a composition is a developed skill. To help develop this skill, look at these examples of balance and imbalance using a variety of leaves on either side of a black line that performs as a fulcrum. As an exercise to further develop this skill, try intentionally forcing a design out of balance. The lack of balance becomes more obvious.

The two leaves are of a similar size, but the leaf on the left has a simple bold form and a very dark-value, low-intensity color as compared to the leaf on the right. These two leaves are out of balance because the dark leaf has more visual weight. If the dark leaf were smaller, it would balance this combination.

The leaf on the left is a neutral green (medium tone, medium value) and the same size as the leaf on the right. The leaf on the right has more visual weight thanks to the strength of its color alone. If it were smaller, this composition would balance.

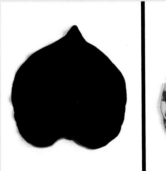

Substituting a leaf with high intensity color and interesting detail for the one on the right balances the two leaves.

Here the leaf on the left has a complex outline, soft texture, and detailed veining. Balancing this is the simple form and high luster of the leaf on the right.

form, color, and texture. If you use more than one of the same elements, you create repetition and rhythm. If you have two different elements, you can create contrast and variety. Contrast becomes an important characteristic in creating balance. The more intense the contrast, the more likely it will catch your attention. If there is too little contrast, you lose the dynamics of adequate contrast and become bored.

Visual weight contributes to balance. Dark, boldly colored, heavily textured elements appear heavier than their lighter, pastel, sleek cousins. Even an object's shape, if repeated by its shadow, can make it appear heavier.

Lines can also affect balance. They can guide a viewer's eye to a central point or away from it. When edges of mowed grass or other strong lines guide our eyes to one side or the other of a garden composition, it may feel out of balance. When a central point is the focus, the composition is balanced. Thus, you can use focal points to balance other elements because they are strong enough to hold a viewer's attention.

And placement of elements can affect balance. The position of one element relative to another can improve the balance of all other design elements or throw them completely off kilter. For instance, say you have a group of elegant, tall, white-barked birch trees on one side of your vertical axis. On the other side—at an equal distance from the axis—you place a short, round, dense pine tree. The birch trees will carry more visual weight as a result of their height and bright color. However, if you move the pine

Keeping visual weight in balance helps to unify the elements of a garden. Large objects, vivid colors, heavy texture, bold patterns, and high contrast have more visual muscle. In this garden, the strong color of the periwinkle blue wall equals the strength of the unique tree fountain, centered in a well-defined pool. Potentially, the base of the fountain, in contrast with the dark pool of water, is the "800-pound gorilla" of the garden. However, the surrounding hedge is bold enough to support that weight, as is the force of the blue wall. The Garden of Little and Lewis, Bainbridge Island, Washington.

tree far enough away from the axis, voila!—the pine tree gains more visual weight, which balances the composition.

Unity

Unifying the elements is one of the most important things you can do when designing a garden. While you can have balance without unity and vice versa, a garden will not feel harmonic or consistent, or create the sense of equanimity you may desire, without the successful use of both.

Unity is all about perception. The Gestalt principles of perceivable organization, proposed by German cognitive psychologists to explain how our brains interpret and organize what we perceive, are based on the idea that our brains have a tendency to simplify what we see. Another way to say this is that our brains tend to perceive the whole as more than the sum of its parts. Our brains interpret what we see in terms of our own way of making sense of the world, according to our own individual cultural and personal experiences. In other words, a brain is more than a camera, since it tries to make sense of what it's seeing. This explains why I overlook the hose lying right in front of me until after I have taken a snapshot. My camera sees the hose, but my mind sees the composition.

This rudimentary explanation of the Gestalt principles will help you understand how to create unity in your design:

- **Simplicity.** We arrange what we see in its simplest form. A succession of overlapping circles becomes one complex shape.
- **Closure.** We see objects as a whole or the sum of parts. We ignore a gap and continue a line. We do not see the leaves, roots, branches, or trunk of a tree. We see the tree. Even if we do

not have a complete picture, our minds fill in the missing part. We complete what we already know.

- **Similarity.** Our minds are inclined to group similar objects together. It is easier for our minds to do this if objects have a similar shape or color. We do not see each deer munching our hostas as separate components but rather as a herd of deer eating our hostas. (I hope that you have no deer eating any hosta.)
- **Proximity.** We are likely to perceive objects near to one another as a collection. We see the forest rather than individual trees.
- **Figure-ground.** We tend to differentiate a shape from a visual field. An object predominates against a background. While our mind sees both the object and the background, it only focuses on one or the other.
- **Continuity.** Once again, our minds want to see a whole rather than each component. In this case, our minds see elements moving in a common direction as a unit (for example, a covey of quail running through a garden or a lengthy stone wall rather than each stone). This explains why we will follow the path of least resistance (or where there is a fork in a path, we will follow the most obvious continuity of the two directions.) The concept relates to intuitive way finding. We tend to follow the continuing concrete walk rather than take the intersecting gravel path.

It is important to look at all of the parts of the garden and see what their relationship or contribution is to the whole design. It is equally important to understand the interaction of parts within the whole if you want to unify your design. The Gestalt principles can help. If I am trying to put my finger on why something does not look unified, referring to these simple principles helps me understand the problem. When you understand a problem, you can fix it.

Time

Mother Nature provides another element to consider in landscape design: time. We see its impact during the course of a day and throughout each season. Time is visible through the durability of exterior elements, architectural and otherwise. We see time as light and shadow, snowflakes and fallen leaves. Time is never more apparent than during the emergence of a flower bud, the elongation of a new leaf, or the colossal growth of a giant sequoia. The design of a garden cannot ignore the critical element of time.

Each season, perhaps each day, alters the balance and unity of a garden. As autumn, then winter, progresses, eliminating leaves and plants, we see the bare bones of the garden. Winter is an excellent time to evaluate how the remaining plants and hardscape work together. If those are balanced and unified, you have a head start on the explosion of bloom in spring.

Each fall, my exuberantly colored *Cercis canadensis* 'Forest Pansy' creates sunshine against a gray sky. After the first hard rainstorm, my deck is wearing the leaves. Mother Nature helps us balance plant material by equally removing leaves from all deciduous plants, keeping the leaves or needles on evergreen plants, and sending perennials back to their roots for a winter rest. What we have to do is to balance the placement of those plants, not only according to their ability to be around for the winter but also

In this quintessentially French garden, the repetition and rhythmic use of the pointy clipped yews and Italian cypress unify the garden, as does the coordination of the whimsical sculpture with the surrounding gravel color. What would happen to this unified landscape design if the owner added a Japanese lantern? Château Val-Joanis, Pertuis, France.

according to how they fit in with our basic design principles.

We see how each season changes the balance within a garden. So too does the balance change from daylight to moonlight. Because at night we cannot see color without light, form and texture play a greater role in the hushed transitions of dawn and dusk.

Design Consistency

One mistake I frequently see in garden design is a lack of continuity or consistency. You may like many things and want to put all of them into your garden. This is about more than chaos versus simplicity. This is about establishing a direction, maintaining a style, and restraint. A good design is not confused.

Style

It is important to include style among the other basic design principles. Style can be formal or casual. If the house is formal, keep the garden formal—at least near the house. If the house is casual, a casual garden will look more at ease.

You need not identify one particular style for your garden if you understand how to combine several styles into one cohesive design or know what to edit. In combining styles, consistency of detail, line, form, and scale are especially important. Styles need not match like a dining set on a showroom floor. Details work together based on whether the scale of one style bears a resemblance to another. Look for what styles have in common. For instance, if a style has predominantly straight, uncomplicated lines, carefully evaluate combining that style with

A casual meadow with a rabbit sculpture as focal point is a considerable distance from the house and its more formal garden setting. The sculpture is appropriate to the overall cottage garden theme of this garden. Garden of Robb Rosser.

one that is detailed and curvaceous. It is possible to do if the objects' scale and detail are in proportion to one another. Combining something like a simple glass table with a set of ornate Regency chairs can be stunning.

However, eclecticism is tricky. Materials can create a common bond. The stainless steel legs on a contemporary chair can work with an outdoor dining table that includes a bit of stainless steel in its design. Colors can also unify dissimilar objects. You can widen your variety of plants if you organize them around a single flower color.

Genius loci and a garden's theme

Beyond the architecture of your home, cultural attitudes, historical perspectives, and personal beliefs will influence your decisions about your garden's style. However, there is one more very important feature to consider: the surrounding environment, known as the *genius loci* or "sense of place" of a garden. Put simply, pay attention to the innate significance of your environment. Discover what makes your site unique. How is it different from neighboring sites? How is it the same?

Considering architecture, culture, history, and beliefs can be overwhelming. Discover threads of each of these that connect with you. This can become the basis of your garden theme. Establishing a garden theme will help you make decisions about what to include or exclude. Begin with any or all of the influences just mentioned and more. Artists may like swirls or glass. Railroad hobbyists may want a large-scale train puffing through their train garden. Philosophers may like symbolism. Just like your site, you are a unique individual. A garden is a place to express your individuality. Why would you want to

The same color organizes different styles of chairs around this table for elegant plein air dining in Provence. Moulin des Vignes Vielles, Eyguières, France. Photo by JJ DeSouza.

duplicate your neighbor's garden? You and your site are not your neighbor or his site.

Your ideas will work well when you put them in the context of your environment. If you live in an igloo, would it make sense to grow palm trees? On the other hand, traveling the logical path does not mean that you cannot have a garden of pure fantasy. Just keep in mind how it fits within your setting. Sometimes there is a fine line between distinctive design and sticking out like a sore thumb.

A good example of a garden suited to its site, architecture, and purpose was in front of a traditional and expansive government building I saw while walking in Paris. Its garden amused me. The garden consisted of intermittently placed, representational human sculptures popping up among lines of waist-high hedgerows. The scale, style, and simplicity of this garden supported the prominent old

building perfectly, without trying to compete with the building.

The inside of your house is not exempt from your genius loci. One of the best clues to what you might like in your garden is right there in your living room. Your interior should relate to your exterior. You can make it happen by paying attention to the furniture styles you use, the fabric and paint colors, and the materials of things like cabinets, flooring, and furniture. If you have a red, black, and yellow rug in your entry area, pull those colors right outside the front door in the form of plant color, pots, finishes, and furnishings. Allow the thresholds at your doors a little transparency rather than letting them act as a blockade. Make your environment read as a whole, not as two separate entities.

Just like the melody, chord changes, and tune of a song must harmonize, so too should elements

The gate is an artistic Thai style. The imaginative topiary bordering it is in keeping with the theme of the gate and the home. Garden of Ron Wagner and Nani Waddoups.

within your garden harmonize, and your garden be in accord with you, your house, and your environment.

Other Considerations Affecting Garden Design

Beyond basic design principles are a few other factors to consider. Function is not exclusive to garden design, but it plays an obvious role if you want your garden to succeed. Fragrance and my personal favorite, serendipity, are considerations more specific to garden design. Although these are perhaps not as important as other factors, they can make a wonderful garden exceptional.

Function

The function of a garden is as important as any design principle. By necessity, function should be a primary driving force in a design. This does not mean you abandon design principles, but it does means that your layout must work. There should be a synergistic relationship between function and design. A design cannot be exceptional unless it also functions well. This means circulation flow, adequate space for activities, and materials that wear well. This is why designers place so much emphasis on planning space and the resulting layout.

Garden function and design must also respect new science and discovery. Issues such as sustainability, biodiversity, the economy, climate change, and diminishing resources are playing an increasing role in the function of a garden. Change of functions alters the use of space and the patterns of our lives. Nowhere can it be more obvious than in how we use space in our gardens. With new challenges comes new opportunity. See the glass as half full.

Fragrance

We see leaves. We feel their felted or wrinkled texture. We hear them rustle in the wind. But plants in a garden offer us the opportunity to engage our senses beyond visual, tactile, and auditory. Fragrance engages our sense of smell, which according to studies stays with our memory far longer than any of our other senses. Fragrance can work with us or against us in the design of a garden.

It is very useful to know if a beautiful plant has an unpleasant smell. You may want to locate that plant away from outdoor living spaces or a well-traveled path. You will also need to know more about a wonderfully fragrant plant. How intense is the fragrance? Very intense fragrances are best experienced in a more limited time frame, as in walking along a path. A delicate fragrance is better located near a patio or front door, where you have more time to experience it and it will not overwhelm you.

A garden without fragrance would be less inviting, but there are circumstances that might cause you to restrict this feature. Fragrance can exacerbate allergies and asthma. Place fragrant plants thoughtfully in your garden.

Serendipity

While not officially a design principle, serendipity, or good luck, cannot be ignored as a factor that has the potential to impact the design of a garden. One year I planted several highly attractive and unusually colored violas in my garden. Serendipitously, they seeded around, expanding their realm, and created quite a beautiful massed planting. Then serendipity turned sour. The adjacent gravel path offered a charmed life for the violas. A few were delightful, few more a bit cheeky, and the eventual flood became the curse of my path. Serendipity does not necessarily stand the test of time, but there is always a chance it might provide more than an ephemeral effect for which you will be grateful.

Preparing Your Conceptual Plan

By now, you probably have some ideas swimming around in your mind about how to apply basic design principles to your garden design. Through the process of applying these principles, you will develop a preliminary design, known also as a conceptual plan. You may go through many iterations of the conceptual plan, trying on different ideas and concepts, before deciding on the one that works best for you.

At this point, you know the location of each function. You have a tentative layout, your bubble diagram. During the process of layout, watch the lines you draw. Do area shapes align? Minimize a chaos of lines and change direction when necessary. Proportion and scale will come into play when you study the shapes of areas. Is one garden area long and narrow? If you cannot change the space, break it into segments to alter the perception of it as skinny. Later in the design process, you can determine precisely what you will use to create the segmentation. Do you have a blank wall that will be monotonous? Develop several concepts to cover the vertical space. Consider the impact of its color. Does it need to change? Could another texture make the wall more interesting? Can you create an interesting trellis with rhythmic vertical and horizontal lines? Use basic design principles to develop conceptual solutions that respond to each space, separately and as an entire design. This is how you establish your conceptual plan, the draft for your final design.

Once you have your framework, you are ready to add furnishings, plants, irrigation, lighting, hardscape materials, and *style*.

Designing the Hypothetical Garden

The Conceptual Plan

Applying basic design principles to the bubble diagram for the hypothetical garden, I make decisions and develop a conceptual design.

First, I add circulation to the plan going the entire route around the house. I watch the lines and the shapes that they create. I offset the route to the house from the front sidewalk so that the route is not quite so direct. This makes the trip to the house feel a little more leisurely and not like you have to run right in the door. It sets a welcoming mood through its generous width. The main walk from the city sidewalk becomes a central axis with the water feature, tree, and bench adding visual weight to offset the driveway. The water feature functions as an auditory and visual focal point on the axis between the bench and the walk to the driveway.

The rain garden is on either side of the central axis and acts to unify both sides of the garden. The route over the rain garden can become a bridge. The rain barrel in the back garden can have an overflow that connects to the rain garden underground. With the right choice of plants, the rain garden can act as a screen for the entry garden.

I extend the bonsai area with the idea that a structure to support the bonsai may also disguise the HVAC unit without inhibiting its function. This minimizes the amount of variety surrounding the entertaining area and prevents it from feeling chaotic. The bonsai unit balances the herb garden on the other side of the entertaining space. The herbs offer fragrance to the entertaining area and other accent plants will provide some height variation for interest.

Seating in the fire pit area will create an interesting rhythm carrying the eye around the focal point of the fire pit. I add height to planting beds surrounding the putting green and provide privacy from the neighbors with an overhead trellis at the fence.

I resolve functional issues—some having to do with elevation, others with shape—as follows:

- The rain garden will need to have sides sloping down toward the middle and can blend with the other planted areas on either side.
- The leafy greens garden and the herb garden are extended to fill otherwise vacant space and maintain a sense of continuity. I add dashed lines to remind me to segment the long, narrow space with columnar plants or art.
- A fence with gates is added around the dog run.
- A dynamic structure to enclose the garbage is added to divert attention from the expanse of driveway.
- The fire pit seating area is made square rather than round.
- I decide to plant herbs around the grill to soften the patio.
- I try curvilinear shapes for the putting green

but in the end keep it rectangular. There are enough functions and detail in the back garden without adding curvaceous distraction. The green can be used as the path to the greenhouse, depending on what is used for turf.
- I decide I do not like locating the hammock within an area of activity (the putting green). There does not seem to be a logical place for it. Should it be in the design at all?

I make these additional design notes to myself to consider as I choose finishes and furnishings for the garden:

- Consider an ornamental rain barrel to prevent an eyesore.
- The meditation bench in front should also be an inviting place for guests.
- The expanse of fence behind the fire pit and the dining area should be disguised somehow.
- Art should be placed in the garden to provide focal points from certain windows in the house.

The conceptual plan for the hypothetical garden applies basic design elements and resolves functional issues.

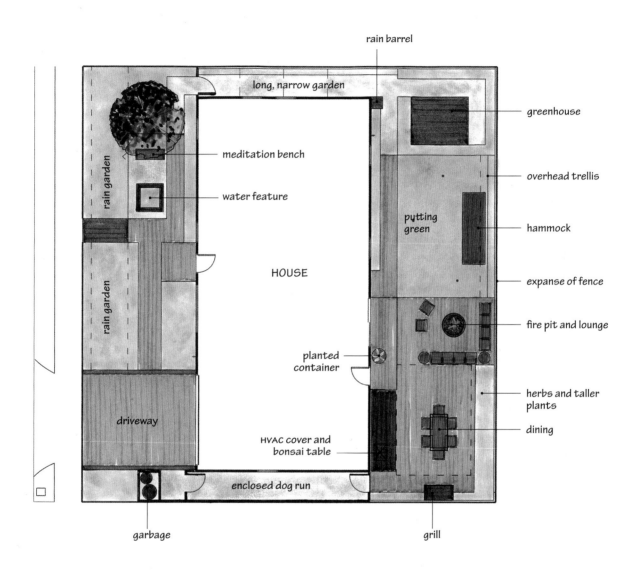

rain barrel

long, narrow garden

greenhouse

meditation bench

water feature

overhead trellis

putting green

hammock

expanse of fence

HOUSE

fire pit and lounge

planted container

herbs and taller plants

dining

HVAC cover and bonsai table

rain garden

rain garden

driveway

enclosed dog run

garbage

grill

N

0 1'   0   10'

0   5'

Finishes and Furnishings

6

Selection as a Process

Now you have a conceptual plan that provides the basis on which to select your finishes and furnishings. This is the time that most draws your attention to reality, because now is when you remind *design* it needs to follow a *budget*. The process of selection commonly begins with hardscape finishes, which are the materials for horizontal surfaces like paths and vertical surfaces like retaining walls. If you have furnishings (furniture and accessories) you will reuse, keep those in mind as you select the finishes and any additional furnishings. By the end of this chapter you will have a plan for your finishes and furnishings.

An enormous variety of finishes and furnishings is available today, especially with access to the Internet. Having a theme for your garden will help you make decisions, as will the architecture and interior of your home, which should have a major influence on the style of finishes and furnishings you select for your garden. You listed the materials significant to your house when you documented your site. Now they provide direction to select finishes, tables and chairs, and art.

It is also much easier to make decisions when you are equipped with an understanding of criteria for evaluating each finish or furnishing. Whether you are selecting materials for paving, vertical surfaces, edging, water features, overhead structures, storage spaces, or furnishings, consider these criteria:

What you will learn:

- criteria to evaluate finishes and furnishings

- which finishes will work best for your garden

- how outdoor furniture will suit your needs and style

- how to select accessories for your garden

This photo shows multiple types of concrete in one installation. The designer skillfully differentiates functional areas using the paving material. The green-colored concrete divides two functional areas in the garden and leads to another garden beyond. Garden of Michael Schultz and Will Goodman.

- **Safety.** Not all materials have safety as an issue, but among the materials that do are paving, edging, and overhead structures. You should review these for the safety of their finish, fabrication, and/or installation. Pay particular attention to the safety of materials in areas where you or a landscape maintenance contractor will need a wheelbarrow or where a wheelchair must go.
- **Security.** Review applicable materials such as fencing, gates, and/or hardware to make sure they provide the level of security you require.
- **Aesthetics.** Evaluate the appearance of all

materials for style, color, and finish, not to mention how they all look with anything you already have (like your house) and how they look with each other. Whether you will see a material as a horizontal surface or a vertical surface will influence your selection. Its orientation may cause you to consider a heavier texture or a different material or another color.

- **Durability.** All materials have a life expectancy. Stainless steel is virtually indestructible, while bamboo might last several years, depending on its application. Generally, you pay more for longer durability. Consider how long you plan

A fountain merrily bubbles away, providing a soothing background to a lounge area. Garden of Michael Schultz and Will Goodman.

to stay in your house in relationship to durability. If you can take an item with you should you move, get the most durable item you can afford. You may also consider that a less expensive item purchased to meet functional needs in an earlier phase of your garden can be replaced later with a costlier but more durable item.

- **Maintenance.** The ease of keeping a finish in good condition should be a primary concern. If you do not have the time to put a finish coat on a wood deck or furniture when they need it, wood should not be in contention as a material for use in your garden. If you know you will be using a pressure washer to clean a brick patio, reconsider using sand or gravel in between the bricks.

- **Sustainability.** Because of climate change, the level of sustainability of anything you buy should be of great concern. Manufacturers use such a broad array of practices that you should expect to encounter some dilemmas. It is not as straightforward as you might hope. For instance, teak can only grow in certain climates, usually meaning that it has to travel quite a distance. Weigh its use of transportation energy against its ability to regrow quickly, its being plantation grown, and its durability. See "Evaluating degrees of green" for things to consider.

- **Price.** Always purchase the best you can afford after you have evaluated all other criteria. Never take price at face value, though.

Evaluating degrees of green

Here are some questions to ask about an item's degree of sustainability:

- Where did the item originate? The distance it travels to get to your house is of concern. Obviously, the shorter the distance, the less energy its transport uses, reducing greenhouse gases spewed into our environment.

- Does this product limit how much new material it takes from the earth? What is the percentage of recycled postconsumer waste (what people throw away when they are done using an item) contained in this item?

- Is the material a renewable resource? Is it biodegradable? How much postconsumer waste does this product generate?

- Can this item be recycled into the same thing or at least something else? Ideally, it recycles to the same product.

- How long will this item last before you have to replace it? Sometimes you can justify purchasing something less renewable if it has a very long life span.

- Is the manufacture or fabrication of this item sustainable? How much energy does it use to produce it? How much waste is generated by its production? How does manufacture of this item affect our natural resources: soil, water, air, trees?

Sometimes a more expensive item has a much longer life span. If you know an item will have to be replaced every five years, how expensive is this item compared to an item that costs twice as much but lasts twenty years?

Landscape Finishes

Some finishes you decide to use may involve a drawing so that either you or your contractor can fully understand how to construct it and price it. In some cases, a fabricator will create it off-site and install it for you. How will you communicate what you want to them? If you have a photo or a drawing, you will need to provide sizes, and in some cases details, to have it constructed properly. You can discuss the details with the fabricator to develop solutions.

One of the biggest mistakes I see in design is overlooking the details of an intersection of two different materials. All materials have a rate of expansion (under heat) and contraction (under cold). Putting two materials together means you need to allow a little extra space for them to continue to expand and contract at their normal rates. Be cognizant

The copper in this arbor (inspired by a Chinese furniture book) will develop patina over time, while the bamboo will deteriorate. The rate of the bamboo's decline will depend on weather conditions. The chartreuse green leaf and deep red ornamental glass finials near the top will remain unchanged for the length of its use. Designed by the author for the author's garden. Copper fabrication by Mike Lindstrom. Blown glass by Andrew Holmberg. Complete assembly by Gordon Young.

An artist created this copper and steel birdbath with recycled materials. The item was purchased at an annual recycled art fair. Author's garden.

of raw edges, such as the side of a piece of wood. If you choose to expose them, will you need to finish them? Pay particular attention to butt joints, where one material simply adjoins another material at their edges. The simplest intersections are often the most elegant. However, I have seen a tremendous amount of thought go into a detail to make it appear simple.

The extensive variety of paving materials available means that you should be able to find something that will fit into your budget and serve your purposes. Each paving material has a specific degree of slip resistance, expressed as a co-efficient of friction. The higher the co-efficient of friction, the better traction you will have and the less likely you will be to slip on the material. For example, rubber on wet concrete has a co-efficient of friction of .6, while rubber on dry concrete has a co-efficient of 1.0—almost twice the resistance of wet concrete. Some materials have a greater difference between wet and dry, meaning they could be considerably more slippery when wet. Usually the smoother the surface, the more likely it is that it will be slippery when its degree of wetness increases. There are coatings that you can apply to a surface to improve its traction—but coatings usually increase a material's maintenance because they generally need to be reapplied at some regular interval.

The category of structures covers a vast array of outdoor construction. Arbors, decks, pergolas, gazebos, retaining walls, guardrails, stairs and stair railings, fencing, and much more require some amount of engineering to assure they are safe and will not collapse once installed. That is why building codes exist. Structures can be built of stone, concrete, metal, wood, glass, and more. Manufacturers and vendors introduce new products regularly. Investigate! You never know what you might find. Following is some basic information about often-used, standard products.

These different materials are elegantly joined. Garden of Michael Schultz and Will Goodman.

Natural stone

Natural stone is the finish of choice for many people, but it can also be one of the most expensive. The advantages of natural stone are its beauty and ability to last for a very long time. Inside the Emperor's Garden within the Forbidden City in Beijing, China, ornamental landscape boulders and stone paths are hundreds of years old. Worn areas where foot traffic typically falls describe the durability of stone.

Selection. The largest selection of stone will be at a stone yard. There they will usually have some sample installations, large boulders, wire cages containing a measured amount of stone, and places where you can obtain small quantities. Stone can be precut to a square or rectangle or it may be a free-form flagstone for paving. Depending on the type of stone, it may come in different thicknesses. Precut stone that comes in tiles may also be gauged (have a uniform thickness), making it easier to install. Masons (contractors who specialize in masonry installation) usually install thinner stone (1 to 2 inches) over concrete (sometimes called a rat-slab). The thicker stones (3

There can be quite a difference in stone color between dry and wet. Pay particular attention to this if you plan to seal the stone.

inches or more) are installed with or without a concrete base. More recently, stone that has been precut to use as a veneer has become available. Sometimes it is prebacked as tiles, increasing the ease of installation. You will find stone as boulders and gravel, for horizontal and vertical surfaces, and for nearly any application you can imagine.

Origin. The origin of your stone may be a factor in your choice. Some stone comes from as far away as China, India, and South America. This information may also tell you something about the stone's durability outdoors. There are stones that should be restricted to an indoor installation. Stone native to your area will look more natural in your garden.

Finishes. You can purchase stone in a variety of different finishes. A natural finish will generally have a fair amount of variability to the surface. If you need to reduce that variability, the stone will need to be cut and finished. Some available finishes are polished, flamed, and honed. Each of these finishes has a different sheen and slip resistance. Before you decide, test each one by walking on it—wet and dry.

Colors. Stone also comes in many colors. Be sure to wet the stone if you are selecting it on a dry day to see how the color changes. This will also give you a good idea of the color if you plan to seal the stone after installation.

Installation. Installing stone can be a do-it-yourself project if you have the strength, some basic skills, and knowledge. However, masons generally do the best job of installing stonework. This is one reason installing stone is expensive, particularly if you hire a quality mason. Many of the best masons could be called artists, because they are expert at seeing the proper orientation of the stone and understanding how to cut it to show the stone to its best advantage.

They should also know stone's structural characteristics, density, and ability to absorb water, important items to know for most applications.

There is an ancient method of installing smaller stones or pebbles called pebble mosaic. These are patterns of pebbles installed in either sand or mortar. When properly installed, a mosaic will last for a very long time. Pebble mosaics are a hardscape tradition in many different countries around the world. Almost any pattern you can imagine can be a pebble mosaic. Your only limitation is color and size of stones available to you. The size can limit the detail within a given pattern, so if you decide to include a pebble mosaic in your garden, find out what is available to you before you finalize your design.

Maintenance. Natural stone is usually very easy to maintain, particularly if you have opted not to apply a sealer. Sealers require periodic reapplication, depending on the recommendation of the manufacturer and your specific conditions. The more extreme your conditions, the more frequently you will have to reapply the sealer.

Price. Mid-range to expensive. Availability, origin, demand, and ease of installation will impact the cost of natural stone.

A lovely pebble mosaic installed as part of a fire pit area has as much hypnotic potential as the fire itself. Marcia Westcott Peck Landscape Design.

Concrete pavers, retaining wall systems, and cultured stone

A wide array of sizes, shapes, and colors of concrete pavers, retaining wall systems, and cultured stone is available.

Selection. Pavers come in varying thicknesses. Make sure that the thickness works for the type of paving you have in mind. Some pavers are made specifically to improve permeability of an installation. This enhances drainage and reduces storm water runoff by allowing the water to absorb into your soil.

Retaining wall systems come in variety of styles and textures. There are systems designed for ease of installation, but a contractor (or you) will still need to know the basics of retaining wall construction. Water pressure can easily cause a wall to fail if it is installed improperly. If the wall is more than a certain height, you will probably need to get a permit and have the wall engineered to assure proper construction. You need drainage behind a wall and footings to support the wall. Also, the wall will likely need some degree of *batter*, or slant in the direction of the retained soil.

Cultured stone, a concrete product made to look like stone, is a fairly recent introduction. It is similar

A curvaceous dragon breathes life into a circular pebble mosaic. This ancient, multicultural symbol corresponds with the circle of time, represented by the inner circle planted with thyme. Designed by the author for the author's garden. Installed by Jeffrey Bale.

to stone that is precut and perhaps prebacked to use as a veneer. Some products imitate real stone more successfully than others do. Usually the better the imitation is, the higher its cost.

Installation. Almost any landscape contractor can install pavers with relative ease. It is important to first install a well-packed, sound base according to the manufacturer's recommendations; following the manufacturer's instructions will help maintain the warranty of the product. Pavers are usually easy for do-it-yourselfers to install, too. You can set pavers on sand or mortar in place. Retaining walls need more expertise and, as mentioned earlier, their installation may need to meet local codes.

Maintenance. Concrete pavers and retaining wall systems are usually easy to maintain. If you live in an area of the country where moss grows easily, you may have to consider using a pressure washer occasionally to keep it at bay. Many manufacturers produce permeable paving products, but you may have to weigh the benefits of permeability against maintainability. If you must install your pavers with mortar or polymeric sand, creating an impermeable surface, then make sure you resolve how to capture runoff water or guide it to a safe place.

Poured-in-place concrete

Concrete can be poured horizontally for patios or vertically for retaining walls and other things like seating, fire pits, and more. Vertical concrete may need to be engineered, will usually require steel reinforcing, and can be the base for other materials on top of it, like stone or brick.

Selection. Concrete comes in several different textures and colors. The broom finish is a standard, inexpensive finish that provides good traction. You

can also have patterns imprinted into concrete that mimic the look of natural stone; rectilinear patterns appear more convincing. Concrete can also be smoothly polished or textured with stone aggregate at the surface. Permeable concrete is also available, but as an emerging technology, will need thorough investigation.

Color. There are several ways to color concrete. Powdered pigments (known as integral colors) can be mixed into concrete in its liquid state. This technique colors the entire material. Integral colorants usually result in a grayer, less intense color. Another

Concrete pavers are an excellent alternative to black asphalt paving. They reduce the driveway's heat gain and, without mortar, improve site drainage. Garden of Mark and Terri Kelley. Design by Vanessa Gardner Nagel, APLD, Seasons Garden Design LLC.

way to apply color to concrete is to cast colored powder over concrete during its installation. This usually results in a little brighter color. The most intense coloration of concrete comes from concrete stain that is brushed or sprayed on. Often, applicators will spray a mix of colors with stunning results. The latter two coloration methods require a sealer to minimize scratching of the concrete. In both cases, the pigment penetrates only into the top surface of the concrete. Installations usually combine two of these methods to improve the aesthetic longevity of the color. Colored concrete fades over time, depending on its degree of exposure to sun, although sealer will extend the life of the finish.

Installation. When installed correctly, concrete has a well-compacted gravel base and usually rebar reinforcing for larger areas. Either you or your contractor will have to install temporary frames to contain the concrete while in its liquid state. Finishing is everything in concrete. The better the final finish, the better your installation will look and wear. Many do-it-yourselfers can do this type of project if they take the time to learn proper installation methods.

Maintenance. Concrete is usually very easy to maintain, especially if you apply a sealer as the sealer's manufacturer recommends. The sealer helps prevent stains and surface degradation from wear and

Here is a contemporary garden installation in progress. The concrete retaining walls required engineering and were poured in place to retain soil before installation of the rest of the garden.

weather. Sealers involve periodic reapplication. Investigate sustainable options.

Price. Concrete costs range from low to expensive, depending on who installs it, the final finish, if and how it is colored, and the overall square footage. The more area you cover, the less you will pay per square foot.

Gravel

Gravel always has a nice crunchy sound to it and provides good drainage if it is not too tightly compacted.

Selection. Gravel comes in various sizes, types of stone, and with or without fines (tiny stone particulate). For instance, quarter-minus gravel is ¼-inch-sized gravel with fines. Whenever gravel's description includes *minus*, the gravel includes fines. Different descriptions of gravel exist. Your area may have its own vernacular, so discuss the application and size of material with your rock yard. Fines allow gravel to compact and stay in place. Quarter-minus has a fine texture that is often preferable to ⅝-minus. Do not use pea gravel as a paving material. It travels, meaning it will be nearly everywhere other than where you want it. The stones are rounded and do not compact. It is a more difficult material on which to walk, something that would be challenging for a person with a cane or in a wheelchair, and for a wheelbarrow.

As people become more interested in sustainability and recycling, they uncover unconventional types of "gravel." One that I have seen is recycled ceramic fragments that were tumbled in a concrete mixer. This type of gravel is probably better suited to a limited area unless your great aunt willed you a huge collection of old dishes or you can find them in a local thrift store at excellent prices.

Gravel is an honest material, used in many locales around the world. It is especially useful to allow water to percolate through the soil on your site. This designer artistically combines it with a beautifully installed stone wall accented with blue glass orbs. Garden of Michael Henry and Barbara Hilty. Design by Barbara Hilty, APLD, Barbara Hilty Landscape Design. Stonework by Chris Randles, Emerald Stone Masonry. Blown glass by Andrew Holmberg.

Installation. To keep gravel in place, it helps to have a compacted base of a larger gravel size (¾ inch to 1½-inch minus). You will need to select an edging material to contain the gravel. Then it is just a matter of shoveling the gravel into a wheelbarrow and placing it where you want it, at least 4 inches deep after compaction. Use landscape fabric as an underlayment to minimize the downward migration of gravel and to minimize deep-rooted weeds.

Maintenance. Gravel takes a bit more time to maintain because seeds love to germinate in it. Naturally, most of them will be weeds, although I get terrific germination of things like *Aquilegia* in my gravel paths. When that happens, I transplant or compost them and repair the path. I also use a weed torch to keep weeds from commandeering my paths. I have sprayed distilled vinegar on weeds, too. This technique works pretty well on most weeds but not all. It is the very rare occasion when I resort to anything more serious and only because I have no other means to control a weed party in the middle of my path.

Price. Gravel is one of the least expensive materials you can use. However, it can still be an elegant *and* utilitarian material.

Wood

Lumber is rarely used for anything below ground level unless it has been pressure-treated, a chemical method that renders wood resistant to deterioration. (But note that pressure-treated wood and old railroad ties are unsuitable for use around edible plants, because the chemical in the wood can leach into surrounding soil.) Wood chips make a terrific path, particularly if the chips are a rot-resistant wood such as cedar or redwood. Certain types of wood chips have the additional benefit of slow deterioration and insect resistance. Slices of rot-resistant wood logs make lovely "stepping-stones" through a woodland,

although over time they will deteriorate. You can also use vertically placed short logs to retain a low level of soil, a popular technique in Japanese garden design.

Selection. Newer, sustainably harvested woods, certified by the Forest Stewardship Council, are making their way into the market as outdoor lumber. Keep in mind the shipping factor that might add expense and use more energy. Wood composite products that look like wood, cut like wood, but last longer than wood are another option. Find out whether the wood composite you are considering meets structural requirements. You may need to use another structural wood product in combination with a composite material.

Installation. Installing a wood deck or arbor involves knowing something about structure. Make sure that your work meets code requirements, intended to keep your construction intact and safe. Installing raised beds made with wood or a wood composite is an easy beginner's project that typically does not need to meet structural codes. However, if you add a seat to the top, you want to make sure that it is structurally sound.

Maintenance. Real wood requires regular maintenance, but it is so beautiful many people are willing to do the maintenance it takes to keep it looking good. It may need occasional pressure washing, cleaning, or sanding before being refinished. You can stain or paint wood any color you wish, which is a big plus. If you want to apply a coating to pressure-treated wood, talk to your paint vendor about a suitable product; pressure-treated wood does not take stain or paint in the same manner as standard wood. Composite wood is popular because it needs virtually no maintenance except occasional cleaning.

Price. Real wood is moderately priced. Composite wood can cost twice as much or more.

Metal

Metal is generally used for railings and vertical surfaces, and very rarely as paving except in special circumstances. On occasion, you will see metal used for stairs or as a bridge from one area to another, with the metal pierced for drainage and to provide traction. Steel and copper make wonderful arbors, pergolas, and gazebos, with nearly any design a possibility. Combined with other materials like wood or glass, metals make a beautiful addition to multimedia garden structures or garden art.

Selection. Metals come in either sheet form or pipe in a variety of gauges. Gauge refers to the metal's thickness. The lower the number, the thicker the metal.

The fabricator will determine the gauge depending on the application. The more structural the application, the thicker the metal will need to be. Cor-Ten steel begins with a rusted appearance; in a suitable gauge it can make a spectacular, slim, retaining wall. Copper will oxidize, turning a darker brown, and will eventually have some bluish turquoise streaks or patches.

Installation. Metalwork typically involves on-site measurements and off-site fabrication. An installation may come in segments and then be pieced together at the site. Fabricators generally, and preferably, install their own work.

This Cor-Ten steel retaining wall and raised planter makes a stunning backdrop to plants. Photo by Cameron Scott.

Maintenance. Because metals oxidize (react to air), with few exceptions, they may need to be maintained. This is your choice. The process of oxidation is often desirable because it gives some metals a beautiful patina. There are products on the market that will coat metals and prevent additional oxidation, but you have to apply them repeatedly to continue the effect. You can also have metals powder coated with any color; this prevents further oxidation and does not require reapplication. Also, consider the environment in which you live. Salt air can oxidize metals more quickly.

Price. Metals are usually moderately costly to expensive, depending on the finish, the gauge, and the amount of labor to fabricate a piece. If the metal gauge is slim and the metal is allowed to oxidize, it can be inexpensive. Hot rolled steel is cheaper than cold rolled steel, although the fabricator will have to contend with the "hardcoat" or outer layer that retards rust. Evaluate the use, as well as the initial and eventual appearance of the metal. Rusting steel may look great, but if you create an arbor with it, you will have rusty drips all over the paved surface below.

Edging

Edging comes in different materials and can keep areas neat and distinct.

Selection. Three different types of linear edging are on the market: wood, steel, and plastic. Wood, in the form of bendable board (commonly called benderboard), can degrade over time, even when it has been pressure treated; pressure-treated wood just takes longer to degrade. Coated steel has a minimal thickness, tends to be a choice edging because it lasts a long time, and is not particularly obvious when installed. Plastic is popular thanks to its low cost and is readily available; however, plastic has a tendency to heave out of the ground during freezing weather, get out of its original alignment, or develop

Steel edging divides two different materials and hardscape from a planted border. Created by Laura M. Crockett, Garden Diva Designs.

a wobbled appearance, particularly if it is improperly installed.

Stone can also make a beautiful, naturalistic edging, whether cut or not. Even pavers turned on their side can make a good edging material. Unconventional materials like the bottoms of upturned bottles can create interest and a chuckle in otherwise lackluster places. Investigate other recycled materials.

Installation. Any linear product requires some sort of staking to keep it upright and in place. It is relatively easy to do. Stone needs to be placed in a way that looks good, requiring more skill and muscle. Pavers on end are also easy and fast to do. All require a few pieces of equipment, like a level, mallet, hammer, nails, stakes, and a shovel to do a little excavating.

Maintenance. Wood edging will need to be replaced periodically as it deteriorates. Composite wood might be an alternative; however, it may act a little like the plastic if it is thin like benderboard. Plastic edging may need reinstallation periodically if it gets out of alignment or heaves during freeze-thaw cycles.

Price. All the edging materials except stone are relatively inexpensive.

Mulch

Mulch is an important component of any garden because it helps keep weeds out, retains moisture in the soil, can prevent roots from freezing (depending on where you live), can decay in place adding nitrogen to the soil over time, and makes your garden beds look tidy. Numerous mulches are available, often depending on where you live. If you live near abundant pine forests, you may have easy access to pine straw; if you live where redwood trees and cedar proliferate, mulch from those trees is readily available. Compost is especially good as mulch because it

feeds your soil the minute you put it on the ground. Quite a few different composted mulches are available, often including the composted bark of local trees. Mulch colors can vary; I prefer varieties that match the color of the native soil.

I often use my own version of lasagna layering to keep down weeds. If I want to get an area under control before I plant it, I wet the area thoroughly (or

Quarter-ten gravel mulch wicks away moisture from the crowns of plants during winter, keeps their roots cool, and minimizes water use during summer. Joy Creek Nursery, Scappoose, Oregon.

wait for rain), then layer cardboard or newspaper on top of the soil, thoroughly soak the cardboard or newspaper, and finish with a 2-inch topping of compost. I modify this method if I already have plants in place. Instead of the cardboard, I usually use four layers of newspaper (with soy-based ink) around the plants, soak the newspaper, and add compost. When I do this where soil is compacted with lots of clay over the winter, I usually have soil that is much more friable by spring. Worms love paper products. They wiggle up through the soil, take bits of the paper back down with them, and aerate the soil in the process.

Another terrific mulch is a gravel product called quarter-ten in my area of the country. Rockeries screen this gravel through a #10 filter to obtain the required size. It contains no fines. I have also used pea gravel as mulch, although its pebbles are a little larger. Both pea gravel and quarter-ten perform as a wick around the crown of plants, keeping moisture from rotting the crown by providing good top layer drainage. I have used gravel over newspaper, too. Remember that the identification of stone products may be unique to your area.

Furnishings

If you have furnished the inside of a house, you have some idea of what furnishing the outside of your house entails. Tables and chairs, pots and containers, and art are the usual garden furnishings. I would also consider nonelectrical lighting as furnishings.

Garden furniture

If you have existing furniture that you want to reuse, now is the time to evaluate its condition. Does it need refurbishing to look its best? Can a powder-coating company give it a new finish to extend its life? This evaluation can also apply to recycled furniture that you find. If you know you want to purchase new furniture, you have an expansive selection to choose from. If you are eliminating existing furniture, try to sell it or give it to a charitable organization for recycling.

Will the style of your existing furniture suit your new garden? If you purchase new furniture, you need to establish some parameters before you head out into the marketplace. One parameter is to apply the style or styles that will be suitable for your garden. If your garden will be contemporary, stay with furniture in a contemporary style. If you will have a cottage garden, consider something like the new weather-resistant wicker styles. You can create an eclectic look if you know how to make that work and if it is appropriate. Again, the major clue is your house and its interior. Recall the discussion about proportion and scale and other "Design 101" tips.

The great outdoors can be hard on materials, so a thoughtful evaluation of what will work in your situation is in order. If you live in a hot, dry climate, you will need materials that can resist the UV rays of the sun. If you live in a humid climate, you will be fighting moss, mold, and mildew. You may need to over-winter upholstered seating indoors during the winter, even if the manufacturer says their furniture will endure outdoors.

Upholstery. Natural fibers do not work well outdoors unless you use them only temporarily and then bring them indoors. If you want to leave upholstered pieces or fabrics outdoors, use a fabric made for that purpose—generally polypropylene, polyester, or nylon. Try to find fabric that uses recycled material, because most synthetic fabrics begin with petroleum. Outdoor fabrics are weather resistant but not bulletproof; some care is still in order. Always read the literature provided by the textile company. Fabric that has the pattern woven into it will usually last longer than a printed fabric (you can tell a printed fabric because the other side of the material is lighter than the primary side).

The good news is that more textile mills are making fabrics for outdoors, so the colors and patterns available are increasing. They can make a big statement in a garden, with or without flowers.

Functionality. Whatever you purchase has to function well, or it is money wasted. If a dining chair will be turned frequently to face a nearby fire pit, does it swivel? Look at the paving on which tables and chairs will be set. If you put a pointy-legged chair on grass—guess what?—you will sit a little lower soon. Use legs that will sit well on grass without piercing it. Also, how easy is it to slide a chair on your selected paving? Sometimes selection is a back-and-forth process. Do not allow a chair to drive the decision of what paving to use—unless it is a valuable existing chair.

Construction. The construction and design of furniture can make the difference between a piece that lasts one year and one that lasts ten years. Pay attention to construction materials, joinery of the same material, and the details of combining several materials. For example, take note of whether wood is joined with a butt joint or a dovetail (a unique interconnection) joint; check out whether welded metal has clean welds or sloppy ones.

Mobility. You may use outdoor furniture for more than one function. If you plan to move it around, consider how mobile it is. Is it too heavy for the person who will usually have to move it to the other side of the garden? Then it is the wrong chair. Would it help if a table had wheels to move it? Do you have a route through which you can move furniture without running into a fence and damaging both furniture and fence? Does that narrow little arbor you

In this colorful array of outdoor fabrics, notice the repeated patterns in different colors (known as colorways). Textile mills often make groups of fabrics that will coordinate with each other. Make sure the fabric you select suits the use you intend. All fabrics courtesy of Sina Pearson Textiles. Sunbrella is a registered trademark of Glen Raven Inc.

so love need to be wider for furniture to be wheeled through?

Comfort. If furniture is not comfortable, it rarely gets used. If a piece is oh-so-gorgeous but uncomfortable, it is art, not furniture. If you want to stay outside and enjoy your garden, you need comfortable places to sit combined with tables that are at the right height to eat and talk comfortably. Test drive your furniture before you buy it so that you know it will be comfortable. Have I used the word *comfortable* enough? You must do this; otherwise, you will just be jumping out of your chair at every opportunity to pull that weed across the garden.

Human factors. *Ergonomics* and *anthropometrics* are two words important to the furniture industry and designers, but they also affect you. They are important because people come in a range of sizes and need to relate appropriately to their furniture. For instance, pay attention to the depth of seating. If people have to sit too far back in a chair in order to get comfortable, they may cut off the circulation behind their knees. Are tables at the appropriate height so that people are not sitting scrunched and hurting their backs? Does the lounge chair bend at the place where you bend?

Shading. If you have a built-in shade structure, purchasing umbrellas or another type of shade structure may not be necessary. However, if you purchase this as a furniture item, make sure you understand how long the fabric will last, whether it is fade-resistant or fadeproof, and whether it can bend or move easily with the movement of the sun or wind. Anchor it well with an appropriate base or hardware or you will be chasing it after every gust of wind.

If you plan to work with a designer, you will have access to a wider selection of fabrics and furniture that are sold only to the trade. You will also have the ability to specify using your own material (COM— customer's own material) on many furniture pieces. This service allows you greater flexibility to have just the right colors and patterns. Ask your designer if you can pay for their time and then have them give you a great discount on what you purchase through them. Some designers will only write specifications for furniture, which you would then purchase through a vendor or retail store. In that case, designers will charge you for their time and may help you negotiate a better deal with the vendor.

A cozy chair tucked near the house offers shelter and a view of the garden. Garden of Richard and Elizabeth Marantz.

It is frustrating that there are many wonderful pieces of furniture to specify but not enough places to go and try out a sample. Most people like to sit in a chair before they buy it, or see how it feels to sit at a table. This is when a picture is really not worth a thousand words. When the manufacturers have representatives or showrooms only in limited locations, you may need to travel to the closest location to try a piece before you buy it. Do this if you need to and you are purchasing expensive pieces of furniture that you expect to last a long time. Maybe you can do a little sightseeing while you are there.

Once you have selected all of your furniture, you may have a collection of marketing sheets with photographs given to you by sales representatives. You can ask any sales representative or manufacturer for them. If you cannot get promotional photos, you can take your own photos, or sometimes the sales representative will take one for you. Assemble the photos and evaluate all of the pieces (including your existing pieces). Does everything work well together?

Pots or containers

Pot and *container* are interchangeable terms that mean essentially the same thing. If you are thinking "pots are pots," you need to know that not all pots are equal. Artisans create pots using several different materials. They fire ceramic and terracotta pots in kilns. The higher their firing temperature (called cone temperature in the trade), the less porous they become. Limited porosity allows them to stay outdoors during colder temperatures without flaking or cracking, because there are fewer areas to trap moisture. Moisture expands in trapped pores and damages pots. Some of the most weatherproof ceramic terracotta pots come from Vietnam and Italy.

Concrete pots are rugged and can take tougher weather than most ceramic and terracotta pots. They are cast in a form and can be duplicated identically, as long as the concrete formula does not change.

The same is true of any metal. Iron is very heavy, while zinc and copper are lighter in weight. Metal pots transfer cold and heat faster to the roots of plants; consider that when you are selecting plants for a metal pot, or move the pot to a more sheltered location if you have a special plant in mind for it.

Carved stone pots are very heavy and expensive. Even smaller pots can be difficult to move. However, stone has an interesting characteristic that most pots

Even if *Aeonium* 'Zwartkop' is not freeze resistant, this terracotta pot from Impruneta, Italy, is. Planting an upright plant in a carved container such as this allows both to shine. Author's garden.

do not have. Stone can store water without cracking or flaking. It also is excellent at keeping roots cooler, which is important if you do not want to water the plant frequently.

More recently, pots have become available that look like heavier pots but are made of lightweight fiberglass or plastic. Some of the imitations are very convincing. Certainly, they have their place when you really need a pot to look heavy but you want the ability to move it easily, with or without plants.

Some of the pots mentioned can stay outside in almost any kind of weather, but you will need to protect others. Follow the manufacturer's instructions to extend the lifetime of your pots. Sometimes

This glazed pot stays out in any weather. Consider installing plants that are equally durable, such as *Juniperus scopulorum* 'Snow Flurries' inside such pots. Setting the pots on gravel improves drainage. Author's garden.

installing "pot feet" or using another method to raise a pot slightly off the ground will improve the pot's ability to withstand some frost.

Generally, the weight of containers is not an issue because they are placed on the ground. However, it becomes an issue when a container is placed on a deck or roof that may not be designed to take the additional dead weight. If you have any doubt whatsoever, consult an engineer to calculate the maximum amount of weight your site can sustain.

As in the selection of your furniture, use the style of your house, your interior, and your garden as a guide to the selection of your containers. If your house is a colorful restored Victorian, you have the flexibility of allowing your pots to be a little more ornate to work with the detailing of the house. You can also use the colors of your house as inspiration for the selection of your containers.

Garden art

Art in the garden can be as simple as an elegant birdhouse on a pole or as splendid as a Henry Moore sculpture. Art is truly in the eye of the beholder.

If you are going to purchase new art, the world is at your doorstep and you can select or have an artist fabricate site-specific pieces. If you have existing pieces that you want to use, you should design places in the garden to accommodate those pieces.

Begin by inventorying the art pieces you plan to use before you make final decisions about where or if you will use them. Take photos of each piece; note overall dimensions and if there are special installation criteria to secure them in place. You may discover that some existing pieces will not work well in your new garden. If so, you may wish to sell them and apply the cash to new art.

As far as selecting new art, one of my clients is a good example of how things too often go awry. The phone call went something like this:

Client: "I just found a wonderful piece of art for the area near the front door, but I need your opinion before I buy it."
Me: "Great! What does it look like?"
Client: "I'll send you an email with a link."

I went to the email, linked to a Web site with some nice art, and saw the piece that had captured my client's heart. The client's desire was to create a garden in the character of a Pacific Northwest mountain retreat, with clean lines, considerable stone, and a voluptuous selection of plants. Imagine my surprise when I opened the link to see an African, contemporary piece. This austere, minimalist piece of art had no relationship to the garden already installed. Its scale felt flimsy compared to the beefy stone hardscape. It might have worked in her modern interior. Here was the main issue: the contemporary, refined interior was not the same style as the requisite naturalistic setting of the exterior. I had to break the news to my client gently.

Selection aside, placement is one of the most critical issues related to art. You want the placement to frame the art and allow the art to take precedence as the focal point it will be. If the environment does not frame the art but instead overwhelms it, the setting is out of proportion to the artwork. There are logical places where art works very well. The end of a path is a perfect location because people traveling the path will have something of interest to lure them forward. It will make the walk seem shorter if it is a long path. Somewhere in the middle of the view from a window will often work as another location. Watch for the direction in which you will view art: straight ahead, from the top, from the bottom, or from its side? What will its orientation to light be? Does it need light behind it to deliver its best effect?

Finish and Furnishing Selection

Realistically, things change during the design process. The hypothetical garden is no different. While I was laying out the actual furniture in the space, new ideas came to me, and I, as the "owner," changed my mind.

I decided that this very busy "owner" would not have the time to use the hammock more than three times a year, so I removed it from the conceptual plan. I made a note that the overhead trellis and dining cover will probably require a special permit to comply with local codes.

Finishes

The hypothetical garden needs the following finish materials:

- horizontal hardscape (walkways, the stone bridge, patio surfaces, caps of planters, fire pit, and water feature), selected on the basis of color compatibility with the home's exterior color, ease of maintenance, and durability
- vertical hardscape (raised planters, fire pit, and water feature)
- a greenhouse
- edging, where it applies
- fencing and a gate for the dog area
- a garbage shelter
- a built-in bonsai display

I usually determine the hardscape materials first, because that is the largest surface in relationship to the house. I select bluestone paving for all horizontal surfaces, except for gravel as a material for the greenhouse area, the north and south paths, and the meditation area in the front. Having gravel as a different material provides a subtle way-finding cue to keep visitors on the path to the front door. Vertical hardscape surfaces will be a multicolored stone that blends the bluestone paving with warmer tones on the house. Edging, where it is required to keep grass or gravel where it belongs, will be powder-coated steel.

I decide to construct the greenhouse of recycled materials. The construction and materials will depend on what I find at a salvage center. The surround of the HVAC unit and the bonsai table will be an ornamental box of perforated, powder-coated steel. The perforation is necessary to allow for airflow to the HVAC unit. This box may relate to the art proposed for the fence on the opposite side of the dining area. All of the fencing, the gates, and the garbage shelter will be varied-width cedar in a simple, regular horizontal pattern. The rhythm created by both the wood fencing and the bluestone pavers, in combination with the repetition of the vertical stone, will tie the entire garden together. I am relating the language of the landscape to the language of the house.

The hardscape finishes plan locates the finishes I have selected for the hypothetical garden.

The horizontal hardscape material will be bluestone, except where I have noted quarter-minus gravel.

The vertical hardscape material will be a variably colored stone, except where I have noted the material to be wood; there are many varieties available from an assortment of areas. This stone coordinates well with the bluestone and the existing stone on the house.

The wood fencing, gate, garbage shelter, and overhead structures in the hypothetical garden will be cedar and similar in material and design to the fencing at the end of the path in this lovely side garden. Garden of Kristien Forness, owner of Fusion Landscape Design, LLC.

136

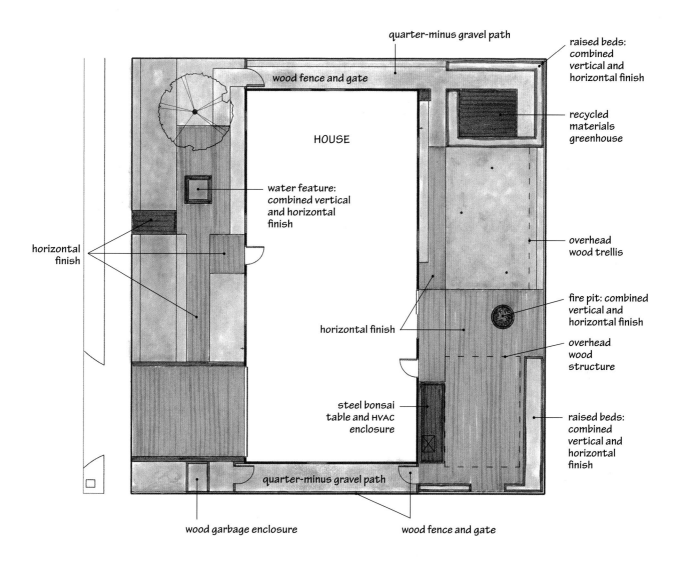

quarter-minus gravel path

raised beds:
combined
vertical and
horizontal finish

wood fence and gate

recycled
materials
greenhouse

HOUSE

water feature:
combined vertical
and horizontal
finish

horizontal
finish

overhead
wood trellis

fire pit: combined
vertical and
horizontal finish

horizontal finish

overhead
wood
structure

steel bonsai
table and HVAC
enclosure

raised beds:
combined
vertical and
horizontal
finish

quarter-minus gravel path

wood garbage enclosure

wood fence and gate

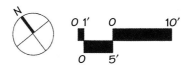

N

0 1'   0   10'

0   5'

Furnishings

On the layout of the hypothetical garden, I have the following pieces of furniture to select:

- dining table and chairs
- meditation bench
- lounge chairs and sofas
- side tables

I need to select outdoor fabrics for the upholstered pieces, as well.

I begin my furniture search by looking for contemporary pieces that will combine well with the architecture and interior of the ranch-style home. I prefer manufacturers that use sustainable materials and that manufacture and distribute as sustainably as possible. However, it is not always possible to find furniture or fabrics that will work with the design that meet those criteria. As more manufacturers increase their sustainability, this will become easier to do. I know I want to keep the table very simple and have some chairs that are comfortable but interesting. I want at least one seating style to make a design splash—perhaps sculptural in nature. I decide to use sofas as some of the seating, because they will seat the required number of people and provide a place for an afternoon snooze in the garden. A side table or two will hold refreshments.

On the conceptual plan, I also locate areas where containers and art make sense. I need one container and three pieces of art plus some flat panels on the fence in the entertaining space. These will tie in with the style of the house (ranch style) and its interior (eclectic contemporary with Asian accents). I show one piece of sculpture for the sake of concept. I will hunt for site-specific art or have some particular material in mind and find an artist to create it.

The dining table will be sleek, contemporary, and simple to set off the chairs; weather resistant; and a dark, rich color. Photo courtesy of Kettal.

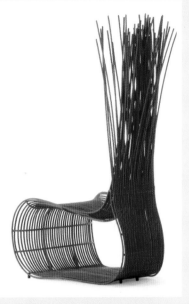

The dining chairs must be comfortable, elegant, and weather resistant. Photo courtesy of Kenneth Cobonpue.

The lounge chairs at the fireplace will serve as accents—as sculpture—yet be comfortable; they will be colorful and weather resistant. Photo courtesy of Kenneth Cobonpue.

The side tables must be weather resistant and coordinate with the lounge seating. Photo courtesy of Dedon.

I want the lounge sofas at the fire pit to be upholstered, comfortable, and weather resistant. Photo courtesy of Dedon.

The upholstery fabrics need to be suitable for the outdoors, fade and mildew resistant, water repellant, and in bright, cheery colors that coordinate not only with the furnishings and the hardscape but also with the home. All fabrics courtesy of Sina Pearson Textiles. Sunbrella is a registered trademark of Glen Raven Inc.

The planting container needs to be very simple, large, and freezeproof, and to pick up color from the seating upholstery.

The concept art piece for the kitchen garden must have a design related to the location of the kitchen garden and be freezeproof and colorful. Sculpture by Margie Adams.

I would like the bench for meditation to be comfortable yet supportive, provide room for up to two people, add sculptural interest to the front garden, and be weather resistant. Photo courtesy of Kenneth Cobonpue.

I would like flat panels that are graphically interesting and that help disguise the fence. Their color should integrate well with the other furnishings. Art and design by Ketti Kupper. Photo by Ashley Elizabeth Ford.

Locations of furniture, art, and pots are noted on the hypothetical garden's furnishings plan.

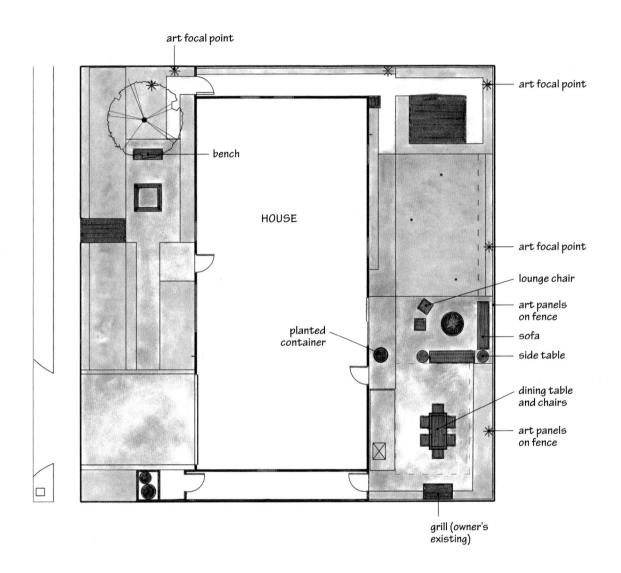

art focal point

art focal point

art focal point

bench

HOUSE

lounge chair

art panels
on fence

sofa

side table

dining table
and chairs

art panels
on fence

planted
container

grill (owner's
existing)

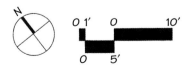

N

0 1'   0   10'

0   5'

Irrigation

Conserving Water Resources

Good design depends not only on plants but also on how you plan to help them survive. Irrigation is necessary if you do not match your plants to your climate and conditions. The number of people who are choosing plants to minimize the need for irrigation is increasing as our climate, resources, and economy fluctuate and as water becomes a more and more prized resource. However, even people who have large portions of their garden planted with drought-tolerant plants often have a small area near the house or the hose bib for a few water-loving plants.

Some say that thinking about irrigation before selecting plants is the cart going before the horse. However, I believe that if you do not think about your water resources before you select plants, you are doomed to continue the mistakes of the past. Now is the time to decide how much water you can afford to budget for your garden. As you review this chapter, keep this in mind. Your water budget will help you decide which plants you will have in your garden later. If you coordinate your water resources with the plants you select, you will have a more successful garden and use less water.

One of the best ways to reduce how much you pay for water is to have plants that can survive without summer irrigation. Fall planting usually gives plants a head start for the following summer because they take advantage of winter moisture to establish their roots. (This concept does not necessarily work well with borderline hardy plants.

What you will do:

- determine the best way to irrigate your garden
- gather pertinent information for irrigation design
- determine an irrigation budget

These homeowners were determined to eliminate any lawn from their front garden. Undeterred by what the neighbors might think, they pulled together a wide variety of plants that tolerate drought. Now their neighbors ask them about their plants. They created more interest with less lawn. Garden of Bonnie Bruce and Michael Peterson.

143

Plant those in the spring to allow their roots the blessing of warm soil to establish their roots before winter.) Native or xeric (drought-tolerant) plants may require water the first year or two, but they should need only a little water during subsequent summer scorchers, if at all.

The Best Way to Irrigate Your Garden

You need to decide which irrigation solution is best for you. You may choose to have your entire garden on an irrigation system. Perhaps you divide areas and water with an occasional sprinkler and some hand watering. You may decide it is better to use a drip irrigation system, or you may select plants that will thrive with overhead sprinklers. If you do not have a lot of time for hand watering or money to install an irrigation system, think about putting in a garden that does not need summer water at all (at least after the first two years). Temporarily use soaker hoses on timers during the two-year period, if necessary.

A critical decision will be how to deliver water to your plants. If you water overhead by either hand watering or using a sprinkler, many plants will respond with a fungal disease such as black spot, rust, or mildew. Many irrigation installers like to install

This pop-up sprinkler head is located in an unobtrusive way.

Extended spray heads often need to be near the front of a border to deliver water properly, making them more obvious than a soaker hose.

systems that have pop-up sprinklers that throw water all around your plants. This might work well with a lawn, but it does not usually work well with shrubs and perennials. Plants grow and can block other plants from receiving water from a sprinkler head. Newer ground-hugging soaker systems deliver water to each plant and minimize water loss through evaporation. Less water used equals more money in your bank account. A drip system is least likely to cause erosion. This type of irrigation system allows gardeners to change plants easily, as new varieties come on the market or to replace worn or less successful plants.

Speaking of money in the bank, compare the cost of an irrigation system with the cost of losing your new plants to dehydration. Although automatic irrigation systems are not cheap, installing one may be the best insurance to keep plants alive. In fact, if a contractor supplies your plants, chances are they will not guarantee the plants without automatic irrigation. An excellent reason to have an automatic irrigation system is that the system uses a controller, which regulates the amount of water. That said, it is not unusual to see people set their systems to deliver too much water and kill plants with kindness.

Irrigation system specialists design irrigation systems in zones. Zoning helps maintain sufficient water pressure by keeping the amount of water to a

This irrigation system at the Bellevue Botanical Garden's Northwest Perennial Alliance (NPA) border is exposed during the winter. The system is a soaker hose set in a regimented layout—approximately every 18 inches, intended to get water to any plant that needs it and designed for flexibility in changing out plants. The border is on a slope, which means good drainage but potential erosion. Soaker hoses help minimize erosion.

minimum within a given area. The controller dictates how many zones you can have on your system. The larger your garden, the more zones you might need. Controllers also need to accommodate how frequently you water and when you water—usually in the early morning. Be wary of irrigation installers who want to water every plant equally. Not all plants are equal.

Select plants and consider irrigation concurrently. Using plants with similar water requirements in the same area will reduce the need to customize irrigation around each plant. While it is possible with some drip systems to adjust the emitters around each plant, you need to recognize that as plants grow you will not always be able to see whether each emitter is working. Often you discover that the amount of water is inadequate when you see your plant on death's doorstep.

If you decide that half of your garden will be drought tolerant and the other half will be irrigated, have your irrigation system designed to have the drought-tolerant half watered separately so you can turn it off as plants become established and grow large enough to survive periods of dry weather. You might want to leave the irrigation in place so you can water the area should a heat spell stress the plants. You could manage such an area independent of the irrigation system, also, with soaker hoses and a timer connected to your hose bib.

Things to Find Out for Irrigation Design

The layout of an automatic irrigation system is important because major equipment will need to be located in specific areas. There will be valves and a backflow preventer near your water meter, to start with. As pipes are laid out to deliver water to the various zones, additional valves and valve boxes may

be needed. This depends largely on the size of the area you will irrigate. But regardless of their number, valves and valve boxes take up space and need to be worked around. If you are mindful about this in advance, you can avoid having a valve box or a main pipe protruding in the exact spot where you want a glorious piece of art.

Find out whether you have access to a well or an underground cistern, or must use city water. Once you decide the source of your water, document its location. If you use well water, you may need to evaluate the quality of the water before it goes into your garden, particularly an area of edible plants. If you are using it for your house, this should not be an issue. If you have city water, your budget may drive your decision about the amount of water you will use. If you can collect rainwater, restrict your water use to what you can collect or plan to supplement with additional irrigation.

Your water pressure will also dictate how to design your irrigation system. Usually an irrigation installer looks for at least 60 psi (pounds per square inch) to assure there will be adequate pressure to maintain an even amount of water to each sprinkler head or drip line.

Local jurisdictions—your county or city—regulate irrigation systems. You will be required to have a backflow device installed as part of your irrigation system. This device prevents a backflow of gray water into your house system. You may need to have it inspected regularly (usually annually) to assure legal compliance. Regulations may require that you file a certificate once per year, with fees to an inspector and to your local jurisdiction.

Your Irrigation Budget

The quality of irrigation systems varies. Do not skimp on things that are difficult to replace, like underground pipes and equipment. Purchase a controller that has as many zones as you can afford, because it will be easier to adjust or add on later if you need to. The less you have to trench, the less you will have to pay. The more complicated your system, the more expensive it will be. If an automatic system is not affordable, design around that idea or combine automated watering with hand watering. Otherwise, use a hose and a sprinkler—with a timer to prevent overwatering.

Adding Irrigation to Your Plan

To add irrigation concepts to your plan, begin by identifying where your water enters your property (usually at the water meter, if you have one) and where you want to have your controller. Then determine the various zones you will want. You may have raised beds in one area that you prefer to irrigate

separately. You will want to irrigate the lawn separately from the borders. If you know you will want to turn off certain areas after two years, or only irrigate those areas sporadically, make them a separate zone. Areas that need the same type of irrigation may be able to be in the same zone, if it is not too large. If it is a large area, you will need more than one zone to cover it, because water pressure will drop if you exceed a recommended distance thanks to the friction of water traveling through a pipe.

The important thing is to identify the type of irrigation you want and how many zones you would like to have, in addition to where you want the controller located. This will help your installer meet your needs more easily. Consider minimizing sprinkler heads in plant borders. Plants grow, cover up the sprinkler heads, and then die from lack of water. Soaker hose irrigation works much better, because it is always at the soil beneath the mulch.

An installer packs in soil around a sprinkler head to assure a firm, sturdy installation.

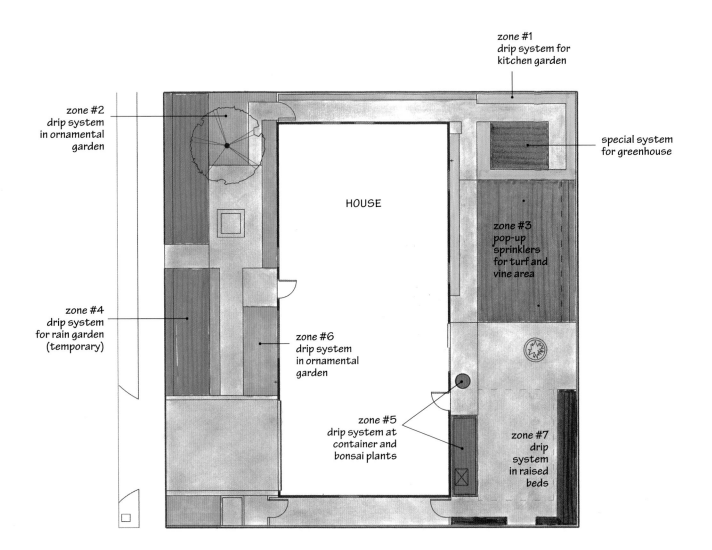

zone #1
drip system for
kitchen garden

zone #2
drip system
in ornamental
garden

special system
for greenhouse

HOUSE

zone #3
pop-up
sprinklers
for turf and
vine area

zone #4
drip system
for rain garden
(temporary)

zone #6
drip system
in ornamental
garden

zone #5
drip system at
container and
bonsai plants

zone #7
drip
system
in raised
beds

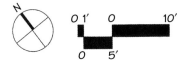

N

0 1'   0   10'

0   5'

Designing the
Hypothetical Garden

Irrigation Concepts

For the hypothetical garden, it is important to keep the use of water to a minimum. I decide to use soaker-type irrigation that keeps the water near the soil and off foliage. Ideally, I will locate the controller in a well-lit, dry place, such as the garage. This way I can easily see to adjust the controller and can do it under cover, a feature I will especially appreciate if I need to turn it off at night or during a rainstorm.

I make sure that I can easily access the on-off switch to the irrigation system before winter. Water needs to be flushed from the system before freezing weather sets in, to prevent pipes from bursting. One more thing: I decide to add an extra zone to the controller to accommodate future modifications. Changes to the garden can alter the type of irrigation or redefine zone requirements.

Irrigation concepts are shown on the hypothetical garden plan.

Plants: A Structural Perspective

8

The Important Role of Plant Structure

Now that you have a rough idea of the layout of your hardscape, you need to think about what truly makes your outdoor environment a garden: plants. Plants play an essential role in their interchange with the built environment. Their significant function could cause you to alter the layout of your hardscape. This is one reason design is described as a process. The design process continues between conceptual plans and the final plan, and often on through construction.

Your conceptual plan shows where you located the planting beds. You know the location of your primary views and possible focal points. From certain windows or doors, at the ends of paths, from patio seating, these guide you through your garden or to your front door. You may not know whether a focal point will be a plant or a piece of art. Now is the time to decide.

A plant's structure can inspire emotional response. You can use this to your advantage in your garden to set a mood. When I want to give an area a sense of humor, I consider using *Sequoiadendron giganteum* 'Pendulum'. That plant with its upright but circuitous form is so unusual that it invites the nickname of "Dr. Seuss plant."

You can also use the form of a plant to fill a functional need in a plant composition or in the overall layout of your garden. For a planting bed to be successful, it helps to spend some time planning, versus the other method of haphazard placement and selection.

What you will learn:

- the importance of plant structure within a design scheme
- plant structure types
- how to use the structure of plants in your design

Two specimens of *Thuja occidentalis* 'Emerald'.

151

Thrillers, Spillers, and Fillers

The concept of "thrillers, spillers, and fillers" is not new, but it is an excellent way to envision the use of plants, not only for containers but for the garden in general.

Thrillers

Plants with the boldness to be a focal point are thriller plants. They are the plants toward which your eye zooms in a group of plants. They can be dense plants with an interesting form, plants with strong color, or plants with bold foliage.

This spectacular container illustrates the use of thrillers, spillers, and fillers. Included within the pot are the tall central plant *Hedychium longicornutum*, along with *Begonia boliviensis*, *Solenostemon scutellarioides* 'Juliet Quartermain', *S. scutellarioides* 'Freckles', *S. scutellarioides* 'Kiwi Fern', *Cuphea ignea* 'Dynamite', *Tradescantia pallida* 'Purple Heart', *Acalypha wilkesiana*, *Phygelius* 'Passionate', *Cordyline* 'Cardinal', and purple ornamental cabbages. Design and photo by Bruce Bailey.

For example, these plants act as thrillers:

- *Phormium tenax* 'Atropurpureum'
- *Ligularia dentata* 'Britt Marie Crawford'
- *Rheum palmatum* var. *tanguticum*

Ligularia dentata 'Britt Marie Crawford'

Phormium tenax 'Atropurpureum'

Rheum palmatum var. *tanguticum*

153

Alchemilla mollis

Spillers

A plant used as a spiller creeps, falls, and overflows by nature. It can be a ground-covering shrub, perennial, annual, or vine. It can be evergreen or deciduous. What they all have in common is their ability to cover ground or tumble over the edge of a container.

Here are some plants that act as spillers:

- *Alchemilla mollis*
- *Geranium* 'Ann Folkard'
- *Hakonechloa macra* 'Aureola'

Hakonechloa macra 'Aureola'

Geranium 'Ann Folkard'

154

Fillers

Frothy and airy, filler plants permeate and unite thrillers with spillers. Their form is less defined, as they fill crevices and surround other plants in the composition. They often unite color by providing a flower color that might match a vein in one leaf or an entire leaf of another. Alternatively, they can provide a little background to showcase the flowers or leaves of another plant.

Plants that act as fillers include these:

- *Dryopteris erythrosora*
- *Dicentra spectabilis* 'Gold Heart'
- *Persicaria virginiana* 'Painter's Palette'

Dicentra spectabilis 'Gold Heart'

Dryopteris erythrosora

Persicaria virginiana 'Painter's Palette'

Flower structure

In his book *Designing with Plants* (1999), Piet Oudolf assesses the structure of flowers as a means to combine flowering perennials. Spires, buttons and globes, plumes, umbels, and daisies are the focus in his stunning combinations of large masses of plants. He also uses plants, often grasses, effectively as screens and curtains. Some structure in the form of evergreen and deciduous trees and shrubs provides backdrop and framework for an ephemeral succession of different colors, flower shapes, and plant forms.

If you plan to use flower structure, keep in mind that you may only have that structure for two to four weeks on average. The remaining forty-eight to fifty weeks in the year could be missing structure unless you plan for a continuous sequence or provide a strong background. This will hold the composition together in the absence of flowering plants.

Spires of *Veronicastrum virginicum* provide bold structure against a backdrop of *Cotinus coggygria* 'Royal Purple'. Author's garden.

Plant Punctuation

Of the numerous lectures by plantsman extraordinaire Daniel Hinkley that I have attended over the years, one in particular caught my attention. During the lecture, he suggested that vertical, columnar plants act like exclamation points in a garden. This led me to wonder whether the plants could act as other forms of punctuation.

In an article in the *Los Angeles Times*, journalist Emily Green (2008) quotes Los Angeles landscape architect Mia Lehrer as saying, "There is a big difference between strategically placed plants used to moderate the scale of an imposing house or to create a welcoming entrance, and a uniform collar of shrubbery." Ms. Green follows with "Put simply, one is punctuation, and the other is fortification." While the commentary refers to the way in which homeowners traditionally skirt a house with plants, Ms. Green highlights the concept of plants as punctuation to one's house.

Punctuation helps organize and add structure to sentences and paragraphs. Could *plant punctuation* work for assembling plants as cohesively in a garden? Ideally, structural plants should have year-round presence because they help organize other plants. Many of them might be evergreen, or they could have a distinctive deciduous form. Following is a browse through plants as punctuation to make sense of our garden sentences.

Periods

A period ends a complete sentence. Plants that can define the end of a composition have a small, rounded, or mounded form. Sometimes periods can denote a continuation, as in dot, dot, dot (. . .). This application could be a useful garden metaphor where you want to lead someone to another part of the garden or as a transition.

The following plants make good periods because they maintain their tight, rounded forms without much trimming:

- *Buxus sempervirens* 'Suffruticosa' (dwarf boxwood)
- *Rhododendron* 'Ramapo'
- *Pittosporum tenuifolium* 'Golf Ball'
- *Berberis thunbergii* f. *atropurpurea* 'Bagatelle'

Buxus sempervirens 'Suffruticosa' (dwarf boxwood)

Rhododendron 'Ramapo'

Berberis thunbergii f. *atropurpurea* 'Bagatelle'

Pittosporum tenuifolium 'Golf Ball'

Commas

Commas have a more complex function than periods. In writing, they set apart interruptions within a sentence, join independent clauses, indicate a pause, and more. A comma plant should be a plant that plays well with others but is distinctive enough to be easily seen among other plants. As a group of plants, they help hold an area together visually but do not dominate in the way an exclamation point would. They may be bolder in leaf or color than period plants. In a plant composition, these plants need to have a relationship to the plants they divide. Perhaps one area of colorful heucheras (coral bells) includes a solid green heuchera or *Ophiopogon planiscapus* 'Nigrescens' (black mondo grass). The solid green heuchera or ophiopogon becomes the link to the second area, which may include *Brunnera macrophylla* 'Jack Frost' and *Athyrium niponicum* var. *pictum* (painted lady fern).

These plants function as commas, being strong enough structurally to organize plants that are more diminutive:

- *Ophiopogon planiscapus* 'Nigrescens'
- *Helleborus ×hybridus*
- *Brunnera macrophylla* 'Emerald Mist'
- *Athyrium filix-femina* 'Lady in Lace'

Ophiopogon planiscapus 'Nigrescens'

Helleborus ×hybridus

Athyrium filix-femina 'Lady in Lace'. Photo provided by Terra Nova Nursery.

Brunnera macrophylla 'Emerald Mist'. Photo provided by Terra Nova Nursery.

Chamaecyparis obtusa 'Elwoodii'

Ilex crenata 'Sky Pencil'

Exclamation points

Exclamation points give emphasis to a sentence. Writers use them sparingly; otherwise, everything would compete for emphasis. As mentioned previously, exclamation points in the garden tend to be columnar plants with a dense form.

Try these plants when you need exclamation points:

- *Chamaecyparis obtusa* 'Elwoodii'
- *Ilex crenata* 'Sky Pencil'
- *Euonymus japonicus* 'Green Spire'
- *Juniperus communis* 'Gold Cone'

Euonymus japonicus 'Green Spire'

Juniperus 'Gold Cone'

Corylus avellana 'Contorta'

Question marks

A question mark ends a question. Plants that might fit into the category of "quizzical" would be plants that surprise us, inspire our curiosity, or leave us puzzled. The Dr. Seuss plant would fit this category. So too would plants with a weeping, wiggly, interesting, or unusual form. Some plants have a *torulosa* or twisted form. One of my favorites is *Corylus avellana* 'Contorta', better known as Harry Lauder's walking stick or contorted filbert. This type of plant can also act as a focal point if the form is strong enough to stand out among other plants. As an old friend of mine used to say, "It needn't be dull."

These plants function as question marks:

- *Corylus avellana* 'Contorta'
- *Chamaecyparis lawsoniana* 'Wissel's Saguaro'

Chamaecyparis lawsoniana 'Wissel's Saguaro'

161

Chamaecyparis obtusa 'Torulosa'

- *Chamaecyparis obtusa* 'Torulosa'
- *Robinia pseudoacacia* 'Lace Lady' (Twisty Baby black locust)

Semicolons

A semicolon joins two independent clauses or a series of thoughts. Plants that can act as semicolons are similar to those that act as commas. How they are different is that semicolon plants dovetail two adjacent garden areas.

Here are some plants that act as semicolons, knitting plants in many compositions together:

- *Fatsia japonica*
- *Helleborus argutifolius*
- *Mahonia* ×*media* 'Winter Sun'
- *Rosa* 'Radtko'

Robinia pseudoacacia 'Lace Lady' (Twisty Baby black locust)

Fatsia japonica

Helleborus argutifolius

Mahonia ×media 'Winter Sun'

Rosa 'Radtko'

Colons

A colon signals an end to an introduction in a sentence or has a special assignment like dividing numbers. As a plant, a colon acts as a transition from one part of a bed or the garden to another. It could be a variegated plant that helps transition the colors from one part of a garden bed to another. *Osmanthus heterophyllus* 'Goshiki' does this very well. Its evergreen, hollylike leaves are buoyant with color. As a medium-size shrub, it has presence without competing for center stage.

These plants act as colons:

- *Osmanthus heterophyllus* 'Goshiki'
- *Aucuba japonica* 'Picturata'
- *Buxus microphylla* var. *japonica* 'Variegata'
- *Salix integra* 'Hakuro Nishiki'

Aucuba japonica 'Picturata'

Osmanthus heterophyllus 'Goshiki'

Buxus microphylla var. *japonica* 'Variegata'

Salix integra 'Hakuro Nishiki'

Parentheses

Parentheses enclose text to differentiate it from the rest of a sentence. Pairs of plants generally define each side of a path or an entry. Just as in a sentence, parenthesis plants have a special duty to bookend one area from the rest of the space. Garden parentheses could be any plants that have sufficient presence to hold their own among other plants—even two exclamation points. Just as opening and closing parentheses differ, this plant punctuation form need not be identical to the plant it is paired with to perform its function.

Plants that act as parentheses include these:

- *Thuja occidentalis* 'Emerald'
- *Cupressus macrocarpa* 'Wilma Goldcrest'
- *Cornus sanguinea* 'Compressa'
- *Thuja occidentalis* 'Rheingold'

Cupressus macrocarpa 'Wilma Goldcrest'

Cornus sanguinea 'Compressa'

Thuja occidentalis 'Rheingold'

The Supporting Cast

When you lay out the hardscape of your garden, you are setting the stage for your plants. Structural plants and plant punctuation set the stage for the remaining plants. It is no stretch for yet another metaphor to describe the role of certain plants in the garden as the supporting cast. This tends to describe just about anything not covered under plant punctuation. Annuals, perennials, grasses, and indistinguishable shrubs tend to do a great job of filling space and covering soil—all important in the effort to control weeds or act as the adjectives and adverbs to the other more important players. They could also be the fillers and spillers that support the thrillers.

As discussed in the chapter "Design 101," you would not want a whole garden of plants that have only one form or one leaf shape. Remember the need to combine plants for color, texture, and variety, and comply with the other basic design principles. It is useful to know the various shapes of plants and leaves. Then when you begin to combine them, you will understand that something with fine texture like a grass with narrow leaves might be the perfect foil for another plant with bold, lobed leaves.

Plant shapes

In the trade, plant growers, retail nurseries, landscape designers, and landscape architects have their own expressions to describe plant forms. If you know how to describe them in the same way, chances are you will get the plant you are looking for the next time you drop into a nursery or purchase through a catalog. Here are the descriptions they typically use:

- **columnar**: like a column, upright and narrow
- **vase**: like a vase, narrower at the base, upright and spreading toward the top
- **arching**: growing in a series of arcs, usually outward from the center

- **pyramidal**: like a pyramid, narrow at the top and wide at the base
- **mounded**: wider than high, with a rounded form
- **prostrate**: clinging to the ground or very low growing
- **weeping**: upright, then dropping—often to the ground, more pronounced than arching
- **upright**: usually taller than wide, with branches that extend distinctly skyward
- **broad**: wider than tall, not necessarily with a rounded form

Leaf shapes

Leaves grow in a myriad of shapes. Just as plants have botanical names and common names, leaves have scientific descriptions and common descriptions. Scientific language seeks to be as specific as possible in describing the shape of a leaf. For example, a narrow leaf could be described botanically as ensiform, falcate, linear, ligulate, subulate, or acicular. For the purpose of design, I use common descriptions in this list of terms for leaf shapes:

- **narrow** or **broad**: *Narrow* and *broad* are relative terms. Look at the leaf's width in relationship to its length. If the leaf is roughly five times longer than wide, you could call the leaf narrow. If the width and length are nearly equal, it is a broad leaf.
- **grasslike**: A grasslike leaf is a very narrow leaf that can either stand erect or gently arch. Switch grass (*Panicum*) and maiden grass (*Miscanthus*) are good examples.
- **lobed**: Lobed leaves are more complex than their simple cousins. They have multiple points. A maple or oak leaf is a good example, but the form also includes bold leaves like that of rhubarb. The leaf texture varies.

- **dissected**: Dissected leaves are lobed leaves that are very deeply lobed, and often the lobes are narrower. The leaves of cut-leaved Japanese maple (*Acer palmatum* var. *dissectum*) are a good example. The leaf texture is typically fine to medium.

This plant composition shows off several plant shapes: upright, weeping, broad, and mounded.

167

- **fronds**: Fronds typically describe fern leaves. They are distinct in the way that they uncurl from the base as "fiddleheads" in the spring. One is a strap leaf form, Hart's tongue fern (*Asplenium scolopendrium*), while the rest are deeply dissected (for example, painted lady fern, *Athyrium niponicum* var. *pictum*). Leaf texture is usually fine, although some ferns have slightly bolder leaves. Sword fern (*Polystichum munitum*) is a good example of a fern with bolder structure in a garden.
- **scales**: Scales are most often found on conifers and describe particularly the appearance of leaves on junipers, cypress, and false cypress (*Chamaecyparis*). The leaf texture is typically fine.
- **needlelike**: Needlelike leaves are found predominantly on conifers, with pine, fir, and spruce as the best examples.

- **spiny**: There are several types of spiny-leaved plants. Some have leaves that come to a severe point or spine, like a yucca. Similar leaves have a spine at the tip but also have spines or teeth along the edges, like a bromeliad or an agave. Other leaves have spines that poke upward along the top or bottom of the leaf, like cacti.
- **straplike**: Similar to grasslike leaves, straplike leaves are longer than wide. However, the ratio of width to length is shorter. The leaves of daylilies (*Hemerocallis*) and red-hot poker plants (*Kniphofia*) are examples.

Topiary

Who could forget topiary in a discussion of plant structure? Topiary describes a type of pruning that tightly clips living plants into ornamental forms. Most are compact, dense evergreens with small

This plant composition shows off several leaf shapes: needlelike, lobed, and narrow.

A whimsical topiary bird of *Buxus microphylla* var. *japonica* 'Winter Gem' sports a grassy *Pennisetum* tail. Author's garden.

leaves. This type of plant works very well, because the pruning cuts are not as visible. Nearly any shape can create something of a focal point. However, the more fantastical they become, the more likely they are to become a subject of much attention. Topiary is living sculpture that requires dedicated attention to keep the shape. Just one fabulous topiary in a garden can be a major focus.

The garden of Pearl Fryar in Bishopville, South Carolina, became a tourist attraction because no one ever told him there was a limit to what kind of topiary he could create. His convoluted shapes make the carnival at a state fair seem tame. It is a magical wonderland of one man's imaginative garden style.

At Great Dixter, the garden of famous plantsman Christopher Lloyd, eighteen birds formed of yew (*Taxus*) define the peacock topiary garden. The genus *Taxus* includes a number of species that lend themselves well to topiary.

In my own garden, I tortured a *Lonicera nitida* 'Baggesen's Gold' into a peacock to hide our heat pump. To support the image I designed a steel and glass tail and head that a local artist fabricated. Topiary adds an element of whimsy, focal point(s), and framework for other plants within a garden.

Plant Placement

While it is not my intention for this book to be a reference work on designing plant combinations, a quick example about how to mass plants might prove useful. Too often, I see a few pansies lined up as though they were marching in a parade. Plants are not soldiers. The only place it makes sense to create a line of plants is when you need to see a line (as in an alleé of trees along a drive), in a vegetable garden, or in a delineated pattern.

Additionally, I see plants spaced too far apart. It is an article of ancient wisdom that nature abhors a vacuum. Unless you are designing a desert, space your plants so they will touch at maturity and hide bare ground. If plants leave exposed soil at maturity, it invites Mother Nature to introduce her own seeds. Most often, they do not play well with what you will plant. Gardeners call them *weeds*. When weeds work with my plants, I call it serendipity.

I tend to mass plants in elongated triangles because it makes different plants easier to weave together. Odd numbers tend to be the rule of thumb when grouping more than one plant. However, I find that once you exceed five plants, it does not matter. Use the number of plants you need to fit within the planting area. Whenever someone gives me two plants or if I have three plants and one dies, I do one of three things:

- hunt for a third plant
- use them as parenthesis plants
- separate them completely into different areas of the garden

The Planting Plan

On the planting plan, I review where a plant would make more sense than a piece of art as a focal point. In one case, it makes sense to use a container with a plant. I also review the plant compositions for punctuation. I place three large comma plants in front to tie the supporting cast together. Two shade trees act as focal points through windows. Two columnar grasses enclose the entry at the bridge. There are plants or art at the ends of paths to pull the person traversing the path to the end. Where two paths intersect, one focal point is a piece of art, while the other is an exclamation point plant that works well with the art. The exclamation point repeats on the opposite side of the front garden, acting as parentheses.

The back garden already has a bonsai table featuring numerous plants. It also has art panels on the fence and a fire pit. It makes sense to feature the art panels and fire pit by not introducing other art that would compete in that area. Therefore, I add plants to soften the hardscape. A container adds plants where there is patio to soften the hardscape and add a focal point by the door from the house into the backyard. The art at the back of the putting green is a focal point from the dining room window. I decide to use something a little taller close to the fence to minimize the possibility of a golf club hitting it. Vines are used on the trellis to enhance privacy and create a backdrop for the art beneath.

Near the greenhouse, I place parentheses to enclose the end of the putting green. I repeat these exclamation point plants along the east back fence behind the herb garden to introduce plant repetition, add emphasis to the art panels, and soften the fence. These plants also fit the narrowness of the space and provide more height in that area for privacy. On the south side of the herb garden, I place three period plants—dot, dot, dot—to announce to anyone walking through the gate they are about to see the rest of the garden. Thanks to the neighbor's evergreen hedge on the other side of the fence, I do not see a need for additional privacy, so the plants are shorter.

Although the putting green is not *structural* as a plant, I consider using closely mown native grass to prevent weeds and avoid the need to use synthetic fertilizers. I might think about using synthetic lawn, one that features as much post-consumer recycled waste as possible, as a low-maintenance alternative.

The planting plan indicates structural plant placement in the hypothetical garden.

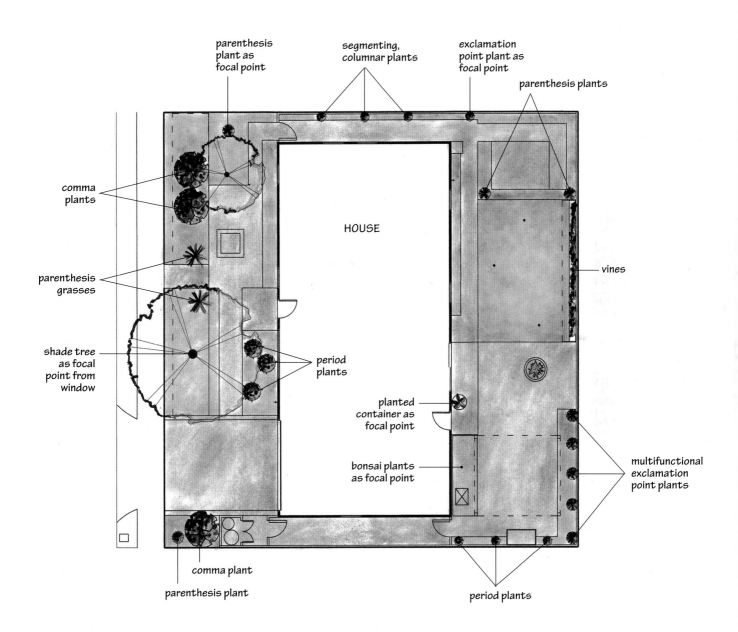

parenthesis
plant as
focal point

segmenting,
columnar plants

exclamation
point plant as
focal point

parenthesis plants

comma
plants

parenthesis
grasses

shade tree
as focal
point from
window

HOUSE

vines

period
plants

planted
container as
focal point

bonsai plants
as focal point

multifunctional
exclamation
point plants

comma plant

parenthesis plant

period plants

N

0 1'   0   10'

0   5'

Garden Lighting

Reasons to Use Landscape Lighting

There are several excellent reasons to have lighting in your garden. Lighting assures our footing in the dark. It allows us to see trespassers, and it allows our friends to see us. Lighting can make a garden sparkle at night and take on an entirely different aesthetic than it has during the day. It invites us to be in the garden longer.

Safety

Night lighting assures us the ability to see where we are going—on a winding path, down a flight of stairs, from parking to the front door. Being able to see where we are going helps keep us safe from physical injury. Consider providing two levels of lighting—a dimmer level for normal use and a brighter level for elderly guests or to use as you begin to age.

Security

There is some debate about whether lighting the garden around your home improves your home's security. Security lighting differs in style from aesthetic garden lighting. It usually involves motion detectors or dusk-to-dawn lighting or some combination of the two.

Most homes have outdoor light fixtures attached near each door, particularly useful at doorsteps. Lighting adjacent to windows and doors allows passersby to see what is happening in those areas, assuming you have passersby. This may deter some criminals and

What you will learn:

- reasons to use landscape lighting
- the various types and styles of outdoor lighting equipment
- the effect of light placement

An adjustable low-wattage fixture aimed slightly upward into Mexican feather grass (*Nassella tenuissima*) gives the grass an exciting glow at night. Home of Maryellen Hockensmith and Michael McCulloch, AIA.

assist your view outside of potential intruders. Some homes have lighting in the soffits near the roof that lights the walls. If this helps light areas with tall shrubs, it may discourage an intruder from hiding there. If you suspect an intruder, a "panic button" that lights the entire yard at once may prove helpful.

Function

Lighting extends the time you can spend in your garden and allows you to see what you are doing at night. This could enable outdoor cooking, conversation, playing of instruments, or perhaps an outdoor game. Most outdoor activities need lighting at night (kissing excepted).

Selecting Light Fixtures

There is a plethora of manufacturers, styles, and types of landscape lighting. It can be inexpensive or costly—and you generally get what you pay for. Knowing how each type works will help you think

Lighting along a retaining wall illuminates a patio at night. Design and construction by McQuiggins Inc.

about the many ways to use fixtures in your garden. Usually, you will need a licensed electrician to install part or all of the system, depending on whether the system uses line voltage or low voltage. You may also need a permit from your local jurisdiction. Usually the electrician applies and obtains the permit for you.

Line voltage versus low voltage

Electricity is essential to landscape lighting. There are two ways to use electricity with your system. Commercial line voltage can be 120, 208, 220, or 480 volts. Commonly, line voltage is what you use inside the house, with the higher voltage dedicated to special uses such as dryers and ovens. Normal residential line voltage is 120 or 220 volts. Low voltage is used to a lesser degree indoors. A transformer reduces 120 volts to 12 volts to create low voltage.

The advantage (and disadvantage) of line voltage outdoors is that the wiring must be buried in a conduit below your freezing level. (Freezing level varies according to where you live.) When you bury wiring in a protective conduit, you are less likely to cut the line with a shovel or short out with irrigation. However, you pay for the trenching and disruption to your property, too.

Low voltage can be touched with a bare hand without consequence, making it easy to install and move. Unfortunately, because low voltage wires are not protected in conduit, there is the risk that either you or your maintenance service may accidentally cut through a wire if you are digging in the area and fail to notice it. In addition, low voltage is only as good as its transformer, the cable (or wire), and the fixtures. If you use low-voltage lighting, pay for a well-built system.

One especially important reason to use proper cable for any lighting system is voltage drop. Voltage drop or "line loss" occurs when the voltage in a circuit falls between the source of electricity and the equipment using the electricity. The wrong type of cable, an erroneous ratio of cable length to number of fixtures, or an installer's inaccurate amperage calculations can cause voltage drop. Succinctly, if you experience voltage drop, your fixtures will not function equally, your lamps will burn out long before they should, and your fixtures may fail. Furthermore, line loss may be in the form of heat, which could deteriorate your electrical connections and distribution system.

Characteristics, style, and aesthetics

Light fixtures are a combination of housing, lamp, and control switch. For some applications, there may also be ballast or a driver. The housing contains the lamp and is what we typically see, unless the lamp is also visible. The housing can be ornamental or very basic in appearance. For outdoor use, it must be waterproof. Fixtures should have a tightly fitted gasket that prevents water from reaching the lamp and electrical socket. Underground or underwater fixtures are particularly vulnerable to leakage.

A creative show garden displays a beautiful lantern within a gazebo, creating a remarkable focal point at night and a siren that could lure a person into the garden. Garden design by Shapiro Ryan Design, Seattle.

Dark skies

There are organizations that focus on minimizing the impact of night lighting by promoting dark skies. Too much light at night disturbs human and wildlife habitat, particularly nighttime ecosystems. Some writers discuss inefficiently designed outdoor lighting and the amount of electricity the light fixtures use. Others assert that overlighting endangers human health and safety. One writer, David Owen (2007), comments that an overlit environment "increasingly deprives many of us of a direct relationship with the nighttime sky, which throughout human history has been a powerful source of reflection, inspiration, discovery, and plain old jaw-dropping wonder."

While some of the concern focuses on how overlighting negatively affects the science of astronomy, as a gardener I am primarily concerned about night lighting's impact on natural habitat. As a landscape designer, I can reduce the danger to our natural ecosystems by designing outdoor lighting in a more responsible manner. I can honor the rules of jurisdictions that do not allow light to spill over onto public or neighboring property.

You can do two things to reduce the impact of lighting in your garden on dark skies: reduce wattage and shield light to keep it from reaching the sky. This means that most lights need to focus downward or have an overhead shield if they focus upward. It means lights should be just bright enough to be effective—no more and no less; this can save you energy and reduce the impact on your budget. Consider these issues as you make decisions about the appropriate type of fixtures and lamps.

Just as your garden style should coordinate with your home, so too should the style of a light fixture harmonize with the architecture of your home and garden. The sweet-looking fixture in the shape of a flower that would coordinate well with a Victorian-style home would look ridiculous on a contemporary-style home. Aesthetically, a light fixture should stand on its own design merit. If it does not look good by itself, its appearance will not improve when you attach it to your house or install it in your garden. If you are not comfortable selecting a light fixture when it comes to its design, either have someone you trust accompany you or hire a professional to help you select fixtures. A good rule of thumb is the simpler the better.

Some amount of adjustability should be included with your system. Your garden will change with the seasons and as plants grow. If you try to hide a fixture with plants, remember that plants change or die.

Cost and value

Some forms of lighting are cheaper at the outset than others, but just because a light fixture is more

Wiring can be fed through a plastic pipe, or sleeve, beneath a concrete walk.

expensive initially does not mean it is uneconomical. For instance, an LED lamp may be the most expensive type available, but the lamp uses very little electricity and has such a long life that you may never have to replace it.

Comparing fixtures and lamps based on life-cycle rather than initial costs makes good economic sense. Paying extra for a better fixture may save you more money in the long run than buying an inferior fixture and having to replace it when it fails. Check into the tests and warranties offered by suppliers. Pay attention to the wire included in an inexpensive lighting kit. It may not stretch much farther than 15 feet or support more than a couple of lights.

The lamp inside the fixture is all important to get the effect you want. Manufacturers continually introduce new lamps. Investigate the possibilities before you select your light fixture. Compare the initial expense of a lamp to its operating expense (watts), the quality of light it produces (color), its beam spread (the spread of light at a given distance), and its expected life. Some fixtures will take more than one type of lamp, although you will usually have to match your selected lamp to specific fixtures. Select your lamp based on your lighting task and then select the fixture. This way you will get the lighting effect you want. Remember that the farther away a lamp is from its target, the less light will reach the target and the more light will spill out away from the target. To confine light to a tighter

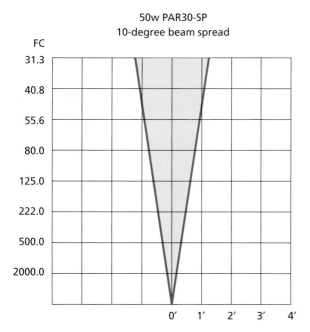

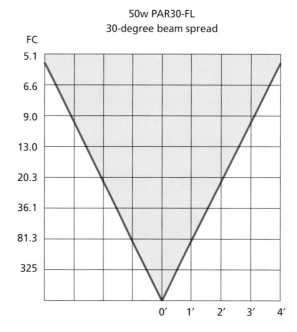

This beam spread chart (where each square represents 1 square foot) shows how the beam spread for the same lamp varies, depending on the lamp's inner construction. One lamp (50w PAR30-SP) creates a narrow spot and the other (50w PAR30-FL) a flood. The numbers along the bottom indicate the distance in feet that each beam can spread. The numbers along the left side of each chart represent the amount of light (expressed as *footcandles*, a measure of light quantity). Notice that the closer the light is to its source, the narrower the beam and the more light there is.

space or to its target, use lamps with a narrow beam spread.

Maintaining your light fixtures is usually as simple as keeping their housings clean and replacing lamps as they burn out. Before you select a light fixture, determine how easy it is to replace the lamp. If you have to unbolt, then unscrew, then twist before you can reach the lamp itself, it can be frustrating. Also, keep in mind how easy it will be to find the lamp at local stores. Can you find the lamp in any hardware store, or do you have to go to a specialty store?

Placing Light Fixtures

How you illuminate the garden and the exterior of your home has an enormous impact on its nighttime aesthetic. It is important to place lighting so it does not shine directly into visitors' eyes—in which case it becomes glare. Glare is particularly blinding at night; as a result of the contrast of surrounding darkness, it inhibits our ability to see where we are going.

Mindfully place the fixtures. For example, think about the purpose of lighting things like the corners

The light source for this bronze Chinese bell is hidden within the structure and mounting of the bell. The light you see graces the delicate detail of the bell and pale blue *Festuca glauca* below. Author's garden.

of your house. Is that what you really want people to see at night? Light fixture placement is critical when you are changing levels. If you are at a higher level, you do not want to look down into a light. If you are going up or down a series of stairs, the light fixtures should be placed so that light will not shine in someone's eyes in either direction. If you are at a lower level and need to look up, you should not have to shield your eyes from a fixture placed high enough to see the lamp inside the fixture. Consider using down lights versus up lights near windows of your house, when you are lighting a special tree. No one wants to look out a window into a glaring light. It is always safer, and kinder to eyes, to see the effect of light, rather than its source.

Good design usually means varying the type of lighting. For instance, lining a path with all path lights is boring. Placing lights in that manner ignores the design opportunity to make a garden come alive at night. Avoid the ubiquitous airport runway layout that is best suited for small aircraft.

It is better not to light all areas equally; in fact, it is more interesting and dynamic to light some areas better than others. Think about the important places that you really need to see first, then second. Prioritize lighting levels. This can also be a very energy-efficient approach. Remember that light can spill from one area to another. A walkway will probably not need as much light as a stairway, but the higher light level at the stair can spill onto the walkway.

Keeping these ideas in mind, I will review the ways you can place light fixtures in the garden.

Uplighting

Uplighting can be difficult to do, but it also has great rewards. A light fixture placed at the base of a tree and aimed to run the light along the trunk and up into the canopy creates a stunning effect. The placement is critical. Place the fixture so that people

walking by the area will not get direct light into their eyes. Lights that shine upward should also be shielded from the night sky. It is important to have the fixtures well aimed at a specific target that will capture all or most of the light.

Downlighting

Downlighting from a house soffit or a tree branch will produce a pool of light on the ground. If you mount several lights overhead in a pergola and hide the source within a plant grown on the pergola, you will have pools of light creating a magical path. Some

A capped bollard light fixture forces light downward onto a corner of a border and spills it out onto the path. Fixture: FX Luminaire. Author's garden.

manufacturers make very tiny fixtures, designed to suspend from smaller branches.

Alternatively, path lights or bollards produce downlight, too. Typically, these are used adjacent to a path, allowing light to spill where feet need to tread.

Grazing

When you want to accentuate wonderful texture (usually of a wall), grazing is the lighting trick to do it. Place light fixtures very close to the surface, either at the base or near the top, and aim the light onto the surface. This creates shadowing at each tiny projection, making the texture much more visible. If you were to light the surface from farther away, it would appear flatter.

Silhouetting

Creating a silhouette can be stunning if the silhouette is understandable and interesting. If the object is overly complicated, the silhouette may lose its impact, which is why you want a silhouette in the first place. This type of lighting makes a very strong statement, so use it carefully for just the right object and place.

Thrown shadow

Shadows can have a breathtaking effect when done well. Tree branches are particularly lovely, but consider art or architectural features. Shadows are much more interesting if they are well defined rather than appearing as an amoebic, unrecognizable blob. You need an adjustable fixture for this technique, because it takes some experimentation with just the right place for the fixture to get the right type of shadow.

Sparkle treatment

A little sparkle at night can be magical, whether you use candles or twinkling electrical lights (or perhaps

An adjustable lamp is situated at the base of this gabion wall in order to graze the stone so that it is visible from the owner's kitchen window and deck at night. Garden of Fran and Sharri LaPierre. Garden design by Vanessa Gardner Nagel, APLD, Seasons Garden Design LLC.

Fiber optic lighting set beneath a rill of colored, tumbled glass twinkles on and off, creating a delightful effect. Garden design by Shapiro Ryan Design, Seattle.

both). Other lighting that falls in this category would be lanterns of any shape or size. They can glow, twinkle, or sparkle. Use this type of lighting as you would a focal point, because a little goes a long way.

Underwater lighting

Underwater lighting is beautiful because it gives water a stunning glow at night. However, you must make sure underwater fixtures are thoroughly waterproof. In addition, if you insert underwater lighting into a fishpond, consider that electrical current in the water may affect the fish.

Preparing Your Lighting Concept

As you develop your lighting plan, identify the features you want or need to see at night. Is there a tree with beautiful bark? What about the amazing piece of art visible across the garden from your dining room window? Is there a path you typically use at night that needs lighting? Definitely plan to light any stairs or steps.

Think about how much light you want on each subject, whether it should be a narrow or wide beam, and where you should place the light to best effect.

A pot and ornamental branches make a striking statement silhouetted onto a wall at night. The light fixture is immediately behind the pot.

Using the same pot as the previous photo but moving the light fixture to the front and left of the pot creates this thrown shadow effect.

Remember all of the different ways to light. Also, consider if you need a clear or frosted lens to diffuse light. Sometimes that is helpful, especially when lighting something with a high sheen, to prevent hot spots. Would bark on a coral bark Japanese maple be more stunning with a red filter on the lens? Would a blue lens accentuate a blue spruce?

As you make these decisions, note them on your plan. Your garden lighting will be far superior to the ubiquitous row of path lights.

This mature *Acer palmatum* 'Sango-kaku' has lost much of its coral bark in the old wood. However, at night a red filter on a light fixture accentuates the hint of remaining coral. Author's garden.

Designing the Hypothetical Garden

Lighting Concepts

Lighting the hypothetical garden involves evaluating the path that visitors should take at night and the ability to easily see the front door while also making the lighting interesting rather than monotonous. In the back garden, I focus primarily on the entertaining area and garden art. The dog run and the greenhouse need some lighting, especially for those nights when there is a question of frost and newbie seedlings stirring to life.

I place the lighting control panel, similar to the irrigation system controller, in a well-lit, dry location that allows easy access and maintenance. The panel will control all lighting zones, similar to irrigation control.

Lighting concepts are shown on the lighting plan for the hypothetical garden.

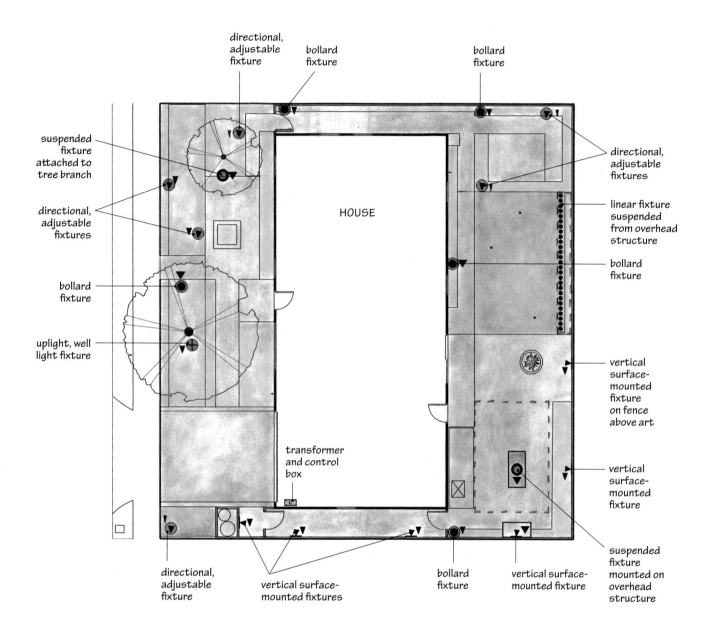

directional,
adjustable
fixture

bollard
fixture

bollard
fixture

bollard
fixture

suspended
fixture
attached to
tree branch

directional,
adjustable
fixtures

directional,
adjustable
fixtures

HOUSE

linear fixture
suspended
from overhead
structure

bollard
fixture

bollard
fixture

uplight, well
light fixture

vertical
surface-
mounted
fixture
on fence
above art

vertical
surface-
mounted
fixture

transformer
and control
box

suspended
fixture
mounted on
overhead
structure

directional,
adjustable
fixture

vertical surface-
mounted fixtures

bollard
fixture

vertical surface-
mounted fixture

Beam spread key

 narrow

 medium

 wide

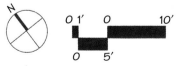

The Final Design

One Last Look

Assembling your final design is a little like laying out your clothes in the morning before you put them on. You evaluate all of your selections before you commit to wearing them for the day. You check to make sure there are no holes in the socks, everything is clean, and the scarf (or necktie) looks right with everything else. Giving your garden design one last look is an opportunity to make sure that you do not wear a black shoe with a brown shoe, metaphorically speaking. You are seeking "gaps and overlaps," as we say in the trade. Once you have reviewed the design, you can produce a master plan and a construction plan for bidding and construction.

A Step-by-Step Review of Everything

The design review should be a methodical, step-by-step process that assures you have covered everything. It starts where you began the design process—at the beginning. The difference between then and now is that you have all of your decisions under your belt. It is an excellent idea to review those decisions one final time before committing to them. The biggest reason is that changes are easy to make on paper. If you make changes after construction begins, you will experience fewer jingles in your wallet because change orders are typically costly and can add up to a bundle of money: *ka-ching*! The more thorough your review now, the less likely it will be that you

What you will learn:

- how to review and edit your design
- what you need before you start construction

An entrancing courtyard where finishes and furnishings are in harmony. Garden of Michael Schultz and Will Goodman.

185

will have to pay for change orders. If you have a sudden bright idea and decide to change your stone type at the last minute, your change order may also include something called a restocking fee. Suppliers charge a restocking fee if they have to take a product back once it has left the warehouse. Restocking fees vary but can be a percentage of your cost or a flat fee. The lesson here is: avoid expensive change orders. Review everything while it is still on paper.

If you have a difficult time comprehending a design on paper, you can do a simple mock-up. Cut out templates for major features and lay them on the ground to get a sense of the layout. Is it too fussy or busy? Do you need more detail? Do you see an overlap or a gap? Just as carpenters measure twice and cut once, you are reviewing for issues to prevent them from becoming headaches. Another method is to stake out each area in the garden. Many of my clients choose to do this and find it immensely helpful. If you decide not to do this, you can always ask

A garden owner stakes out the plan to get a sense of scale.

your contractor to do it for you so you can review and approve the design before construction begins.

Site data

The biggest reason to review site data is that too often during construction, contractors find errors in original measurements, or uncover some overlooked drainage problem, or . . . . I could continue for a week with examples. A garden renovation can be similar to a house renovation. Unknowns lurk where you least expect them. If you thought you knew where the utilities are located when you were documenting your site, make sure now. Err on the side of caution. Call your utility company. Have them mark the locations of each utility, if you need to.

Review your site documentation materials. Does everything make sense? If something looks a little strange, get it sorted out now. Have you discovered anything since you recorded the information? Has anything changed?

As an example of how quickly something can change, my spouse and I used to have a 13-acre forest behind our property. Each spring morning, I opened our door to hear an almost cacophonous chorus of glorious birdsong. In the span of one autumn week, the forest was clear-cut, down to the last twig, for development. The chirping, tweeting, and peeping became occasional chirps the following spring. Not only did it change our experience instantly, it changed our exposure to the sun and created new drainage problems for us. (Humus-laden forests are nature's sponges, absorbing copious amounts of rain.) I planned for garden changes that fall and the next spring after the clear-cut. I moved many shade plants from a portion of my shady woodland garden and created a sunny, drought-tolerant garden. Per legal zoning, the entire development was supposed to be single-story homes. However, to our surprise, our county surreptitiously granted the developer the right to build some two-story homes. He constructed two of the taller homes 5 feet from our property line. Now we are growing new trees to restore our privacy. With a forest of new roofs and pavement, sans sponge effect, we also had to install new storm control methods in response to new winter drainage problems. If your jurisdiction tells you "studies were done" regarding storm water runoff, do not bet the rent that your problems are solved.

If the only change you have had to face since you started planning is that an existing plant that you had hoped to use has died, consider yourself lucky. Record it now. If you originally recorded your information in spring and it is now midsummer, the route of the sun has changed. Walk around your property to see if you would change anything based on where the sun is now. Make a note of it if you think this might change something in the design.

Did you document those phone calls and meetings with your local jurisdiction if you had to contact them? Send them a letter or email confirming your understanding of what you each said and agreed to. It could come in handy later if an inspector makes a decision that does not match what you heard originally.

Garden components

If you have been second-guessing any of the components of your garden, now is the time to fish or cut bait. Either be comfortable with your decisions as

Meadow and forest are nature's sponge. Home of Maryellen Hockensmith and Michael McCulloch, AIA.

they are or change them now. Many people vacillate about one particular thing or another. Typical questions include the following:

- Should we include the trampoline in the garden or should we have a playhouse instead?
- How can we use the space after the children grow up?
- Will one of our children jump or fall into the water feature if it is too large?
- Should we illuminate this tree or a different tree at night?

Here is a question I recommend asking yourself: Are we buying it because we will make good use of it, because we will get pleasure from it for a long time, or because we hope to impress our friends? Indecision is usually born of not knowing or not listening to your inner voice. People may not know if they will use something. They may be unsure of how long something will be useful. Do you have something over which you have been wavering? Is your conscience bothering you about something not being as green or sustainable as it could be? Now is the time to make peace with the little voice in your head.

Adjacency and circulation

Comfort with the location of all your components is important. Does it bother you that one thing is too far away or too close to something else? If you have a better idea of how that might work, change it. Are the paths to get around the garden where they need to be? Are they wide enough? If you sacrificed the width of a path to make something else larger and you are not content with that decision, revisit that now. Life is too short to be unhappy about little things that you have the power to change.

The most common thing that my clients end up wishing they had done differently is listened to me when I told them that a path should be wider. They were confident that 3 feet would be wide enough in certain areas. They discovered after they used the garden for a while that they should have widened the path.

Visualizing the garden layout

Now is the time to test your visualization skills. Envisioning how your garden will look when it is complete is one of the best ways to be confident of your choices. If you have the ability to create a drawing of how you think an area will look, it will help you see how a curved line will look versus a straight line. It will help you see that a circle looks like an ellipse as you approach it in the garden.

Speaking of circles, here is one useful thing to remember. If you join a path to a circle, aim the path toward the center of the circle. Did you ignore the center of a circular element? If you did, you may find that you will feel uncomfortable psychologically around that area. If you are intentionally trying to tweak the comfort level of visitors to your garden, that would be a way to do it. I have seen some fascinating designs where a designer placed a circle off center within an ellipse, or vice versa, as though someone had sliced through a hard-boiled egg. This design was quite dynamic and was successful partly because the attention was on the center of the shape inside the larger shape.

On the topic of combining shapes, have you inadvertently created an acute angle or awkward intersection in your layout? If it does not feel right on paper, it will only feel worse when you encounter the real thing in the garden. Are you trying to join a square and a rectangular area? Rather than placing them so they touch corners, overlap them. Your psychological comfort will be the better for it. Connecting corners to corners creates tension. Recall the discussion about zigzag lines in Chapter 5. This is a variation.

If you are not handy at creating a sketch (and even

many designers are not), there is a simple process that can help you visualize your new garden by locating an object on a drawing from a photograph. As an example, I will use the layout of the hypothetical garden to visualize the meditation bench (A, next page).

First take a photograph, shot straight on (not from the side), of the focus area you wish to visualize. Include some portion of your house or another primary structure in the photograph. In addition, at the corner of the area you want to draw, place a square reference object (such as a cardboard box) with one

visible side perpendicular to your primary structure. Reference your plan as you go, determining the area on your final plan on which you want to focus. My drawing A (next page) shows a 1-foot grid over the area, but you do not need to do this unless you find using a grid easier.

Enlarge a copy of the photograph to approximately 8 by 10 inches. Then tape your photograph to a flat, firm surface, lay some tracing paper over the photograph, and tape the paper to the same surface. (You can use drafting tape or dots that are not

A wider path is more gracious leading to a front door. Save the narrower paths for farther out in the garden. Garden of Bonnie Bruce and Michael Peterson.

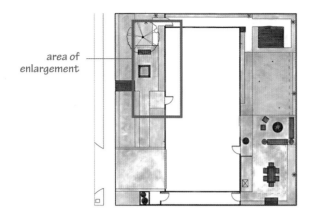

area of
enlargement

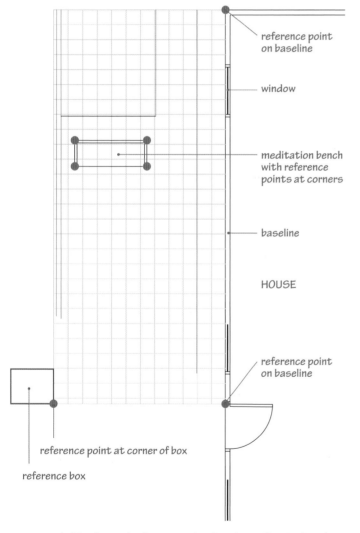

reference point
on baseline

window

meditation bench
with reference
points at corners

baseline

HOUSE

reference point
on baseline

reference point at corner of box

reference box

A. Use the garden layout to visualize the meditation bench.

as sticky as regular tape.) Trace over the things that will be there after you install your garden. You might consider using a drafting triangle or ruler to keep lines straight. If your reference object will not be present after you complete your design, lightly trace that object as well. You can erase it later.

The next step is to find the horizon line and the vanishing point (B). The horizon line is at the height of your eyes when you took the photograph. An easy way to see where the horizon line is located is by looking for the tops and bottoms of any objects in the photograph. The closer they are to the horizon line, the less you see of them. If you were at the beach overlooking the vast ocean, the horizon line would be where the ocean and the sky meet. For the sake of your drawing, the horizon line is straight across your paper, side to side. It is not at an angle.

Vanishing points are on the horizon line. You find a point by following lines perpendicular to where you were standing. In other words, if you stood in front of your house, assume that the front of your house was parallel to you. One side of your reference box is perpendicular to your house. Set a straight-edge (such as a ruler) along the low, perpendicular edge of your reference object; it will lead you to the vanishing point on the horizon line. All lines perpendicular to you from one object will converge on the horizon line, in this case at a single vanishing point. The line where your house foundation meets the ground is your baseline.

To locate the focus area, I draw a line parallel to the baseline through the corner point of the reference box (C). This is the same line, parallel to the house, that creates the focus area. I locate the reference points from the plan onto the drawing along the baseline. Then I draw a line from the vanishing point through each of the base points and intersect the parallel line. Now I have the boundaries of the focus area.

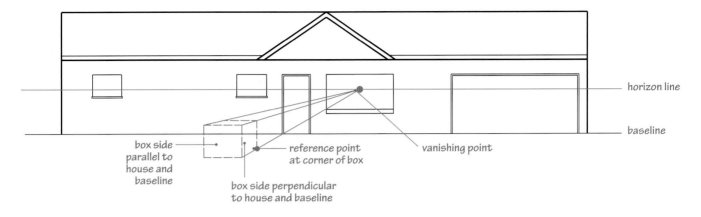

B. Find the horizon line and the vanishing point on the drawing.

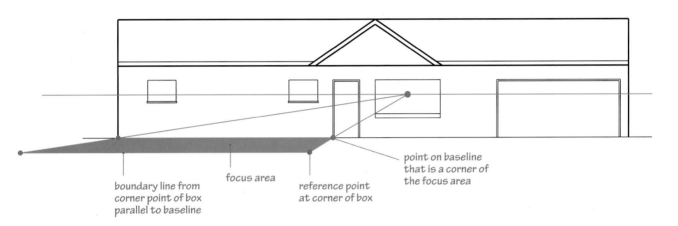

C. To find the boundaries of the focus area using the vanishing point and reference points, (1) locate points on the baseline that relate to the focus area and (2) draw a line from the corner point of the box parallel to the baseline.

Notice that on the hypothetical plan, the bench is close to the boundary line of the focus area. On the drawing, I draw a line just above the boundary line to set the area for the bench (D), estimating the exact location (remember, this is a sketch). Using a lightweight pencil (an H or 2H), I locate all four corners of the bench two dimensionally: (1) draw a line parallel to the baseline to indicate the edge of the bench farthest from the house; (2) locate reference points on the house and baseline that relate to the

position of the bench; (3) use the vanishing point and reference points on the baseline to find the front and back of the bench, the two corners farthest from the house, then the two corners closest to the house.

Now there is a rectangle on the ground plane representing the bench. In order to bring the bench into the third dimension, I will locate points for the height of the seat (E). On the same lines I used to locate the bench corners, I estimate the height of the bench from the baseline. Usually seating height is

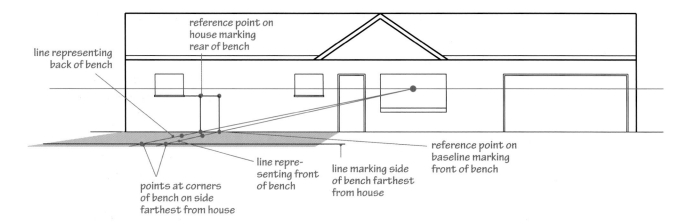

line representing
back of bench

reference point on
house marking
rear of bench

points at corners
of bench on side
farthest from house

line repre-
senting front
of bench

line marking side
of bench farthest
from house

reference point on
baseline marking
front of bench

D. Mark all four corners of the bench by (1) estimating the position of the location of the bench farthest from the house and drawing a line parallel to the baseline to indicate this, (2) locating points on the house and baseline that relate to the position of the bench, and (3) using the vanishing point and reference points on the baseline to find the front and back of the bench, then the two corners farthest from the house.

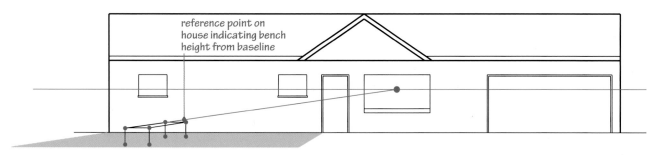

reference point on
house indicating bench
height from baseline

E. To bring the bench into the third dimension, (1) measure up from the baseline and mark on the house the height of the bench, then (2) use that point and the vanishing point to indicate the bench seat and legs.

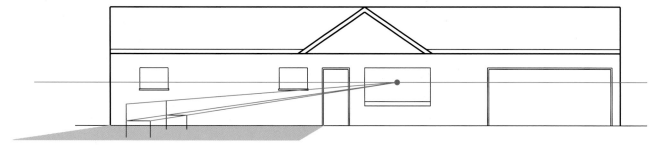

F. Finish the bench by extending the lines representing the back, using the vanishing point.

approximately 18 inches. I know the height of the windowsill on the base plan is about 42 inches from the baseline; using the ratio of 18 to 42, I locate the height along the vertical line. Through that reference point, I draw another line from the vanishing point to a vertical line drawn up from one of my bench leg points. I do this for each of the four leg points and then connect all of the points to draw in the seat of the bench.

I locate the back height of the bench in the same manner as the seat height (F). Now I can use the outline to sketch my chosen bench for the project and have it look fairly realistic.

If you have neither time nor inclination to create a drawing, staking out your new garden may be an easier method. This technique will improve your visualization of how much space you have dedicated to various functions. To get an idea of height, use a few bamboo poles and some willing friends or family members. Locate the bamboo poles to get a sense of structure height. Have your friends or family members stand with arms spread to give an idea of the size of a mature shrub or small structure.

Finishes and furnishings

By now you have a variety of finishes staring at you, especially if you picked up samples and have them parading across your back porch. Did you evaluate all of them based on their function and level of maintenance? Will they work with your lifestyle? How do they coordinate now that you have them all assembled?

One thing to remember is that how you see finishes as samples may not be how you see them proportionately in your garden. One finish may be only 10 percent of the garden. Does your sample reflect that or is it the largest sample you have? Also, remember that you will not see all finishes at the same time. Is it the case that one finish looks peculiar with the rest, but you will see it only next to a single, compatible finish?

Review how each finish intersects with another in each location. Is one vertical and the other horizontal? Sometimes the same finish can look different in different locations because lighting plays tricks. Examine finishes in the position and under the light where you will install them. Do not study them in total shade if they will usually be in full sun. View them vertically if that is how you will see them. If you will typically see a finish at ground level, place it there to observe it. If you view it at arm's length, you might be fooling yourself about how it will ultimately appear in your garden.

Once you have all the furniture assembled, at least on paper, evaluate all of the pieces (including your

The orientation of these two samples of the same finish, one turned vertically and one turned horizontally, makes it appear as though they are different colors.

existing pieces). Does everything work well together? Will your dining chair selection really fit around the table you selected? Can you sit up as high as you want to if you want to read in the lounge chair? Double-check functionality, durability, maintenance, warranties, finishes, pricing—everything—before you pay for it and it is yours.

Evaluate how the finishes of your furnishings look with your hardscape finishes. Are they complementary? Does one finish almost match another but not quite? If so, reconsider one of them, because it will appear as though you tried to match them but could not. It is better to make them either completely different or a shade lighter or darker than have two finishes almost match.

Irrigation

The reason you evaluate irrigation before you select plants is that you need to know your water source and the quantity available before you select plants. However, irrigation and plants are close companions. Usually, it is not until after you select plants that you actually have the irrigation system designed. Before you make the final decision to install the irrigation system, make sure the system is designed appropriately for your planting beds. Irrigation zones should align with the water requirements of each planting bed.

If you are hand watering your plants, make sure you can get a hose to your plants easily. Will you need hose guides in various locations so you do not drag the hose through your plants? Would it make sense to add an additional, remote hose bib?

Plant structure

Among the most important things to revisit in your review of plant structure is whether the plants you selected are hardy in your area. There are numerous books about plants where you can find zone information, or you can browse the Internet for your area. Matching your plants to your zone is not a perfect science. Sometimes plants that are cold hardy in your area may not appreciate excessive winter rain. Or plants that can handle the cold will not handle an ice storm or summer heat and humidity.

Once you have done your homework on your plants' capability of survival, review the structure of your plants one more time. Does it make sense to have an exclamation mark next to the garage door? Remember that strong plant structure calls attention to itself. You may not want attention focused on what is nearby, like the garage door. That location may need plant structure that leads your attention elsewhere.

Lighting

It is difficult to evaluate lighting without having all of the fixtures installed. However, you can get an idea of the effect a light will create by placing a flashlight where you intend to have the fixture located. While the flashlight is restricted to a specific lamp and beam spread, it will still give you an approximation of what you can expect. Carry the flashlight with you around the garden and use it where you are able, especially if you are keeping existing objects (like a large tree). If you are unable to do this because nothing currently exists, visit a public park or a friend's garden at dusk. There, while you can still see to get around and make notes, select objects to light with the flashlight that are similar to those you will have in your own garden. You can also walk around your neighborhood and find examples of what other people have already done, but this might be more time consuming.

You also need to evaluate how the light fixtures will look with all of your other selections. With photos of your light fixtures assembled in combination with your finishes and furnishings samples, evaluate your fixtures based on finish and appearance. Are they what you hoped they would be? If not, change a finish or swap fixture selections now.

In some cases, lighting manufacturer representatives from local vendors may be willing to come to your home after you have installed most of your garden and test various fixtures and placements for you. This proves very helpful to me and to my clients. However, I usually develop a preliminary plan for the lighting in advance, so the electrical connections are already where we need them to be. This program saves my clients some money for my time, because I do not have to decide all of the lamps or fixtures in advance. The in-garden program helps us jointly decide on the lamp, fixture, and placement in situ.

Use of a flashlight at the base of this tree allows a basic evaluation of whether this would be a good location for a light fixture.

A Chance to Edit Anything

Editing is different from reviewing. Editing typically involves removing or replacing something based on design, versus functionality, maintenance, or many of the other issues you reviewed. Editing is all about control. Gardens are really our control over nature. I believe that editing is an ongoing process during the life of a garden, because plants wither and die (they have life expectancies, too) and damage occurs and needs repair or replacement. Weeding is a form of editing. However, an editing process should also occur before installing the garden. While you have been editing all along as you made decisions, you did not have the full array of decisions in front of you until now.

After your review, you probably made a couple of changes. Now with all components assembled, is there anything that sticks out like a sore thumb? The most important reason to edit is to create clarity and simplicity. If something is glaring at you, it probably does not belong or it is out of balance with the rest of the garden.

Using what you learned about all of the design principles, especially balance and unity, evaluate the location of your components, the space they use, paths of circulation, and the location of focal points. To bring the plan into balance, relocate, remove, or replace as needed. Remember, the design is still on paper. Never get so attached to an idea that you are unwilling to change it. Always keep an open mind about design.

If you need a few more opinions, invite interested friends over for appetizers one afternoon. Pin up your plans, set out your finishes and photographs. Then explain to them why you planned your garden the way you did. Ask them for their ideas. Inviting critique is not necessarily easy. However, it is amazing what you can receive in return. They may offer some ideas you never considered. Even then, you will need to accept that things may change during installation. Sometimes you will have to accept an unexpected reality. Certainly, there will be the reality of the garden's evolution over time after its installation.

Once you finalize all of your decisions, revise your conceptual plan to include all the changes. This becomes your master plan. A master plan typically shows all of your hardscape, including patios, paths, water features, fencing, and so on. It also includes

Nothing in this delightful display sticks out like a sore thumb. It all works together beautifully, hinting of the harmony to be found in the rest of the garden. Created by Laura M. Crockett, Garden Diva Designs.

your plants and furnishings. It is a comprehensive plan that becomes your guideline for a construction plan.

Producing the Construction Plan

A plan for bidding and construction typically includes no more and no less information than the contractor needs in order to give you a price and construct the garden. This can be extremely detailed. Anything unclear or missing will usually elicit questions from your contractor before bidding. If anything is left ambiguous, this can mean change orders later, or your contractor telling you that he could not include it in the bid because he did not know what you wanted. It will mean added, unexpected cost.

More information, rather than less, is the best defense. Make sure you have things like dimensions on a plan to tell a contractor how much of an area to cover with a stone patio or how high to make a wood arbor. What is the design of that patio or arbor? Do you have photographs or drawings and sizes you can give the contractor? Have you specified the type of stone or wood? Pretend you are building something yourself. What information do you need to know to do it? That is the information a contractor wants to know, and it should be written down. Be methodical and thorough.

You can identify areas on your plan and create a list of notes to accompany each area, if that makes the information clearer to the contractor. Even if you do the work yourself, if you have adequately detailed each of the items you will construct, it will be easy to figure out the amount of materials needed to build them.

The Master Plan and
the Construction Plan

More than one sore thumb bothers me about the hypothetical garden: the location of the meditation bench, the uncomfortable intersection at the corner of the putting green by the back step, and details of the dog run. I resolve these issues in the following ways:

- I enclose the meditation area in a private courtyard with an ornamental fence and gates. This eliminates my concern that a visitor could unexpectedly disrupt someone sitting on the bench. Because of the addition of the fence and gates, I revise the lighting near the bridge. Instead of specifying fixtures at ground level, I put fixtures on the fence on either side of the entry gate, to light the water feature, and by the driveway gate. I coordinate the materials and design of the fence and gates with the fence that encloses the dog run.
- I also decide to cut around the corner of the putting green rather than have those corners just meet in an uncomfortable intersection.
- I decide that cedar chips would be the best paving material for the dog run. Cedar chips contribute to minimizing fleas and other insects, and they won't stick in a dog's paws and track into the house like gravel. I add some dog-resistant columnar plants to shade portions of the dog run during the day. (Alternatively, I could have designed some shade structures.)

Now the garden feels consistent and unified. All areas function better. The revised conceptual plan becomes the master plan, expressing the final design. The master plan is the basis for my construction plan, which gives dimensions and specifies materials at a minimum. I will also provide adequate notations, details, and perhaps photos to describe construction fully to a contractor. Now I am ready to move forward into construction.

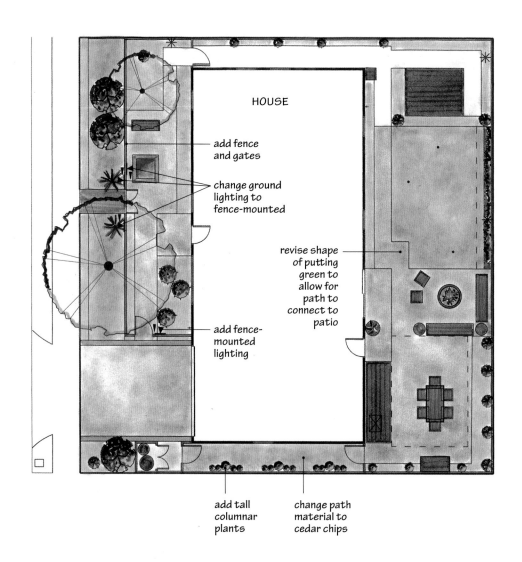

HOUSE

add fence
and gates

change ground
lighting to
fence-mounted

add fence-
mounted
lighting

revise shape
of putting
green to
allow for
path to
connect to
patio

add tall
columnar
plants

change path
material to
cedar chips

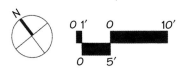

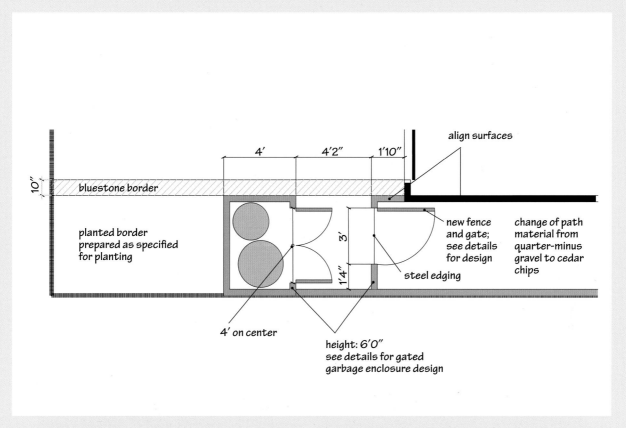

This small portion of the construction plan for the hypothetical garden, showing the garbage enclosure and part of the dog run, displays the type of information that is typically required by a contractor in order to bid on and build a garden.

The revised conceptual plan becomes the master plan, showing the new fence around the courtyard area as well as the revised light fixtures, putting green, and dog run.

Construction: Working with Contractors

A Little Perspective

Unless you have some familiarity with construction, hiring a contractor to install your garden can be the most daunting part of bringing a garden to life. However, with a little knowledge, you can change intimidation to self-assurance.

Before beginning this chapter, I interviewed a group of contractors about specific and common issues that property owners have when they are about to undergo a garden installation. Their responses help me bring both a contractor's and a designer's perspective to share with you, a garden owner or aspiring designer.

In this chapter, I use the pronoun *he* when I refer to contractors. This is not to say that there are not women landscape contractors. However, the vast majority of landscape contractors are male; my apologies to those capable women who are landscape contractors.

Finding and Selecting a Contractor

My clients who choose not to install the garden themselves frequently ask me to recommend someone to help them. Even if you think you will install part or most of your garden yourself, some portion of the work will likely require a contractor's

What you will learn:

- how to find and select a contractor
- about bidding a project
- what happens during phases of construction

Joinery of materials can distinguish a contractor's skills, as well as his thoroughness at coordinating trades. Design by Shapiro Ryan Design, Seattle.

skills and equipment. It helps to know how to look for a landscape contractor and what to consider as you go about selecting the right one for your garden installation.

Getting leads

Word of mouth is probably the most common way for garden owners to find a contractor. Sometimes the referral system gets convoluted, but it does allow clients to find contractors. One contractor mentioned that he acquired a project through referrals conveyed between four interrelated persons before his client heard about him and hired him. If you do not have chatty neighbors to pass along a referral, a contractor installing a project down the block can be handy. Usually contractors put up a yard sign to show that they are the ones installing the garden. Take a stroll by the project to see how it is coming along. Talk to the owners, if possible, about what they think of the contractor—preferably after the project is complete.

Sometimes a qualified landscape contractor is hard to find through the grapevine of family, friends, and acquaintances. When that happens, consider talking to vendors that supply the kinds of products that a landscape contractor might use or talk to a subcontractor that might do a portion of a project for a general contractor. Good examples would be a lighting company that specializes in landscape lighting, a grading company, a lumberyard or stone yard, or an irrigation installer. Vendors or subcontractors can tell you how much business they do with the contractor and have a good sense of how knowledgeable and responsible the contractor might be.

And then there is always the Internet or the yellow pages to help you find a contractor. However, the amount of detail you get that way varies, so it may be harder to sort out which ones might be a good fit for you. This method is a mixed bag unless you can get excellent references.

Local trade organizations also keep lists of quali-

Seeing a contractor's project under construction can give insight. Design and construction by McQuiggins Inc.

fied landscape contractors. Such an organization will often cover a wide area, such as a state or province, but will usually have local chapters. You can commonly find a list of members in your area on the Internet, with contact information and links to individual Web sites. Contractors usually post photos of their best projects on their Web sites. It helps to see a stone fire pit that a contractor has built if you are planning one for your garden.

Screening candidates

If possible, consider selecting a contractor even before your design is complete. You can develop some basic criteria to prequalify a contractor, taking into account contractors' qualifications, references, project approach, and more. In addition, if a small portion of your project is fairly well defined, this can be the basis for obtaining a bid. If you decide to do this, make sure each contractor knows that this is just a percentage of the overall project. Preselecting your contractor can give you the advantage of being able to check in with the contractor for preliminary pricing and general information about materials during the design process.

If you choose to finish your design before requesting bids, briefly discuss your project with interested contractors and set up a time to meet with them. Be prepared to spend some time meeting with several

A swirled stone fire pit with a gabion penetrating its side is an example of a stonemason's work and potentially a good referral. Garden of Fran and Sharri LaPierre. Design by Vanessa Gardner Nagel, APLD, Seasons Garden Design LLC.

contractors to get to know them. Keep in mind that your investment of time now can save you time, money, headaches, or all three in the future. The next few paragraphs offer some things to keep in mind as you interview contractors before you solicit bids from your final list.

Perhaps the number one criterion that people usually think of is the degree of expertise and craftsmanship exhibited by a contractor. Does he or she do good work? What level of good work are you expecting? Contractors' abilities can be very different. Look at details to separate the wheat from the chaff. How do contractors join two different materials? How do they create an outside corner or terminate a run with any material? How well do they finish the installation of a material? Do they apply a coating for waterproofing? If so, how many coats? What is the coating? How long will it last? You can appreciate that this can get complicated.

Getting along with others is an important trait in any person, but it is critical when working with a contractor. This is not just true for the contractor. You are creating a working relationship, so try to discern your compatibility and realize that they are evaluating you on the same basis. Contractors are people, too, and unless a contractor does something to earn your disrespect, respect him as the business owner, craftsperson, scheduling and materials expert, manager of many trades, and people pleaser he tries to be. If a contractor perceives that you may be difficult to work with, he may do any number of things to get you to select someone else besides telling you he does not want to do your project. Examples of gracefully refusing to do a project are giving a high bid or a long period before he can start work. Note, though, that a contractor's schedule may genuinely be very busy, indicating he is in demand for good skills, low cost, or quick delivery (rarely, if ever, all three at once). Contractors will increase project

fees if they think a client is going to need a lot of hand-holding.

Local jurisdictions usually require contractors to be bonded and insured to a stipulated minimum amount. Some contractors exceed the minimums. Always ask what they carry—especially if they forget to tell you. Ask for documented proof, because if there is an accident or either of you overlooks or forgets something, it could affect the success of your project. Make sure they have the financial capability to cover an error.

Jurisdictions vary with regard to licensing laws, just as they do with bonding and insurance. Check your jurisdiction for the legal requirements to be a landscape contractor. Some locales only require posting a bond to become a contractor, while others require passing an exam or multiple exams for various categories of landscape work. Sometimes professional landscape contractor organizations certify their members through peer review. Assure yourself that the contractor you choose has met all of the legal criteria and some degree of professional experience review before he works in your garden. Be wary of contractors who suggest you do not need to get a permit if it is legally required. They may not want to have an inspector review their work, because their work may not be in accordance with codes. That can mean trouble for you later.

One of the best traits a contractor can have is integrity. When I queried the group of contractors, I asked each of them what integrity meant to them. Any client will respect a contractor who has it. Each of them felt that it is important to be honest and reliable. Good contractors want their work to speak for them.

A trustworthy contractor is crucial, because you are not the expert in all of the materials or methods he will use. Even if you are, you may have to depend on a contractor because you do not have the time to do the work. Educating yourself ahead of time helps both of you. Sometimes a garden owner will find a product that the contractor has not heard of because it is new to the market. With a constant stream of new materials advertised by every conceivable means, it is impossible for any contractor to be familiar with all of them. The ability to share what you find and how the contractor handles your shared information may cause you to prefer one contractor over another.

Ask contractors if they have a portfolio of their work through which you can browse. This will give you an idea of the range of expertise they have and how often they have done projects like yours. Some contractors have online portfolios, which are very convenient to review, while others are still catching up with the digital age. This has nothing to do with their capability to install a garden, but it may have something to do with how easily you can get information about them and communicate with them.

Scheduling and installation priorities

Before you arrive at your short list of contractors to solicit bids from, ask each contractor when, in his schedule, he will be able to do your work. A contractor's schedule can be one of the most circuitous things on this planet. He may be responsible for coordinating subcontractors' work if he does not have all the trades under his roof. Mother Nature controls the speed at which he can progress on projects, and he is also dependent on how quickly subcontractors or other contractors become available to work on yours. Weaving trades through a project depends on a number of issues: weather, their relationship with their subcontractors, other projects, project hiccups (expect the unexpected), changes you make after work begins, and more. Sometimes it is a miracle they can complete a project on time and on budget. Often there is a contingency amount inserted into a construction budget to cover unexpected

circumstances, averaging 5 to 10 percent of a budget and even higher if you have a smaller project. Remember that no matter how perfect your contractor may be, it is unusual to have a perfect schedule. Appreciate it if you get it.

If you have a schedule with priorities, be up front with your contractor before you hire him. If the project schedule is particularly restrictive, he may opt out of bidding on your project. This is a situation where your failure to plan ahead sufficiently will not create his emergency—unless he really needs the work. However, emergencies do happen. Let the contractor know why it is an emergency and you may gain his compassion and goodwill.

Access is a key issue for contractors. Contractors generally give priority in their schedule to areas of difficult or limited access. This means they will tackle the least accessible corner of your yard first, which is often the backyard. This is typically counter to what a homeowner would like to see done, but this way you do not need to remove or destroy existing landscaping to access the backyard.

Your responsibilities before bidding

It is important for you to know your limits before getting bids. When most people think of limits during a project, they often think first of finances. However, there are several other kinds of limits to consider. If you think you want to help with the project by doing some portion of it, consider the limits of your time, energy, and knowledge. Your contractor will not appreciate hearing halfway through the project that you suddenly do not have the time you thought you would have. It is not worth risking increased project cost, declining goodwill, and a reduced sense of trust. Relationships do not work as well under those circumstances. Be conscious and honest from the start.

Usually a homeowner has the contractor's responsibilities virtually memorized. However, you will have responsibilities as well. They may be as simple as staying out of the contractor's way or as significant as purchasing of product that the contractor will use. If you choose to accept responsibility for anything on a project, make sure you do it and make sure it is done on time. If you default on your responsibilities, be prepared to have the contractor change your schedule for installation—and not necessarily for the better. If the tools and materials are not available when your contractor has that work scheduled, he has to reassign employees or worse, accept that subcontractors may have another project in the queue that they will start if there is no work for them on your project.

The landscape contractor on this project will need to access the back of the property first through this narrow, uphill area. In some situations a portion of fence may need to be removed in order for the contractor to gain access to the garden area.

The Bidding Process

Once you have a list of at least three contractors with whom you would be comfortable working, you can begin the process of bidding. Make copies of the information you have put together for your project. That should include any plans, drawings, sketches, material lists, and such. Provide each of the contractors that have made your final list with a set of your documents so they are clear about the scope of work you expect. Offer to walk each contractor around your property to allow them to gain an understanding of the lay of the land. This will help them determine a number of things, not the least of which is the best access to the site, where they might store materials during construction, and where potential problems might lurk.

While the contractors are putting their bids together, expect questions. Sometimes questions arise about specific criteria you have in mind or about the materials you have selected. For instance, if you asked them to add 2 inches of soil amendment to each planting bed before planting, one or more of the contractors might ask if you have a specific composition in mind for the soil amendment. They might also suggest using less to lower their bid.

If you agree to change something with one contractor, you will need to notify each contractor so they all provide bids that match. Your goal is to get responses that are as equal as possible. Even with your best efforts, contractors will usually still slip in some creative replies. It is not unusual to have to make a few phone calls to clarify items or to align work descriptions. This is not the time for a fruit salad: apples and oranges do not mix when reviewing bids.

Interesting things happen during bidding that can affect the estimates that you receive from contractors. Dealing with substitutions can be intricate. If you have done considerable research before making a decision on a particular material or product, be wary of suggestions during bidding to substitute something else. The onus is on the contractor to prove that what he is suggesting is as good as or better than what you selected. Often a contractor will suggest something less expensive because it means that his final number may be more competitive. You are better off making each contractor provide pricing for the same thing during your selection process. If you think that the product the contractor suggested is better than your original selection, you can request a change before you sign the contract.

Reviewing bids and awarding your project

When you receive all the bids, review each one for completeness before you start comparing fees and services. Did each of them provide references? Did they provide you with their qualifications? Did they tell you who your contact will be during the course of construction? How well organized is the bid? Can you find everything easily, or do you have to hunt for the details? Check off everything you requested. If something is missing you should call to request that portion or receive an explanation for its omission.

If any portion of a proposal is unclear, call to clarify those items. Be particularly attuned to what is included in the way of services and materials. Some contractors may have a lower price because they leave out a step that another contractor includes. This is not necessarily a bad thing, but it is something you should pay attention to and learn more about. The contractor may have to correct a portion of the bid. Make sure it is in writing and becomes part of the contract.

Time spent checking out references and referrals that a contractor gives you is time well spent. Sometimes a contractor will escort you through another client's garden if he can make an arrangement that

suits everyone's schedule. This is particularly useful when the other project is similar to yours because then you can ask questions that will relate to your project.

Reviewing a contract

Construction should never digress to a finger-pointing contest, but the fact is that it happens too often. Occasionally it is because the garden owner and contractor have expectations of each other that remain unstated. Silence is not golden when it comes to construction and working within the confines of a contract. The more you each communicate at the

Long lead times are common for certain products. Garden art can be one of them. In the riotous garden of Marcia Donahue, she displays some of the art for which she is famous.

207

beginning, the more likely it will be that you will meet each other's expectations. Any good contractor will take great pains to let his client know what it is he will do before he starts. Your contract should clearly state the scope of work. The contract should be sufficiently detailed so there is no question about the work you are paying the contractor to do. Once you sign a contract, the contractor has every right to give you a change order for anything you change. Often the change negatively affects your budget.

Here are the details you should expect to see in a contract:

- the total fee
- how and when the fee will be paid (fee schedule)
- a contract submittal date
- a contract expiration date
- a construction schedule: beginning and ending dates
- a definition of substantial completion
- late completion penalties or early completion incentives (optional)
- your address as the project address, and a description of where the project will be done on site, if it is a partial area of the garden
- who the parties to the contract are
- the contractor's address, phone number, and legal business name
- a description of the scope of work: what is included and what is not (as necessary)
- the area of work or work boundaries
- where staging of materials will occur
- use of utilities (electrical, water, and such)
- a provision that states this is the only agreement between you for this project and any amendments must be submitted in writing
- how changes in the agreement will be handled, particularly if they involve either additional cost or reimbursement
- the state or region that governs the contract
- a place for signatures of all parties legally bound by the contract

A contract may contain additional phrases and sections. Review all of them thoroughly, making sure you understand each item. You should consider including your drawings and sketches or your list of materials as part of the contract. If you have a completion date that the contractor has agreed to meet, include that as part of the contract, noting that acts of God can cause exceptions.

A common fee arrangement is to advance one-third of the fee at the onset of the project. This allows the contractor the ability to order materials for your project. Midway through the project, at some significant completion point, another one-third of the fee might be due. Upon substantial completion, the final one-third of the fee may be due. If you are more comfortable holding a portion back until final details are completed, speak up before signing the contract. Another common fee payment schedule is for the contractor to invoice monthly or bimonthly, depending on the size and complexity of the project, as well as asking for money up front to begin work.

If you have specific materials that you want used on a project and you know there is a long lead time for manufacturing or fabrication, consider noting in the contract that the contractor will order said materials with sufficient time to receive the materials for installation at the appointed time in the schedule. All too often I have experienced a substitution request at the last minute because the contractor did not order the product in time. This is not your fault, so why should you suffer for it?

Occasionally an owner will include an incentive

for the contractor to complete the project early in conjunction with punitive charges if he is late. Usually, this is only used if time is of the essence or the completion date is critical.

What to Expect During Construction

Your relationship with your contractor changes once construction begins. Before construction, you see the contractor occasionally and things seem normal around your house. Once construction starts, expect to see the contractor or his project manager on a frequent basis. Also expect turmoil and anything but normal. Different people may show up on the job on a regular basis as different trades do their work. Secure things you do not want to lose. The possibility of loss or damage of unsecured items increases as the number of trades and subcontractors increases.

Once construction begins, make every effort not to change anything unless it is critical. Scope creep or the incremental increase of new work for the contractor can yield surprisingly large invoices to compensate for the interruption of work. This is not always true, but in my experience it happens often enough that it always raises red flags for me when I see it happening. Contractors are normally pretty good about going with the flow of new directions by their clients, but usually they prefer to stick with the original plans if possible. Client-dictated changes can create havoc with their schedules, cause extra effort recalculating fees, and possibly confuse workers.

Having some familiarity with the phases of construction will minimize the surprise you may get when the power company turns off your power in preparation for installing underground electrical or some other such activity. Usually your contractor will let you know at least a day ahead of time.

Communicating with Your Contractor

Communication is the key to any good relationship. In this case, more is more. When you communicate with your contractor, consider documenting what you said and when. Contractors generally do this as well. It is good professional practice. If you send emails, faxes, or a letter, you should make a copy for yourself. If you phone your contractor, create a written phone record if you made a decision that affects the project's budget or schedule—two things that have the potential to create disharmony if there are inconsistencies. You may think that documentation is necessary only in the case of litigation, but it is also preventative. It will help keep all oars rowing in the same direction.

All of the contractors I interviewed said that email and cell phone are the best ways to reach them at any time before, during, or after a project. Some emphasized that cell phones are better than email, particularly if they are out on a job site. The best times seem to be later in the day because usually they are purchasing materials or coordinating subcontractors or employees early in the morning.

However, that might create an inconvenient situation. Review the major events and potential inconveniences ahead of time to reduce surprises. Following is a description of the major phases of work during construction. Your project may not involve all of them, but generally they will occur in this order.

Site preparation

If either you or your contractor identified a site condition that requires investigation before construction can begin, the contractor will arrange for soils tests and other geotechnical investigations. Generally, he will have a company with whom he works, but he will usually have you pay the company directly and separately from your construction fees.

Your local jurisdiction will require permits for various portions of your project. Demolition, grading, underground work, utilities, and hardscape often require some degree of permitting. This may also involve a review of the work during and after installation by a designated public official.

Among the first objects to arrive on site may be a portable toilet for workers. Expect to see it there until your construction is complete. You can work out the location with the contractor as necessary.

Before work can begin, the contractor will install protection for existing trees or other areas that need protection during construction. The ground around trees needs protection out to the drip line—the line at which the overhanging branches drip water during rain. Additionally, he may install things like a silt fence to prevent soil from eroding into another property or a temporary chain-link fence to protect materials or prevent possible injury to visitors or trespassers.

The contractor will also call the utility companies before work begins to have them mark where underground utilities lie. This is very important for nearly any type of work on your property. Your neighbors may not think to thank you for the electricity they continue to have, but they will undoubtedly mutter your name with unpleasant words if their electricity goes out because your contractor accidentally severed an underground power line. Your contractor will be equally surprised if not shocked.

Demolition

Chances are that things on your property you are not keeping will need to be removed before any other work can begin. Ideally, the removed items can be recycled or sent to a company that can recycle materials. Usually a contractor will have a system of flagging plants for removal, relocation, or to be left in place. Make sure you have approved all the flagging before demolition begins. Otherwise, your favorite tree could become firewood.

Equipment access to the site may be critical, depending on the size of the equipment required. You may also need a dumpster in which to place demolished materials. Recycle as it is possible.

Excavation, site remediation, and grading

Once demolition is complete, excavation, site remediation, and grading can begin. The order of these may vary depending on the scope of the project and the existing condition of the property. Site remediation may entail the implementation of recommendations made by a geotechnical engineer or civil engineer if you have a particularly challenging site, meaning one with steep slopes or drainage problems—or both.

Underground work

Once the land is stable, grading has the land going in all of the right directions, and excavations are complete, the contractor installs the things we pay large amounts of money for but never see. These include the piping for any underground irrigation; plumbing for remote hose bibs, for outdoor showers and sinks, and for water features or pools; gas lines; and wires and cables for electrical and telecommunication equipment, including outdoor lighting. Underground tanks for propane or a water storage system may also be included.

One important thing to consider when excavating for a large tank is where all the excavated soil will go. You can pay to have it removed from the site but it makes more sense to use it on the site. One of the best things that ever happened to my garden was a large

Before the contractor lays a flagstone patio, he installs a drainage system for the retaining wall on the right. Design and construction by McQuiggins Inc.

pile of soil left over from filling the space vacated by the removal of an oil tank. That berm became the separator between our parking area and the main garden. The berm developed into a rock garden that contains tough but attractive plants.

Hardscape

When the contractor begins hardscape installation, you finally begin to see the first increments of your design efforts. Concrete foundations, concrete or stone retaining walls, and/or patios and walkways of concrete, stone, or pavers will appear. The contractor will also install other items of concrete or stone, like pools or water features, columns for fences, preparations for an outdoor kitchen, and bases for garden art.

Next to appear will be wood or metal fabrications—fences, gates, arbors, gazebos, pergolas, and more. To prevent damage by heavy equipment needed to install any other items, fragile artwork of these materials generally will be installed last. For instance, the contractor may delay installation of a multimedia work with glass or with delicate moving parts to just before planting.

Equipment

Next up in the construction schedule will be the installation of equipment. The contractor may have installed some equipment earlier (like pumps for a pool or water feature or irrigation controls). However, now is when equipment for areas like an outdoor kitchen or the playground will arrive and be installed. The contractor may also install surface irrigation in the form of a drip system while he is installing other equipment. It is not unusual for specialty equipment (like outdoor kitchens) to be installed by specialists identified or provided by the manufacturer. Your contractor may just be the coordinator of this type of installation.

Planting

Planting is the time when your garden truly begins to feel like a garden. Plants will arrive by the truckload, usually beginning with larger items such as sod for lawn, trees, and large shrubs. Contractors usually install turf in the form of either sod or seed after they install the plants, to avoid making a mess of the new turf. First, the contractor lines out the plants before planting. This is your opportunity to review the arrangement and make sure the plants on the ground match the ones on your plant list. You may also want to review proper planting methods so you can check to make sure he installs your plants correctly. Most contractors will plant woody shrubs and trees with their crowns about an inch high so that when the plants settle, the crown will not sink below ground level. If this were to happen, it would smother the crown and kill the plant quickly. I see this happen more than it should, which is why I mention it.

Sometimes contractors have employees who are not well educated about plants. They purchase the right genus (the plant taxonomy classification below

Lining out plants on a project prior to their installation. Garden of R. Scott Latham and Beth Woodrow. Design by Barbara Hilty, APLD, Barbara Hilty Landscape Design. Photo by Barbara Hilty.

the level of family but above species) but get the species (the smallest unit of classification for plants) wrong. This could mean you get a vastly different plant from what you wanted. Alternatively, contractors may have a plant broker purchase plants for them. They have innumerable resources for plants and are usually good about notifying the contractor that a plant substitution may be necessary if you cannot wait. Sometimes my clients have to wait until spring for a few plants to arrive because the contractor installed most of their garden in the fall, when

plants are less available. Nurseries let their inventory of plants get lower toward autumn so that they will have fewer to care for over the winter. A few contractors also their own nurseries to ensure the plants they typically like to use on a project are available to them or the designers with whom they work.

Final touches

One of the last things installed in a garden is lighting. Major wiring may already be underground if you needed or opted for standard line voltage. If all

A substantially completed project is one in which nearly everything is done. Usually there are a few items left to do, and certainly, cleanup is yet to be done. Design and construction by Eckelman Architecture and Planning. Garden design by Vanessa Gardner Nagel, APLD, Seasons Garden Design LLC.

of your lighting is line voltage, the only thing left is to install the fixtures and flip the switch. However, if you opted for low-voltage lighting (the most common type of garden lighting), the contractor will need to place the cables around the garden. He will run cables through underground sleeves or pipes when crossing driveways and walkways before installing the fixtures. Plan to take some time one evening to fine-tune the position and direction of garden lighting with your contractor. It is also not a bad idea to ask the contractor to include a little extra wire for each light, because it will give you a little more flexibility when you adjust the placement of each fixture.

Mulching is another of the final tasks of a garden project. You should have already decided how many inches you want and have selected the material. Make sure the contractor does not install mulch too close to woody tree or shrub trunks. Some perennials are also susceptible to crown rot. Some nurseries and plant specialists recommend a small type of noncompactable gravel around the crowns of these plants. I use primarily quarter-ten gravel plus compost in my own garden. The gravel has made the

difference in plants surviving versus succumbing during severe winters. On occasion, I also recommend well-aged, small particle, local wood chips. Just be sure the chips are aged or they will rob your soil of nitrogen as they decompose.

Although a good contractor will clean up each day after work, the very last task, but not the least, is cleanup. Beyond sweeping scattered mulch or leaves off the walks, it means making sure that mortar has not dripped onto stones, there are no scratches on painted or stained surfaces, the equipment operates correctly, and so on. Even on the best of projects, there may be small items that need correction or repair. Generally, the contractor will set up an appointment to review the project for problems and create what the trade calls a punch list of tasks. Once the contractor completes these tasks, he considers the project finished. This also signals his final invoice and your final payment for the project. All of the contractors I spoke to make every effort to take care of problems that may arise after project completion. Good contractors want your garden to function perfectly for you. They love having satisfied clients because it speaks well of them.

The Construction Schedule

For the hypothetical garden, I created an oversimplified construction schedule to demonstrate how the start dates of tasks are staggered and how some tasks overlap.

TASK	WEEK 1	WEEK 2	WEEK 3	WEEK 4	WEEK 5
Mark utilities	•				
Demolition: remove old sidewalk and plants	• •				
Mark new layout; excavate for new walkway	• •				
Install irrigation and wiring for lighting		• • • • •			
Install edging and base material for new walkway			• • •		
Install new walkway material			• •	• • •	
Amend soil in planting beds				• •	
Install new plants and mulch				• •	• •
Install and adjust light fixtures					• •

This simple construction schedule for the hypothetical garden shows the timeline for tasks.

After Construction

Completing the Garden Installation

Once the contractors are gone, peace and quiet reign once again. Now you can progress into the home stretch. Just as a room inside your house would be unusable without furniture and inhospitable without accessories, so too would your garden be just as unfinished. Now you are ready to install your garden art, place your outdoor furniture, and plant some decorative pots.

Installing garden art

The installation of some pieces of art is as simple as poking them into the ground. However, even that should have a rhyme and a reason. If it is that simple, make sure the height of your art piece is what you want it to be in relationship to its surroundings. If it needs to be plumb or level, use equipment to make sure it is. If an angle is intentional, you have a greater margin of error and the freedom to estimate it.

Some other pieces of art, like large pots, will need to be placed on a level surface. In some cases, you will need to create that level surface before you place the item because the ground is not already level. You can set a large concrete paver or stone first, tamp some gravel, or pour a concrete pad if necessary. A wonderful pot placed catawumpus always looks a little odd. Use a level to make sure your surface is level. If it is, your piece of art should be, too.

What you will learn:

- how to install garden art and planted containers
- crowd control techniques and garden etiquette for a party or open garden
- strategies for a successful garden party or open garden
- suggested maintenance to prepare for an open garden

A beautiful pot does not require plants. This focal point pot draws attention to the knot garden on the other side of the path. Garden of Dulcy Mahar.

Then there are larger pieces of art that for whatever reason need secure anchoring. The trick is to anchor the art without damaging the piece and in such a way as to prevent its theft, particularly if it is in the public view. Art museums and galleries are experts at this. In addition, the artist can usually recommend the best way to install the art securely. Depending on what it is (because it could be almost anything), I would consult a gallery owner for her or his recommendation. Usually if the piece is inordinately heavy, the weight alone is a deterrent. If it is something you salvaged and recycled, you may feel less concerned about its value and could anchor it directly into concrete, in much the same way as you might install a fence post. There are many creative ways to secure art. Investigate to find the best way for your garden art.

Arranging outdoor furniture

Arranging your outdoor furniture is not rocket science. Most of the arrangement was already determined when you drew your garden layouts and created rules of thumb. However, it is my experience that without a crystal ball to see precisely what

This garden art was easily installed: just set it on the ground. Garden of Dulcy Mahar.

Eremurus ×isabellinus 'Cleopatra' intermingles with a spectacular red steel sculpture. From a balcony, the top of a stair, and the far side of the garden, this piece makes a visible hub for the garden. Garden of Michael Henry and Barbara Hilty. Design by Barbara Hilty, APLD, Barbara Hilty Landscape Design. Sculpture by Ivan McLean.

something will look like, people experience occasional surprises during installation.

Sometimes it is necessary to just slightly change the angle of something or move pieces a little closer together or farther apart. Sometimes a chair color clashes with a flower at certain times of the year or the texture of a woven piece of furniture just does not read properly against the foliage texture behind it. Occasionally the scale of a piece of furniture is not right. Designers are paid to think of these things ahead of time and are used to considering these issues. However, they are not perfect, just educated.

Red wicker chairs fit right into this setting, which includes an outdoor area rug with red in its pattern. Plants in this area include *Rosa moyesii* 'Geranium' (with its early summer red flowers and fall red hips) and *Cercis canadensis* 'Forest Pansy' (with its red leaves). Author's garden.

The unexpected will happen, especially when you think it will not. Do the best you can to plan ahead. Change what you need to change at the time of installation or live with it unless it will make you crazy.

Planting containers

You have innumerable choices for arranging plants inside containers. Every conceivable plant has spent or will spend time ornamenting a pot. The general wisdom is to place plants cheek by jowl in a container so it is as full and fabulous as possible. Generally speaking, I enjoy lavish displays of plants within containers. However, I also appreciate the display of a single plant in a container, particularly as a focal point but sometimes repeated in a row. It is a minimalist approach. It is serene. It can be equally as fabulous as an extravagant planting.

When you plant your pots, consider where you plan to place them. Do you want to achieve stimulation or do you want tranquility for you and your guests? How appropriate is it to the area where you are placing the pot? If the area is one of casual conversation, you may want the larger-than-life explosion of color and form to stimulate that conversation. If you are more interested in thought provocation, a more studied, quieter-colored planting or singular plant might be in order.

Will you put a more-or-less permanent plant in a four-season container? Perhaps a more architectural approach to the plant will look better and be easier to maintain. It is common to create vibrant displays with plenty of annuals that will last through the summer. If you use pots to disguise something you do not want to see, the pots may need to contain permanent screening plants.

Make sure your containers are appropriate to the time you have to water them. Small pots need frequent watering unless you are growing cacti. Give plants adequately sized pots so the plants do not rapidly outgrow them. If you have any doubts as to the size needed, ask your favorite knowledgeable nursery person. He or she will be able to give you advice about the eventual size of the plant and the speed at which it will get to that size.

I need to say one last thing about placement. If you are placing one or several large containers on a deck, rooftop, or other structure aboveground, reassure yourself with an engineer's calculations if necessary that the structure will hold the weight. Ensure that your gatherings will remain lively without the surprise of a structural failure. You can reduce the weight of the containers considerably by using lightweight potting medium and other lightweight materials below the root mass areas. In fact, many new lightweight containers are on the market now, some looking just like real terracotta or ceramic. Some manufacturers colorfully recycle post-consumer waste, too.

The Garden Party or Open Garden

Whether you choose to open your garden to the public or guests from your garden club for garden viewing or decide to have a party in the garden, no doubt you will want your event to be successful. There is more to consider beyond installing potted plants, art, and furniture.

Creating ambience

Creating ambience is an art. There are quite a few things you will need to have for your open garden or party, while other things are just nice to have. If your event is late in the day and into the evening, you will need lighting—possibly beyond the outdoor lighting for the garden. To set a particular mood or theme, consider using some ornamental, fun lighting over or around the main gathering areas. Candles are

nice as long as you can set them out safely without a problem with wind. Luminarias (candles in adequately sized paper bags with sand in the bottom) in Spanish-themed, or other, gardens are particularly beautiful, although not practical for all times of the year. You can use other containers of varying materials if you want, as long as they work well with the heat of the candle fire. Hurricane lanterns would be one alternative. Remember to limit your light to your property.

In addition to lighting, you may wish to provide other ornamentation to create the right atmosphere. Functional art for tables in the form of tablecloths, dishes, pitchers, bowls, flowers, or fruits and vegetables all contribute to the feeling of a party. One

A small brunch setting is coordinated to celebrate the old blooming rhododendron. Author's garden.

party I attended in Guadalajara, Mexico, years ago was set within the stone walls of an old hacienda. The walls that surrounded us were lined with tea lights that glimmered everywhere we looked. At the center of each table was a magnificent (and large) candelabra decorated with flowers, lemons, and greens. Dessert was served with considerable pomp and circumstance on long boards paraded before the guests. Large blown glass gazing balls (said to keep flies away) adorned the boards along with the desserts. The gazing balls reflected each flicker of tea light and candle. It was spectacular and unforgettable.

Music is another important ingredient of setting a mood and creating a theme for a party (or open garden). Music for an open garden would generally be a little more laid-back and relaxing. Classical guitar or new-age piano makes wonderful open garden music. Party music can be just about anything you want that makes you feel good and upbeat, without being too loud and obnoxious. Remember, you will be in a garden, so take that into consideration. Close neighbors will thank you, but they will thank you more if you invite them, too.

Whatever you decide to do, it is okay if the garden is not perfect. Nature has a hand with gardens that makes perfection nearly impossible. Do your best with garden maintenance and then go with the flow. Sometimes the most interesting gardens have an area under construction. It is a wonderful learning opportunity for guests.

Crowd control techniques

Controlling a group of people is usually more critical the greater the number of visitors and the larger your garden. You cannot be everywhere. Avoid signage if you can because it is usually an eyesore in a garden. Generally, you are trying to prevent people from going places you do not want them to go or attracting them to places you do want them to go. Here are a few techniques that I have used for an open garden that also work well for a large party:

- Place a large planted (or not) pot or piece of heavy garden art in front of a path where you do not want your guests to wander. It should be large enough that it would be difficult for a person to get by, if at all. If the area is wider, you could use two pots of gorgeous plants to support a bamboo pole.
- If you have a fragile chair that you would not want broken, place a special potted plant or piece of art on the chair as a display.
- If you want to attract people to a certain area of the garden, you could place flags, lights, a fabulous windsock, or another creative item

A beautiful but fragile bamboo chair displays a special pot that prevents anyone from sitting in it. Author's garden.

there as an attractant. While balloons would also be a solution, take responsibility for keeping them grounded. Do not let them wander off into the stratosphere where they could do environmental damage.

- Use bright colors to attract peoples' attention. Coordinate with an area of the garden or your home.
- If you are guiding people along a path to a party destination, make the beginning of the path obvious with the use of an arbor, columns, large lanterns, or planted containers on each side of the path. Then repeat something ornamental along the path that relates to the beginning of the path. You could repeat colors, materials, or forms, for example, as long as it is obvious.

- If you must use a sign, say what you need to say as gently and tactfully as possible. "Please" and "thank you" are always tactful. Loud colors may feel like you are shouting. If you use signs to identify plants, do so discreetly.

Open garden etiquette

A guest behaving badly is a nightmare that no garden host should have to endure. Seeing your favorite plant squashed beneath the foot of an errant guest who just had to step into a flower border to sniff a flower could anger the most restrained host. Many botanical gardens display guidelines or rules to visitors in hopes they will comply. They seek only to have guests respect the sanctity of the garden and enhance the experience of all who visit.

For a homeowner it may feel a bit odd to hand out

Open garden guests browse the plants and discuss plant identification, garden design, and more. Garden of Michael Schultz and Will Goodman.

222

a sheet of garden etiquette guidelines. You hope that people will just *know* how to behave in a garden. The truth (always stranger than fiction) is that some people are clueless about how to respect a garden. For an open garden I would not feel shy about stating my expectations for behavior if I felt there was any doubt about visitors. This is particularly important if you are opening the garden for a public viewing.

If you are inviting fellow garden club members, you might expect better behavior. Even then, there is no guarantee.

Feel free to adjust the list in "Garden Etiquette for the Uninitiated" to your wishes. If I distressed you when I listed small children, it is not because I do not love and adore small children. I do! However, I do not love children pulling leaves off my plants, eating

Garden Etiquette for the Uninitiated

You can always research a botanical garden's expectations of etiquette. They may have a longer list than mine. However, for the average garden owner the following list of expectations for garden guests should be adequate.

- Stay on paths or mowed lawns. Do not step into garden beds or water features. Climb only stairs.
- Leave flowers, plants, and their parts for all to enjoy. Do not assume it is okay to snip a piece of a plant. Ask the host about the plant and where he or she obtained it. Perhaps the host will snip a piece for you if it is not easily available.
- Do not ask a garden host to use the restroom unless he or she has indicated that restrooms are available.
- Leave plant labels in place.
- An open garden is not a professional photo shoot. Do not use a tripod to take photographs. Monopods may be permitted if the host agrees. Do not ask other visitors to move out of your photo range. Be patient and wait until they move on.

- Maintain a respectful distance from wildlife, if found, in the garden.
- Be cautious in tight garden areas with your umbrella, handbag, and camera to not damage plants.
- Turn off cell phones and other noise-generating equipment. Respect others' right to quietly enjoy the garden.
- Do not eat in a garden unless your garden host offers refreshments.
- Never leave litter in a garden. Take it out with you or place it in a bin that the garden host provides.
- No smoking allowed. Cigarette butts near certain plants can spread tobacco mosaic virus. And secondhand smoke not only is unpleasant, it also kills.
- Small children, pets (unless a guide dog), and play equipment are not allowed.
- If you make unfavorable remarks in a garden, assure yourself that the host will not hear you. If you have favorable comments, make sure the host hears you.

poisonous parts of plants, or breaking a piece of my glass art and cutting themselves. Children investigate. That is their nature. While their parents preoccupy themselves with identifying a plant or chatting about a plant they have not seen before is when little ones run amok. When children visit my garden with their parents during a party, we are all generally in one area, so it is easier to keep an eye on them than when they are wandering about during an open garden. Warning parents that you have poisonous plants in the garden helps, too.

Strategies for success

Successful parties are usually successful for a few reasons: remarkable people and conversation, scrumptious food and drink, and awe-inspiring ambience. In any case, people feel welcomed and esteemed. Here are a few suggestions for making an open garden a success, followed by a list of suggestions for making a garden party a success.

Strategies for the open garden

- **Announcement.** Generally speaking, an open garden is announced via the news media or your garden club. It is not unusual to plan well in advance, as early as December of the previous year, to have your garden listed in an open garden booklet. If it is in a publication, up to a month of lead time may be required, depending on the publication.
- **Ambience.** Simple is best, often just a greeting table (beneath shade) with a guest book where guests may leave comments for you about your garden. Consider having a vase of flowers from your garden on the table to give a hint of what visitors are about to see. Remember that people are there to see your garden and admire,

discuss, and learn from the garden's design, its plants, and its art.
- **Food and beverage.** Something simple like iced tea, water, or lemonade to drink and a special cookie or appetizer is an unexpected treat.
- **Trash receptacle.** Provide a receptacle for trash near where food and beverages are served.
- **Restroom.** A restroom is not necessary, but you may want to keep it clean just in case there is an emergency.
- **Garden access.** Guests generally access the garden directly for an open garden. There may be an obvious gate or entry, but if not, set the greeting table somewhere near where people will enter your garden.
- **Music.** Music is not necessary but is very pleasant to have. Play music that is soothing and compatible with visitors strolling through your garden. Having live music is a special treat, especially if the instrument is a harp.

Strategies for the garden party

- **Invitation.** Make the invitation as comprehensive as possible so guests will know date, time, place, dress, and anything else expected of them or that they might expect from you.
- **Ambience.** Your ornamentation can be as elaborate as you have time to create. Keep it complementary to the garden and exterior of your house. Simple elegance is always in good taste and often the easiest to accomplish. A few well-chosen ornaments special to the party may be all you need. If you have the time, energy, and budget, guests will appreciate your enthusiasm.
- **Food and drink.** You can provide all of the refreshments yourself or have a potluck. If you provide the refreshments, consider grilling

outdoors so you can be in the garden with your guests. Make food ahead of time that you can easily bring from indoors. Minimize food that requires freezing or refrigeration, or wait to bring that type of food until you know people will be ready to eat it. Consider whether you will want vegetarian options. Fresh, local food is especially welcome in a garden setting. After all, that is where you grow food.

- **Trash receptacle.** Provide a receptacle for trash near where food and beverages are served.
- **Restroom.** Make sure your guest bathroom is clean because it will be used often during a party. Put out a basket of beautiful soaps, extra toilet paper, an elegant hand towel (with a garden theme, of course), and a box of tissues. Scented candles are a nice touch, as are some fresh flowers from your garden.
- **Accoutrements.** Fabric tablecloths and napkins are particularly nice for table settings; beautiful dishes, glassware, utensils, and table decorations are a welcome complement. Avoid paper and plastic if you can, particularly if you have a smaller group. It is a more sustainable option.

A large garden party congregates around the pool and the food, with the garden creating a magnificent setting. Home of Maryellen Hockensmith and Michael McCulloch, AIA.

- **Party access.** Will everyone come through the house or directly into the garden? Give people advance notice on the invitation of how to get into the garden.
- **Music.** Music, background or dancing, is de rigueur for a party. Play music that is suitable to the age of your guests, or something that all ages will appreciate if your guest list includes multiple generations. If your guests are more interested in conversation, provide soft background music that is relaxing but not sleep-inducing.

Maintenance Preparation for the Open Garden

Open gardens are opportunities for plant nerds to congregate, gasp, and ogle plants. When I am preparing for an open garden, I stash large black nursery pots around our more than half-acre garden. I tend to weed as I make daily rounds through various areas. The convenient black nursery pots become repositories for my collected weeds until the last minute, when they disappear to the compost pile. Depending on the time of year of your open garden, sometimes a

This dazzling garden provides enjoyment all year. Garden of Bruce Wakefield and Jerry Grossnickle.

load of well-aged compost can help cover up and kill small weeds. Handy tools such as a hori-hori, a Cape Cod weeder, or a scuffle hoe can make quick work of even the most deeply rooted weeds. Sometime a pad for the knees comes in handy, too.

Of course, you knew I would mention that you should water your garden well ahead of time (assuming your garden requires adequate water to look good). You can water the pots the morning of the open garden. Make sure there is no reason for limp plants.

Along with weeding, deadheading spent flowers will keep your plants looking tidy. The bonus is that it will also encourage more flowers. A handy pair of secateurs will also help you keep dead branches pruned, brown leaf tips clipped, and the occasional itinerant plant corralled.

You brought your garden to fruition. You inaugurated it with an open garden or garden party. Now enjoy it to its fullest. If you were not a gardener before your garden installation, chances are you may be more interested in gardening now. I hope so. Your garden will require maintenance to look its best. Think of it as nurturing your garden in return for nature nurturing you all year long. Sometimes an area will require a full-scale overhaul. Plants die for many reasons or have winter dieback. This gives you an opportunity to try something different next time.

In my own garden, I make certain to have unveiled, expansive winter views. Even then, I cannot see from indoors many places beyond the vanished deciduous foliage or where perennials sleep for the season. Curiosity forces me to get out and see what is happening. It keeps me connected to the garden, our community, and to the earth.

If you expected to see a photo of the completed hypothetical garden, I need to remind you that it is hypothetical. The best photo of the hypothetical garden lies in your imagination. Let your imagination continue to inspire you throughout the year.

Bibliography

Alexander, Christopher, Sara Ishikawa, and Murray Silverstein. 1977. *A Pattern Language: Towns-Buildings-Construction*. New York: Oxford University Press.

Alexander, Rosemary. 2009. *The Essential Garden Design Workbook*. 2nd ed. Portland, OR: Timber Press.

Alexander, Rosemary, with Karena Batstone. 2005. *A Handbook for Garden Designers*. London, England: Casselli Illustrated.

Anderton, Stephen. 2009. It's time to see the bigger picture in your garden. *Times Online*, May 30. http://property.timesonline.co.uk/tol/life_and_style/property/gardens/article6387981.ece.

Brookes, John. 1991. *The Book of Garden Design*. New York: Macmillan.

———. 2002. *Garden Masterclass*. London, England: Dorling Kindersley.

Ching, Frank. 1975. *Architectural Graphics*. New York: Van Nostrand Reinhold.

Colman, David. 2003. Havens; Out in the garden, a reputation blooms. *New York Times*, July 11. http://www.nytimes.com/2003/07/11/travel/havens-out-in-the-garden-a-reputation-blooms.html.

Eck, W. Joseph. 2005. *Elements of Garden Design*. New York: North Point Press.

Glass, Penny. 2002. What do babies see? Lighthouse International *VisionConnection*, Summer. http://www.lighthouse.org/medical/childrens-vision/what-do-babies-see.

Green, Emily. 2008. All hemmed in. *Los Angeles Times*, February 7.

Healing gardens nurture the spirit while patients get treatment. 2002. ACS News Center, July 24. http://www.cancer.org/docroot/FPS/content/FPS_1_Healing_Gardens_Nurture_the_Spirit_While_Patients_Get_Treatment.asp.

Hemenway, Toby. 2009. *Gaia's Garden: A Guide to Home-Scale Permaculture*. 2nd ed. White River Junction, VT: Chelsea Green.

Hobbs, Thomas. 2004. *The Jewel Box Garden*. Portland, OR: Timber Press.

Julius, Corinne. 2007. In the name of art? *The Garden*, May. http://www.thinkingardens.co.uk/corrine's%20piece.html.

Karlen, Mark, and James Benya. 2004. *Lighting Design Basics*. Hoboken, NJ: Wiley.

Kellert, Stephen R., and Edward O. Wilson. 1993. *The Biophilia Hypothesis*. New York: Island Press.

Kingsbury, Noel. 2005. *Gardens by Design*. Portland, OR: Timber Press.

Lovejoy, Ann. 2001. *Organic Garden Design School:*

A Guide to Creating Your Own Beautiful, Easy-Care Garden. Emmaus, PA: Rodale.

McAlester, Virginia and Lee. 2003. *A Field Guide to American Houses.* New York: Knopf.

McDonough, William, and Michael Braungart. 2002. *Cradle to Cradle: Remaking the Way We Make Things.* New York: North Point Press.

Meadows, Keeyla. 2002. *Making Gardens Works of Art.* Seattle, WA: Sasquatch Books.

Miller, Naomi. 2001. Can lighting help people with aging eyes? Naomi Miller Lighting Design Web site. http://www.nmlightingdesign.com/topics/index.php.

———. 2004. Light and health: The new drugs. Naomi Miller Lighting Design Web site. http://www.nmlightingdesign.com/topics/LightAndDark.pdf.

Oudolf, Piet, with Noel Kingsbury. 1999. *Designing with Plants.* Portland, OR: Timber Press.

Owen, David. 2007. The dark side: Making war on light pollution. *New Yorker*, August 20. http://www.newyorker.com/reporting/2007/08/20/070820fa_fact_owen.

Pergams, Oliver R. W., and Patricia A. Zaradic. 2008. Evidence for a fundamental and pervasive shift away from nature-based recreation. *Proceedings of the National Academy of Sciences* 105 (February 19): 2295–2230. http://www.pnas.org/content/105/7/2295.full?sid=ec9ddc59-f066-4357-ab6e-ebf74b2848d0.

Pickering, Craig. Gestalt design laws: Seeing is believing? http://www.squidoo.com/gestaltlaws.

Reid, Grant W. 2007. *From Concept to Form in Landscape Design.* 2nd ed. New York: Wiley.

Rossi, Ernest Lawrence. 2004. *A Discourse with Our Genes: The Psychosocial and Cultural Genomics of Therapeutic Hypnosis and Psychotherapy.* London: Kamac Books.

Timiras, Paola S. 2007. *Physiological Basis of Aging and Geriatrics.* 4th ed. New York: Informa HealthCare.

Tolle, Eckhart. 1999. *The Power of Now: A Guide to Spiritual Enlightenment.* Novato, CA: New World Library.

Williams, Robin. 1995. *Garden Design: How to Be Your Own Landscape Architect.* Pleasantville, NY: Reader's Digest.

Woy, Joann. 1997. *Accessible Gardening: Tips and Techniques for Seniors and the Disabled.* Mechanicsburg, PA: Stackpole Books.

Index

Acalypha wilkesiana, 152
accessibility, 69, 73
Acer palmatum var. *dissectum*, 85, 167
Acer palmatum 'Sango-kaku', 182
adjacency diagram, 71, 75
Aeonium 'Zwartkop', 133
afterimage, 80
agave, 168
Alchemilla mollis, 154
allée, 169
allergies, 19, 51, 110
Allium christophii, 87
ambience, 18, 220–221, 224
American Nursery and Landscape Association, 22
American Society of Landscape Architects (ASLA), 22
Americans with Disabilities Act (ADA), 19, 33, 69
analogous, 82
Anderton, Stephen, 15
angle of repose, 38, 47
anthropometrics, 132
Aquilegia, 126
arbors, 29, 119, 127, 211
architect's scale, 30–31
architectural details, 26
architectural styles, 26–27

Asplenium scolopendrium, 168
asters, 83–84
asthma, 19, 51, 110
asymmetry, 27, 102
Athyrium filix-femina 'Lady in Lace', 159
Athyrium niponicum var. *pictum*, 158, 168
Aucuba japonica 'Picturata', 164

backflow device, 146
balance, 9, 90, 101–107, 195
  formal or informal, 101–102
barbecue grill, 67–68
beam spread, 177, 194
Begonia boliviensis, 152
Beijing, China, 120
Bellevue, Washington, 81
Bellevue Botanical Garden, 81,145
bench, 65–66, 113, 140–141, 189, 191–193, 197
benderboard, 128
Berberis thunbergii f. *atropurpurea* 'Bagatelle', 157–158
bidding a project, 201–202, 205–207
biodegradable natural fabric, 48
Biophilia Hypothesis, The, 91
Bishopville, SC, 169
Boboli Gardens, 46–47

bocce ball court, 54, 60
borrowed landscape, 36
Boutet's color circles, 82
bromeliad, 168
broom finish, 123
Brunnera macrophylla 'Emerald Mist', 159
Brunnera macrophylla 'Jack Frost', 158
bubble diagram, 71, 74, 76, 111
budget, 14, 20–21, 34–35, 56–58, 73, 93, 115, 119, 143, 146, 176, 205, 209
Burt, Deborah, 15
Buxus microphylla var. *japonica* 'Winter Gem', 168
Buxus microphylla var. *japonica* 'Variegata', 164
Buxus sempervirens 'Suffruticosa', 157

cabbages, ornamental, 152
cacti, 168
Callicarpa bodinieri var. *giraldii* 'Profusion', 85
carbon footprint, 30
catmint, 51–52
CC and Rs (covenants, conditions, and restrictions), 19

cedar, 129, 136

Cercis canadensis 'Forest Pansy', 85, 106

Chamaecyparis, 168

Chamaecyparis lawsoniana 'Wissel's Saguaro', 161

Chamaecyparis obtusa 'Elwoodii', 160

Chamaecyparis obtusa 'Torulosa', 162

change order, 185–186, 196, 208

Château Val-Joanis, 43, 89, 95, 106

cherry trees, 84

chicken coop, 54

children, 49–50

Children's Hospital and Health Center, San Diego, California, 15

Choisya ternata Sundance (= 'Lich'), 83–84

chroma, 80

circle segments, 90

circulation diagram, 72

circulation factor, 62, 63, 67

cisterns, 46–47, 146

closure, principle of, 105

codes, building,19, 52, 55, 119, 123, 135

co-efficient of friction, 119

colon plants, 164–165

color, 10, 94, 98–99, 103–104, 109, 129, 155, 166
  basic concepts of, 79–87
  in lighting, 177
  in construction materials, furnishings, and decor, 29, 111, 116, 120–121, 126, 128, 219, 222

colorways, 131

COM (customer's own material), 132

comma plants, 158–159, 171

complementary, 82–83

composted mulches, 129

conceptual plan, 111–112, 114, 135, 138, 151, 197

concrete, 20, 23, 44, 57, 99, 115, 119–120, 122–125, 133, 217–218
  colored, 123–124
  foundations, 211
  masonry units, 21
  pavers, 122–123, 217
  permeable, 123
  sidewalk, 26, 105

consistency of design, 107

construction plan, 197, 199

Consumer Product Safety Commission, U.S., 50

containers, 130, 133–134, 138, 141, 170, 219–220, 222

contingency, 205

continuity, principle of, 105

contract, 205–206

contrast, 81, 86, 90, 94, 99, 101, 104

Cordyline 'Cardinal', 152

Cornus sanguinea 'Compressa', 165–166

Cor-Ten steel, 127

Corylus avellana 'Contorta', 35, 161

Cotinus coggygria 'Royal Purple', 156

county extension service, 38

croquet lawn, 54

Cuphea ignea 'Dynamite', 152

Cupressus macrocarpa 'Wilma Goldcrest', 165

cut and fill, 34

cut-leaved Japanese maple, 167

cypress, 168

dark-sky lighting, 176

daylilies, 168

decomposed granite, 57

deer-resistant plants, 36

demolition, 210

Dicentra spectabilis 'Gold Heart', 155

dining area, 60, 71, 98, 136

downlighting, 179–180

downspout disconnection, 44

drainage, 26, 37–38, 44, 46, 57, 122, 125, 127, 130, 134, 186–187, 210–211

drip system, 146, 148, 211

Dryopteris erythrosora, 155

dusk-to-dawn lighting, 173

easements, 19, 31

Emperor's Garden, 120

engineering fabric, 48

equilibrium, 101, 103

Eremurus ×isabellinus 'Cleopatra', 218

ergonomics, 132

erosion, 47–48, 145

Erythronium californicum 'White Beauty', 45

Euonymus japonicus 'Green Spire', 160

Eupatorium purpureum, 98

evergreen foliage, 36, 106

excavation, 21, 210

exclamation point plants, 160–161, 171

existing conditions plan, 25, 29, 34, 36, 40, 48, 59

false cypress, 168

Fatsia japonica, 162

fee payment schedule, 208

fencing, 37, 119, 135–136, 196, 211

fiddleheads, 168

figure-ground, principle of, 105

fines (in gravel), 57, 125

fire pit, 38, 54, 64–65, 67, 88, 112–113, 123, 135, 137, 170, 203
  rule of thumb, 60
  furnishings near, 131, 139

Florence, Italy, 46–47

focal point(s), 69, 94–98, 104, 107, 111, 135, 151–152, 169–170, 175, 181, 195, 217, 219

footings, 122

Forbidden City, 120

Forest Stewardship Council, 126
fragrance, 110–111
fronds, 168
Fryar, Pearl, 169
function, 61–62, 66–68, 71–74, 110–111, 131, 174, 193, 197, 214

Gallup Organization, 22
gaps and overlaps, 185
garden art, 15, 127, 134, 182, 207, 217, 221
garden
  components, 43, 61, 65, 187
  theme, 108
  parties, 10, 217, 220–222, 224–225
Garden Conservancy Open Days Program, The, 10
garden lighting, 22–23, 111, 173–176, 181–182, 197, 213–214, 220
gas lines, 211
gazebo(s), 19, 29, 55, 119, 127, 175, 211
gazing balls, 221
genius loci, 108–109
geotechnical, 34, 39, 210
Geranium 'Ann Folkard', 154
Gestalt principles of perceivable organization, 105
glare, 178,
global warming, 43
Goethe's color wheel, 82
grading, 34, 44, 202, 210
gravel, 56–57, 102, 117, 120, 124–126, 130, 136, 214, 217
gravel paths, 105, 110
grazing with light, 180
Great Dixter, 169
Green, Emily, 157
Greenbrae, California, 15
greenhouse, 53–55, 63, 67, 74, 76–77, 93, 113, 117, 135–137, 148, 170, 182
grid paper, 30–31
grilling, 61
grilling rule of thumb, 60
ground sulfur, 38

groundwater table, 44
Guadalajara, Mexico, 221
guardrails, 119

habitat, 35–37, 176
Hakonechloa macra 'Aureola', 154
Halberg, Francine, MD, 15
hardscape, 26, 34, 111, 115, 135–136, 194, 196, 210–211
  and balance or mass, 93, 102, 106
  and plants, 151, 166, 170
  in existing conditions plan, 40
Hardy Plant Society of Oregon, 10
Harry Lauder's walking stick, 35
Hart's tongue fern, 168
healing gardens, 15
Hedychium longicornutum, 152
Helleborus argutifolius, 162–163
Helleborus ×hybridus, 159
Hemerocallis, 168
heuchera, 158
Himalayan blackberries, 25
Hinkley, Daniel, 157
horizon line, 190
horizontal plane, 101
horseshoe pit, 54
hose bibs, 31, 143, 211
hose guides, 194
hostas, 105
house style worksheet, 28
hue, 80–81
humidity, 37, 194
hypothetical list of garden components, 67

Ilex crenata 'Sky Pencil', 160
Impruneta, Italy, 133
Integral colorants, 123
intensity of color, 80–82, 103
iron sulfate, 38
irrigation, 46, 111, 143–147, 149, 174, 182, 194, 202, 211

Julius, Corinne, 14

Juniperus communis 'Gold Cone', 160–161
Juniperus scopulorum 'Snow Flurries', 134

Kellert, Stephen R., 91
kitchen garden, 9, 53, 140, 148
Kniphofia, 168

landscape architects, 166
landscape contractors, 10, 123, 201–202, 204, 206
landscape designers, 9, 166, 176
lasagna layering, 129
leaf shapes, 166–168
LED lighting, 177
Legacy Good Samaritan Hospital, 16
Lehrer, Mia, 157
life-cycle costs, 177
light fixtures, 174–180, 194–195, 199
Ligularia dentata 'Britt Marie Crawford', 153
line, shape, form and space, 87, 90
line loss, 174–175
line voltage, 174, 213–214
Lloyd, Christopher, 169
Lonicera nitida 'Baggesen's Gold', 169
low-voltage lighting, 174, 214
Luther Burbank Home and Gardens, 97

Mahonia ×media 'Winter Sun', 162–163
maiden grass, 167
Marin Cancer Institute, 15
masonry, 120
mass, 90, 93–94
Master Gardeners, 10
master plan, 197–199
McDonough, William, 20
Meadowbrook Farm, Pennsylvania, 94

measuring, 25, 29–34
metal fabrications, 211
microclimates, 26, 37
Miscanthus, 167
monochromatic, 82
mosaic, pebble, 121–122
motion detectors, 173
movement, 90, 98
mulching, 214
mycorrhizae, 38, 48

Nassella tenuissima, 99, 173
native plants, 25, 35, 45, 93
Nepeta ×faassenii 'Walker's Low', 51
neutral zone, 98
Northwest Perennial Alliance (NPA) border, 145

Obama, Michelle, 43
open garden, 10, 217–219, 223–224, 226–227
Ophiopogon planiscapus 'Nigrescens', 158–159
Osmanthus heterophyllus 'Goshiki', 164
Oudolf, Piet, 156
outdoor
    dining area, 60, 65
    furniture, 115, 218
    kitchen, 211
    showers and sinks, 211
    upholstery, 37, 130–131, 138
overhead trellis, 55, 135, 137
Owens, David, 176

packed gravel, 48
Paeonia suffruticosa, 85
Panicum, 167
parentheses plants, 165–166, 171
parking, 19, 23, 44, 48–49, 173, 211
parterre garden, 90
pastel, 80
patio(s), 26, 55, 81, 92, 112, 117, 123, 135, 170, 196, 211

pattern, 100
Pattern Language, A, 59
paving materials, 119
peacock topiary garden, 169
pea gravel, 56, 125, 130
Pennisetum, 168
percolation test, 39, 44
Pergams, Oliver R. W., 16
pergola(s), 26, 119, 127, 179, 211
period plants, 157–158, 171
permeable pavers, 48
permit(s), 19, 35, 52, 55, 122, 135, 174, 204, 210
Persicaria virginiana 'Painter's Palette', 155
Pertuis, France, 43, 89, 95, 106
pets, 23, 51
Phlox paniculata 'Nora Leigh', 98
Phormium, 99
Phormium tenax 'Atropurpureum', 153
Phygelius 'Passionate', 152
pine, 129
Pittosporum tenuifolium 'Golf Ball', 157–158
plant
    brokers, 213
    placement, 169
    punctuation, 157, 166
    shapes, 166
    structure, 151, 194
planting, 9, 35, 93, 98, 110, 143, 151, 169
    containers, 133, 219
    and contractors, 199, 206, 212–213
    plan, 170–171, 199
planting beds, 151, 194
play structures, 50
point survey, 31
poisonous plants, 19, 51, 224
polymeric sand, 123
Polystichum munitum, 45, 168
pop-up sprinklers, 145
porous concrete, 48, 57
Portland, Oregon, 16

power lines, overhead, 39
precast paving, 20
preliminary plan, 195
prequalifying a contractor, 203
pressure-treated wood, 126, 128
Primula, 13
proportion, 90–91, 93, 101, 106
proximity, principle of, 105
punch list, 214
punitive charges, 208
putting green, 63, 66–67, 112, 170, 198–199

quarter-minus gravel, 56, 125, 137
quarter-ten gravel, 129–130, 214
question mark plants, 161–162

rain barrels, 46–47, 63, 111, 113
rain chain(s), 46
rain garden(s), 44, 46, 53, 63, 67, 76–77, 111, 148
rainwater collection, 46
rainwater harvesting, 46
raised beds, 9, 19, 126, 137, 147
recycled, 117, 125, 129–130, 136–137, 170, 210, 220
red-hot poker plants, 168
redwood, 129
repetition, 90, 96, 98, 101, 104, 106, 136, 170
restocking fee, 186
retaining wall(s), 48, 55, 58, 65–66, 115, 119, 122–123, 127, 174, 211
RGV color wheel, 38
Rheum palmatum var. *tanguticum*, 153
Rhododendron 'Ramapo', 157–158
Rhus typhina 'Bailtiger', 84
rhythm, 90, 96, 98, 101, 104, 112, 136
rise and run, 33–34, 71
Robinia pseudoacacia 'Lace Lady', 162
Roosevelt, Eleanor, 43
Rosa moyesii 'Geranium', 219

Rosa 'Radtko', 162–163
rot-resistant wood, 126
Rousillon, France, 100
Rudbeckia, 83–84
rules of thumb, 59–61, 169, 176

safety, 19, 50, 69–70, 116, 173
Saint Rémy-de-Provence, France, 23
Salix integra 'Hakuro Nishiki', 164–165
San Diego, California, 15
Santa Rosa, California, 97
scale, 90–91, 93–94, 101, 108–109
schedule, 21–22
security, 19, 116, 173
semicolon plants, 162–163
sequence, 90, 98
Sequoiadendron giganteum 'Pendulum', 151
shade (dark value), 80
silhouetting, 180
similarity, principle of, 105
simplicity, principle of, 105
site
    plan, 29
    preparation and remediation, 210
    requirements, 44
    survey, 29, 39, 44, 48
slip resistance, 119
slopes, 25–26, 30, 33, 38, 44, 46–47, 55, 65, 69–71, 145, 210
soaker hoses, 144, 147
soil, 26, 38
Solenostemon scutellarioides 'Freckles', 152
Solenostemon scutellarioides 'Juliet Quartermain', 152
Solenostemon scutellarioides 'Kiwi Fern', 152
sparkle treatment lighting, 180–181
split-complementary, 82–84
spray chalk, 30, 32
stairs, 33, 70–71, 73, 81, 89–90, 119, 127, 173, 179, 181, 223

stakes, 30, 32–33
steel rebar reinforcing,
Stenzel Healing Garden, 16
stepping-stones, 57, 126
Stilgoe, John, 15
stone paving, 57
storm water collection system, 44, 46
straw blanket barriers, 48
style, 107–109, 111, 115–116
substantial completion, 208, 215
substitutions, 206
subsurface water, 38
subtle way-finding, 69, 136
surveyors, 25, 31
sustainability, 20, 110, 117, 125, 138
symmetry, 29, 101

Taxus, 169
Taxus baccata 'Fastigiata', 97
terracing, 38, 48, 73
texture, 9, 90, 99–100, 102, 104, 111, 116, 166, 180, 219
thrillers, fillers, and spillers, 152–155, 166
thrown shadow lighting, 180
Thuja occidentalis 'Emerald', 150, 165
Thuja occidentalis 'Rheingold', 165–166
time, 90, 106
tint (light value), 80
tone on tone, 99–100
topiary, 109, 168–169
topography, 73
Tradescantia pallida 'Purple Heart', 152
transition, 90, 98
triangulation, 30–31
Trillium grandiflorum, 45
Trillium kurabayashi, 6
turning radius, 48
Twisty Baby black locust, 162

Ulrich, Roger S., 91
underground
    tanks and bladders, 46
    utilities, 39, 210
    work, 20, 210
underwater lighting, 181
unity, 90, 105–106
uplighting, 179
urea, 38
utilities, 20, 31, 35, 39–40, 44, 48, 51–52, 186, 210

value of color, 80–82, 103
vanishing point, 190–192
variety, 90, 100, 104, 166
Veronicastrum virginicum, 156
vertical plane, 101
videophilia, 16
visual scale and weight, 81, 104–105
voltage drop, 174

walkway(s), 56, 69, 73, 99, 135, 179, 211, 214
water feature(s), 22, 36–37, 55, 58, 63, 67, 76–77, 111, 113, 115, 135, 137, 196–197
    construction, 211
    safety of, 188
water pressure, 123, 145, 147
water treatment facilities, 44
wheelchair access, 70
Wilson, Edward O., 91
wood
    chips, 126, 198, 214
    composite products, 126

xeric plants, 144

yucca, 168

Zaradic, Patricia A., 16
zones
    irrigation, 146–149, 194
    lighting, 182

V ✓